A popular puzzler: A young man and his father were in a traffic accident. The father was killed and the young man seriously injured. In the hospital, on the operating table, the young man was readied for surgery. The surgeon cried in recognition, "My God, this patient is my son!"

Who was the surgeon?

(See page 259)

Anatomy class, 1897, Western College and Seminary, Oxford, Ohio (now defunct)

Women
and
Medicine

BEATRICE S. LEVIN

The Scarecrow Press, Inc.
Metuchen, N.J., & London
1980

Library of Congress Cataloging in Publication Data

Levin, Beatrice.
  Women and medicine.

   Bibliography: p.
   Includes index.
   1. Women in medicine. 2. Women in medicine--
Biography. 3. Women's health services. 4. Women in
medicine--United States. 5. Sexism in medicine--
United States. I. Title. [DNLM: 1. Health services.
2. Physicians, Women. 3. Physicians, Women--Biography.
4. Women. W84.1 L665W]
R692.L49   508'.8042   80-12705
ISBN 0-8108-1296-7

Copyright © 1980 by Beatrice S. Levin

Manufactured in the United States of America

To Dr. Estelle Ramey,
of Georgetown University School
of Medicine, and to other women
doctors who have sought to
liberate us all.

"Her inward sympathy with a
doctor's and a surgeon's work
grew stronger and stronger,
though she dismissed reluc-
tantly the possibility of
following her bent ... since,
after all, her world had
seemed to forbid it."
--Sarah Orne Jewett,
A Country Doctor (1884)

ACKNOWLEDGMENTS

To my husband, Franklyn, for his patience, support, and love.

To the staffs of the Jesse Jones Medical Library, the Houston Public Library, and the Winter Park (Florida) Public Library.

To Roberta Fenlon, Estelle Ramey, Janet Travell, Marie Valdes-Dapena, Helen Hittner, Florence Sabin, Helen B. Taussig, Niles Newton, Barbara DuBois, and all the other women who so graciously helped me with this book.

Special thanks to Jo Manton for permission to quote from Elizabeth Garrett Anderson (Methuen) and to Margery Scott-Young, who was a kind hostess on my tour of the Rachel Forster Hospital in Sydney, Australia.

Passages in Chapter 4 from Office Hours: Day and Night, by Janet Travell, M. D., (copyright © 1968 by Janet Travell, M. D.) are reprinted by arrangement with The New American Library, Inc., New York, New York.

TABLE OF CONTENTS

Part I

"THE
DINOSAUR
IS
TWITCHING"

"THE DINOSAUR IS TWITCHING"

1. Phantom Symptoms and Put-Downs

Life is a thriller, all right, girls. All we have to do to prove it is to go for our annual physical checkup and have the doctor recommend x-rays to detect breast cancer. Next day's headlines report that the x-ray procedure known as mammography sometimes induces the very cancer it is supposed to detect.

What's more, in the summer of '76 a woman doctor, Carol M. Proudfit, warned against routine prescription of estrogen. Dr. Proudfit maintained that women treated with the sex hormone are risking uterine cancer to about the same degree as pack-a-day cigarette smokers risk lung cancer. Researchers have found increased incidence of cancer in the endometrium, the lining of the uterus, and have associated it with estrogens. While not all studies agree, the estimated risk of cancer associated with estrogen treatment is up to 7.6 times higher for women treated with estrogen, and the risk may be increased with length of time on medication. Yet women going for yearly physical examinations often walk away from the doctor's office with a prescription for estrogen--particularly if the women are facing menopause. Researchers have concluded that regular dosages of estrogen may increase the risk of breast cancer!

The real shocker, of course, is the investigations that reveal that the synthetic hormone D.E.S., diethylstilbestrol, which was prescribed in the late 1940s and early 1950s to prevent miscarriage, is a possible cause of vaginal cancer in the daughters of women who took the drug.

The effects of D.E.S. were discovered when Dr. Arthur Herbst began noticing a surprisingly high incidence of vaginal cancer among young women patients; the doctor found seven cases in Boston. This kind of cancer had been rare; the only common denominator discovered was that all the women were in their early 20s and had mothers who had had difficulty in carrying a pregnancy to term. These moth-

1

ers were among approximately 2 million women who had taken
D. E. S., and--listen to this!--most doctors now agree the
drug had little or no effect in preventing miscarriages.

Have doctors, then, given up entirely on prescribing
D. E. S. ? Not at all. They are still offering the drug as a
highly effective "morning after" pill to prevent pregnancy if
taken by a woman within 72 hours after intercourse. Women
also walk out of doctors' offices with prescriptions for D. E. S.
for correcting hormonal imbalance during menopause, and
there is evidence of a possible connection between D. E. S.
and cancer of the uterus.

In Houston Dr. Marjorie Horning has been particularly involved in studying the transfer of drugs from a pregnant
woman to her child. When she began this work in 1968, Dr.
Horning said, "The impression was that the placental barrier
protected the fetus from the drugs the mother took. " Her
research revealed that "essentially every drug" taken by a
pregnant woman reaches the fetus. She found that drugs
taken by a nursing mother will reach the child through the
breast milk.

Dr. Horning, professor of biochemistry at Baylor College of Medicine, has recently been awarded the Garven
Medal, presented by the American Chemical Society to wom-
en for distinguished service to chemistry. Dr. Horning and
her husband Evan were also honored with the Warner Lambert
Lecturership for outstanding contributions in developing techniques for studying how drugs are broken down and used by
the human body. Today Marjorie Horning's work affects patients everywhere, but when she began her research, she
faced all the barriers that women had to face three decades
ago. She worked as an unpaid aide in the University of
Pennsylvania lab in Philadelphia because women simply were
not hired for lab work. She had graduated from Goucher
College, a women's school in Baltimore, in 1938, and she
received an M. S. and a Ph. D. from the University of Michigan. Eventually she and her husband came to the Institute
for Lipid Research at Baylor.

The discrimination Dr. Horning experienced has been
the universal situation until recently. The traditionally conservative American Medical Association had long blocked the
equality of women in the profession, and a woman doctor at
a meeting of the A. M. A. publicly pronounced that organiza-

tion "prehistoric!" She added, "But the dinosaur is twitching!"

In the 1976 academic year men continued to outnumber women four to one in medical-school enrollment, but there are strong indications that the disparity between the sexes is at last narrowing.

In 1976 there were only 12 women doctors in all of Wyoming, 14 in Nevada and Montana, 17 in Idaho, 15 in North Dakota, 17 in South Dakota. These professional women often suffer from feelings of isolation. Large Midwestern cities in the '70s were losing qualified physicians to more glamorous sections of the country. Doctors move because they want a better-equipped hospital or proximity to other physicians for consultation or companionship. Doctors abandon industrial states, rural areas, and urban ghettoes to practice where life is easier in middle- or upper-income areas in coastal cities or in bedroom communities.

Proposals for tax incentives to lure doctors to ghettos and rural areas where they are most needed may not get physicians to these locations, but encouraging women to join the Armed Forces and educating them to become doctors will; for these women, as we have seen, may marry doctors and form teams to serve where social isolation has made service intolerable for a lone doctor.

Women in the '70s were rebelling against discrimination against them both as patients and as doctors. Dr. Estelle Ramey, speaking in Mexico at an International Conference of Women in June 1975, observed, "The outstanding thing about women in health care is that even in those countries where women make up the majority of the doctors, they do not occupy the key, decision-making posts." Speaking out against discrimination on another occasion, Dr. Ramey said, "I believe that men are just as capable as women in medicine. No one ever refers to 'Men doctors' or 'men scientists'-- yet I am always identified as a 'woman scientist.'"

Consumer-oriented groups were examining the chances of a woman in the United States having to undergo a hysterectomy, and the probability worked out to 45.3 percent. Statistics revealed that women who are members of health-maintenance organizations--that is, prepaid group plans rather than fee-for-service plans--have only a 16.8 percent probability. Women were up in arms about the possibility that hysterectomies and breast surgery were being performed unnecessarily.

Women were examining how they were being portrayed in medical magazines; the drug advertisements pictured female patients as excessively neurotic and anxious, or elderly insomniacs, eager for tranquilizers, estrogen, pain-killers, or anti-depressive drugs. Such advertisements were regarded by sociologists as a betrayal of the confidence of women patients. Women have accused drug laboratories of waging campaigns directed at physicians mainly to promote the sale of drug approaches to control stress.

How do doctors regard women patients? The question stirred two psychologists at California State University/Northridge, Dr. Linda Fidell and Dr. Jane Prather, to study ads in medical journals for four years. "We never saw a woman doctor pictured. We saw young pretty female nurses. We saw female patients who were housewives and unskilled workers. We saw patients who were important executives. The women patients were in ads for stimulants or tranquilizers; the men were in ads for medicine treating specific diseases."

Doctors, the psychologists concluded, tend to take male patients' symptoms more seriously than those of female patients. Dr. Fidell said that 48 percent of American women over 30 are on mood pills at some time. When a man goes to a doctor he is given medicine for his illness, but a woman is given a tranquilizer. A woman may tell the doctor not only her physical symptoms, but her emotional reaction to the symptoms as well. A man just talks about what hurts him. That doesn't mean, adds Dr. Fidell, "that women are more hypochondriacal than men."

Ruth Cooperstock, a sociologist in Canada, in 1971 asked doctors to describe "the typical complaining patient," and 72 percent referred to a woman. Only 4 percent referred to a man. Women "complain"; men "describe symptoms" (Cooperstock). *

In 1979, in other research conducted at the University of California/San Diego Medical School, Dr. Lawrence

---

*Citations in parentheses refer to the Bibliography.

Schneiderman reported that a man who complains of headaches, for example, probably gets a more extensive examination than a woman with the same symptoms. The physicians in the study were all male, and the medical study lent
support to women's claims that doctors do not take them
seriously; in this study male doctors reacted differently to
similar symptoms described by men and women by doing a
more extensive medical workup on male patients. This sys-
tematic study compared records from a total of 181 doctor
visits by 52 married couples (104 patients). For headaches,
chest pains, dizziness, fatigue, and back pain, male patients
received closer attention from family-practice physicians who
were members of the U. C. S. D. medical faculty. These five
medical complaints are equally common among men and wom-
en and may signal more severe problems. Schneiderman
concludes that the doctors, "by doing fewer kinds of physical
tests for organic disease in women are expressing their belief that these complaints are likely to be psychosomatic. "

Women who make appointments with the doctor may
have very real illnesses; they may also have psychosomatic
illnesses that cause very real pain. They deserve to be
treated seriously.

In May 1979, in Sweetwater, Texas, an 83-year-old
Spanish-speaking woman was hospitalized and x-rayed for the
first time. X-rays revealed the calcified remains of a fetus,
about three months developed which may have been 70 years
old. *

The fetus was approximately four inches long with
identifiable limbs. The patient had complained to the physicians of abdominal pain and vomiting. Though she was married, she had never had children, and through seven decades
the fetus had remained in her abdominal wall, until the
Sweetwater doctor removed it surgically. How many doctors
must have ignored this poor woman's "complaints" during
those 70 years!

Breast surgery and breast feeding have contributed to
greater interest in medicine among women.

In no area are women doctors more needed than in

*Houston Chronicle, June 3, 1979, Sec. 3, p. 32.

research for reducing the death rate from breast cancer.
When former First Lady Betty Ford and the Vice-President's
wife, Happy Rockefeller, within a brief period both had to
have breast surgery, the nation's attention was focused on the
seriousness of the problem.   Over 70,000 women in America
learn they have breast cancer every year.   A thousand undergo surgery for breast cancer every week.   Some 30,000 will
die of that cancer.   The operation may involve radical mastectomy, the removal of the breast and surrounding tissues.
The surgery is disfiguring, and many women respond with a
sense of lost femininity and worth.

Here is a research field where women doctors must
be involved, for these women can well imagine the suffering
and psychic misery of those who undergo full-scale surgery.
Dr. M. Vera Peters of Toronto's Margaret Rose Hospital
urges simpler surgery for early breast cancer "in order to
preserve the patient's morale."

For certain of Dr. Peters's patients in whom early
diagnosis has been made, "lumpectomy" is preferred--that
is, the removal of the cancer only rather than the entire
breast.   Dr. Peters claims that the operation, which is followed by radiation therapy, offers some patients the same
survival rate as radical mastectomy.   Of 81 women upon
whom radical mastectomy had been performed between 1955
and 1965 over 70 percent were alive five years after the operations.   Dr. Peters paired each of these patients by age
and other pertinent factors with 81 women who had only
lumpectomies.   Comparing the two groups' survival rates,
there were only slight differences each year, and after five
years 71.6 percent of the lumpectomy patients were still
alive.

Other doctors are questioning radical breast surgery,
viewing it as absurd and archaic.   Women's-liberation groups
support the movement toward less radical surgery, contend-
ing that women should have some decisions about what is done
to their bodies.   The United States is the only country where
doctors still cling to the century-old technique.   In such
countries as Denmark, Italy, Sweden, and England, doctors
have given up the procedure for several decades.   Some
women patients who have the lymph glands removed develop
unsightly, painful swelling of the arm until the fluid that the
glands normally drained finds other channels into the blood-
stream.

Doctors must consider the quality of life left to a woman

who loses a breast. Just postponing death is not enough.
Women who delay seeking treatment for fear of losing a
breast, say Italian doctors, may come more promptly to the
physician when they know that an alternative to breast removal exists. One of my most sophisticated friends said to me
after her breast surgery, "The first time I saw myself naked
in a mirror, I nearly went berserk!"

In the '60s few reconstructive operations of breasts
after mastectomies were even considered possible. Most
physicians were interested only in removing the breast and
curing cancer. When reconstruction attempts finally began,
doctors used silicone implants, which produced a poor imita-
tion of the natural breast. The newest technique in the late
'70s is a method of reconstructing breasts by transferring a
flap of muscle (and sometimes the skin attached to it) from
the back to the breast area and then implanting a silastic gel
bag to give the breast shape. The surgery lessens the
severe emotional and psychological shock of losing a breast.
Many women who have had mastectomies are asking for
breast reconstruction. Reconstruction can begin about six
weeks after the mastectomy, and can be performed regardless of whether the cancer was contained within the breast
or spread to the lymph nodes. Naturally, doctors insist
that therapy for the cancer must take precedence. But many
surgeons believe this is a great advance, a plausible way to
reconstruct the breast. The transfer of the muscle to the
chest, however, may create a scar, so the patient must
realize that she may be trading one defect for another.

Dr. Nancy B. Easterly, a pediatric dermatologist at
Michael Reese Medical Center in Chicago, delivered her
first child in England, where breast feeding was encouraged.
Her next three children were delivered in university hospitals in the United States, where the attitude toward breast
feeding ranged "from total disinterest to undisguised disgust." To encourage greater interest on the part of obstre-
ticians in support of breast feeding, Dr. Easterly organized
a symposium of women physicians who breast fed their own
children. Drs. Nancy Fuery, Michele Ginsberg, Barbara S.
Kirschner, Marilyn Miller, and Jo Zurbrugg all emphasized
the advantages of breast feeding: it is inexpensive, convenient, and promises less diarrhea and respiratory infections.
There would be no bottles to sterilize, no muss or fuss, and
there would be a close interaction between mother and child.

Dr. Carol Weichert of Syracuse, N.Y., is a pediatri-

cian who has breast fed four children of her own; she
claims that women are so fixed on the breast as a yardstick
of feminine desirability they forget its nurturing role.   She
disputes the argument that breast feeding might affect the
marital relationship or cause feelings of jealousy on the part
of the father.   Dr. Weichert urges physicians to encourage
their patients to breast feed their infants.

In the following chapter we will take a look at another
factor that has drawn women to the field of medicine--the
women's movement.

"THE DINOSAUR IS TWITCHING"

2. Doctor, Wife, and Mother

"Let's put women in their place," urges Dr. Jean Mayer, Harvard professor of nutrition, "like for instance, City Hall." Or City Hospital. He says, "Many men go into medicine with Walter Mitty-like dreams of stardom--each one is going to become a famous heart surgeon, a chief of medicine at City Hospital, an Albert Schweitzer among the grateful natives, or the discoverer of a radically new antibiotic...." Women tend to be more realistic. Many men become bored or irritated with the complaints of the elderly. But such unhappiness about feeling useless and a burden speaks to the condition of women in general, and women doctors generally lend a sympathetic listening ear and a responsive word. Women seem instinctively to know how complex the family relationships are when a member of the family is sick and can often bring emotional support as well as medical care. Women don't tend to think of a patient as "that appendicitis in Room 213."

"Women physicians," concludes Dr. Mayer, "can be counted on, I believe, to improve the humanity of the hospital over and above what the nurses can provide, to help do away with the harshness and impersonality of the admission procedure, with the interminable wait to which mothers and children--and low-income wage earners--are subjected daily in the clinics of our large cities."

Medicine needs women to strengthen the profession's concern with the quality of life, the multitude of health-related problems of poverty, lawlessness, crowding, and alienation. The commitment that women physicians make to children's problems, extending beyond physiologic disability into those social and psychological realms so often relegated by physicians to the non-medical area, bring attributes--of concern, of empathy, of heart--that often are in short supply in the world today.

9

At the International Conference of Women in 1972 Representative Martha E. Key of Kansas asked why only 7 percent of the physicians in the United States are women, observing that we have the worst record in the Western world.

In the United States, as in most other countries, healing the ill, attending at childbirth, or caring for the elderly were traditionally regarded as feminine work. Even in our country today 75 percent of the total health-care work force, including nurses, technicians, aides, and hospital cleaning employees, are women, says Barbara Ehrenreich of the Women's Health Forum of New York. She adds that women in health care are concentrated in the low-pay, low-status jobs and are effectively denied admission to the elite. The evolution of Western medicine into a lucrative technological science paved the way for men to take over the profession as it rose in prestige and income (Ehrenreich and English).

For better or worse the women's-rights movement is definitely focusing on the meaninglessness of woman's life, particularly her later life, when many middle-aged women despair, with a despair whose specific character--as Kierkegaard observed, "is precisely that it is unaware of being despair."

Estelle Ramey has enjoyed as successful a marriage as a career. Born in Michigan just as women in this century were about to vote for the first time, Dr. Ramey earned a doctorate in physiology at the University of Chicago after marrying and having two children. Her professional career began as a teacher of chemistry at Queens College in New York in 1938, continued during the War at the University of Tennessee in Knoxville, and after the War at the University of Chicago School of Medicine and the Medical Research Institute of Michael Reese Hospital. She is now professor at Georgetown Medical Center in Washington, D. C. Her husband is a distinguished attorney, their son is a physician, their daughter a lawyer, head of the California A. C. L. U.

"We have so many anonymous women in this country whose talents could move the world," says Dr. Ramey. "In my own family, my daughter-in-law was a student nurse when she and my medical-student son got married 12 years ago. They have one child, and she decided she wanted to be a physician. She now has a reputation as one of the truly outstanding young doctors in the program."

Asked if it is harder for a woman to be admitted to medical school, Dr. Ramey observed, "Curiously, medical-school admissions committees have not had to search their consciences about female discrimination. The percentage of women accepted into medical schools has been almost exactly the same percentage as women who applied. (In 1929 women represented 3.5 percent of all applicants and 4.5 percent of all acceptances. The astonishingly small percentage of women doctors in this country reflects the psychological roadblocks thrown up for girls early in life."

Dr. Rosalyn Yalow, Nobel prize winner in medicine, believes there has been "marked professional discrimination against women and other disadvantaged groups for admission to medical schools ... and strong social pressures ... to discourage women from professional careers."

Unquestionably, women need men to support their militancy in seeking equal opportunity. Volatile, vocal, and sometimes vehement, the women's-liberation movement has the potential to be a terrifying explosive business, making for difficult relationships with men. In its extreme form it could create hostility that could lead not only to divorce between man and woman, but also between woman and the world.

"My boss thought it was fine to have women on the staff of the school, but he didn't expect them to want to advance or to be aggressive. He played the father-figure. But I wanted to be promoted. He would look at his committees and never appoint a woman to a committee or give a woman any control, of course," claimed Carolyn Rozier, professor of anatomy. After three years as a physical therapist Rozier decided she could be more effective in an allied health field where she could work independently, without taking orders from a physician. As a physical therapist, she believed she knew her work and how to evaluate what would help a patient and what was the most effective treatment, but a physician in charge of the patient often would not give her permission to do what she thought best. She believed that the physician resisted the assistant's expertise because he wanted full control of the financial relationship between doctor and patient.

Rozier received an assistantship for graduate study at the medical school in Oklahoma City. As a physical therapist, she was already knowledgeable about anatomy, and she

decided to expand that special area of interest. The head of
the anatomy department wanted only Ph. D. candidates, and
Rozier was one of three women accepted. "I felt confident
in that atmosphere. I was treated as an equal, as someone
who knew something. "

She enrolled in other courses at the medical school
to qualify for a Ph. D. in anatomy. "But we were discouraged
from taking courses with other medical students, courses with
less detail and substance in a medical program which had
been cut from four to three years. As future teachers, we
studied in greater depth, and I put in four years and wrote
a dissertation on work space of the upper extremity of the
amputee. " She became director of physical therapy at Texas
Women's University, Denton.

A cooperative spirit between men and women in total
health care will make the female therapist, anesthetist, or
psychiatric social worker a partner and equal in the care of
patients and erode the Olympian position that American physicians occupy. Dr. Rozier observes that often the pharmacist knows more about drugs than the doctor, but has to fill
the prescription that an even uninformed doctor orders. So,
too, in the case of the physical therapist, the doctor might
do well to listen to the well-trained paramedical worker.

When singer Pearl Bailey observed in a panel of professionals that she had just survived an earthquake and
thought that women, who were mothers and therefore "closer
to the earth, " were more affected by the disaster than men,
Dr. Estelle Ramey replied through gritted teeth: the only
way women are closer to the earth is because "we have to
clean up the dirt of the world. " Resentfully she added that
many men in the audience had come to hear the panel merely to be entertained. Men feel that women aspiring to be
professionals are "sex starved. " But, Dr. Ramey said,
"men in this audience have far more fragile cardio-vascular
systems than the women. Many will die of heart attacks
within three years. " She insisted that she did not want to
put down men. "Most of them have a hell of a time in this
society. But then, so do women. "

What really riled Dr. Ramey in recent years was the
publication of a medical book illustrated with seductive female nudes more suitable to a barroom calendar than to a
textbook. As president of the Association of Women in

Science, Dr. Ramey launched an organized boycott against the publisher. Implied in the Hippocratic Oath that every doctor takes, she claimed, "is an objective, nonprurient attitude toward patients. Examination of a female patient by a male doctor is an objective procedure that does not involve sexuality on either side." The textbook The Anatomical Basis of Medical Practice promoted a "lascivious approach to the study of anatomy" that was, Dr. Ramey insisted, "an obscene denigration of women and indeed of the men practicing medicine." The book, she continued, "was obviously intended to make a lot of money by gingering up a rather dull subject with the fun and games of prurient photographs of leering naked women in seductive poses. The authors smirk and preen themselves throughout ... they use coy undulating nymphs to illustrate anatomical land marks such as the left big toe ... they show no naked men in full manly glory."

The Association of Women in Science, livid over this approach to medicine, could not have chosen a more articulate president than Estelle Ramey.

"The purpose of AWIS," she insists, "was to help women in science overcome the very obvious discriminations in salaries, promotions, and rank that everybody knows about." Then she lets the National Academy of Sciences have it: "It's a very prestigious organization, and if you get elected to it, it's very helpful to you in terms of status in the scientific community, both as to money and rank. But out of about 900 members only 11 are women."

As for the future of The Anatomical Basis of Medical Practice (which was intended for freshman medical students), the book had to be entirely redone. The publisher stopped advertising the book, and the authors took it off the market and out of bookstores.

Estelle Ramey had proven again her belief that "women are a remarkable and marvelous sex: the female of the species, any species, is sturdier than the male from the moment of conception to the last hurrah."

"Stereotypes are bred in the bone of a society, and the stereotype of the woman doctor is a horse-faced, flat-chested female in supphose who sublimates her sex starvation in a passionate embrace of the New England Journal of Medicine.... It takes considerable determination for a young girl to ignore this threat to her image as a desirable woman,

Dr. Estelle Ramey

and only a pitifully small number of women risk it. It's enough to make a cat cry," she concludes.

The bias against women becoming doctors begins "at the time of the baby's birth, when someone asks, 'Boy or girl? A girl? Too bad. Next time it may be a boy,'" observes Jeannette Piccard, widow of famed balloonist Jean Piccard of France. Madame Piccard, an engineer and pilot, insists, "The inexorable separation of the sexes continues through life." In kindergarten little girls are given nurses' caps to play with; little boys receive stethoscopes.

At a seminar in the auditorium of Baylor College of Medicine in fall 1973, hundreds of high school girls heard women medical students tell them, "You can be a doctor! Don't let anyone scare you off." Dr. Christie Saller, a nephrologist in private practice, stated that "a woman going into medicine has to realize she'll frighten some men. But if she has what it takes to become a doctor, then she won't

be upset by losing that kind of man." Like other women
practicing medicine, she finds herself juggling many roles;
she never felt picked on as a medical student, however.
"The prevailing attitude is a matter of proving yourself.
Every physician has to do that."

The important thing, according to medical students
Beverly Siegal and Judy Craven, is not to let school coun-
selors steer you into stereotyped roles as a nurse or therapist or let anyone compromise your goals.

Medical training is grueling, and no doctor remem-
bers it as easy.

In Houston Dr. Jean Liles tried private practice for
a year, then switched to work that allowed more time for
her family. In charge of the emergency room at Hermann
Hospital, she works from seven to seven, four nights a
week. She's not on call the other days. "Beware of boy
friends who try to talk you out of your medical career,"
she advises. She dated a fellow who convinced her to try
pharmacy, which seemed to him more appropriate work for
a woman. She hated it. In the meantime she met and
married a man who encouraged her desire to go to medical
school.

"You need somebody to back you. You have bleak
moments when you think it's not worth the hard work. The
hours are bad, and you're so tired. But my husband was
there saying, 'It's the thing to do,'" Dr. Liles recalls.
Her husband, going after a graduate degree in physics,
wanted his wife to have the same professional satisfactions
as he anticipated. In her senior year in medical school
Jean Liles had a baby. That didn't make life any easier.

"Being in training and having small children is hard,"
recalls Dr. Elizabeth B. Connell of Manhattan. ("If you're
going to be competitive and effective in a traditionally masculine field like medicine, you must be willing to work as
hard and as well as your male associates.) It's destructive
to the image of women in medicine to demand all sorts of
concessions because you have ovaries and have babies."
Connell took her children with her to professional conferences abroad. Now she sees how proud they are of her.

Three generations of women in Dr. Connell's family

Dr. Priscilla Campbell earned a Ph. D. from the University of Colorado school of medicine and is involved in investigating the interaction of cells. She is on the staff of the National Jewish Hospital and Research Center in Denver.

worked outside the home. "It was natural for me to think that a woman's role could go beyond having children and taking care of a house." Both her parents were psychologists, and young Elizabeth was tested regularly to learn her abilities, aptitudes, and interests. After her freshman year in college she worked for a summer in a local hospital and found that medicine had great appeal. She married a fellow medical student, and after graduation they set up general practice in a small town in Maine. Five years and three children later the couple returned to the city for advanced training, he to become an allergist, she to specialize in obstetrics and gynecology.

Dr. Connell published a report in Family Planning Perspectives based on a review of oral contraceptive research from medical centers throughout the world, that concluded that the "pill is a highly effective and generally safe" method of birth control, but not for all women. "With the pill, as with every medication, its benefits must always be weighed against the risks." In the question of cancer risk, Dr. Connell believes that there is "no evidence connecting use of oral contraceptives with cancer of the breast." Indeed, she finds, there's some evidence that the pill may actually be protective against benign breast disease. However, risk of thromboembolism and strokes is confirmed by recent research, with death resulting to approximately three per 100,000 women per year taking the pill. No link was established between pill use and liver problems. For gall bladder disease Dr. Connell found increased risk associated with pill use. There is also the problem some women experience--a slight elevation of blood pressure from use of the pill. As the mother of six children Dr. Connell was interested in the effects of the pill on the fetus, and her report states that this is an area requiring further study.

Despite her active medical career in biomedical sciences at New York's Rockefeller Foundation and as chair of the National Committee of Planned Parenthood, Dr. Connell finds time for swimming, horseback riding, and mountain climbing. She gets a kick out of life. Her children have a view of society and of women's roles they would never have had if their mother had been a homebody.

Dr. Dorothy V. Whipple, a pediatrician practicing in Washington, D. C., observes herself as "Exhibit A--a woman physician who has practiced medicine as well as led the life of a married woman and the mother of a family ...; it is not a rare thing to be doctor, wife, and mother."

In an interview with the author, she shared her feelings about her triple role.

Dr. Jane C. Harnett was a staff physician with the National Jewish Hospital and Research Center in Denver, which has a long tradition of fighting respiratory diseases. Dr. Harnett received her medical degree from SUNY/Buffalo.

About being a doctor, the qualifications are the same whether one is a man or a woman. It requires a certain degree of intelligence; it requires also dedication, a sense of responsibility, and an enjoyment of hard work ...; all of these qualifications are a little bit greater in the girls who actually go through with the arduous medical training. One finds that some men whose talents might be consid-

ered mediocre do succeed in medicine, but mediocre women either do not start on a medical career
or are discouraged and drop out along the way.
As a result, there are very few mediocre women
doctors.

About being a doctor and a wife? There is a
vast difference between being a doctor and a husband and being a doctor and a wife. There are
many things a wife does for a husband--and I do
not mean mechanical chores like vacuuming and
cleaning that can be done by someone else. I
mean truly wifely chores like arranging a good social life, buying gifts, sending Christmas cards,
all the dozens of things that make life run smooth-
ly for a married couple. It takes some degree of
executive ability to arrange life so that the multitude of little things that must be done get done.
I am sure that every working woman, whether she
be doctor or in any other profession, has at times
wished she had a "wife."

There is one more thing about being a doctor
and a wife, and that is the kind of man one chooses.
The husband of a professional woman must be suf-
ficiently confident of himself that he can accept the
wife's profession without threat to his own ego....

Let me remind you that I am not only a doctor,
a wife, and a mother, but also a pediatrician,
which gives me not only a maternal interest in
children but also a professional one.

My feeling is that the first year or two of a
child's life are of great importance for his future.
Anyone who brings a child into the world has the
responsibility of seeing to it that in the early
years the child is well nurtured. There are circumstances under which the care of a baby can be
done well by someone other than the mother. On
the other hand, a few years spent at home by the
highly trained professional doctor need not be considered wasted years professionally. Not only do
the children have a mother's care, but the doctor
herself learns things she can never learn in any
school. She comes to know, because she has experienced, the pleasure of watching a child balance

the top block on his tower; she knows the frustra-
tion of never having a minute to read a book; she
knows the boredom and loneliness of home chores
and home confinement; she may experience the soul-
chilling fear of watching beside a seriously ill
child. . . .

This knowledge is of infinite value to any doctor
who ultimately deals with people. It provides the
basis of an empathy which is an essential ingredi-
ent in the art of medicine. The practice of medicine is not all a matter of biochemistry.

Thus, a few years at home are not wasted professionally; they bring rich rewards in understanding. It is only women who are given the opportunity for this kind of learning.

After children are a little grown up and the
mother goes back to her profession, she continues
to have domestic responsibilities. When she comes
home she needs energy to read stories, to talk, to
listen, to play. The woman who is exhausted after
her day's work and wants to kick off her shoes and
relax will not make a success of her maternal responsibilities. While mechanical domestic chores
can, and should, be delegated to hired help, there
is no delegation of the role of counselor, companion or guide.

Having her babies was the hardest problem of all,
says Houstonian Helen Hittner, who at 32 (1979) is married
to a judge and is the mother of three children ("our treasures"). Regarded by other physicians with enormous respect, she is at the top of her profession, a fellow of the
American College of Surgeons and a recipient of a grant from
the Retina Research Foundation for "Ocular Screening for
Retinopathy of Prematurity." She teaches ophthalmology to
Baylor University pediatricians and has received a special
award for the quality of her teaching.

Although Hittner was valedictorian of her graduating
high school class, she had trouble getting into Rice University, which was slow about enrolling women or Jews. She
graduated Phi Beta Kappa with high honors from Rice but
had trouble getting acceptance to Baylor University College
of Medicine, because it was slow about enrolling women or
Jews. ("I filled two slots for them!" she notes.)

One of three women among 80 medical students in her freshman class, Hittner, together with another woman, was given a fat, bloated, stinking cadaver. The class was started on the study of breasts, a most unusual beginning. Determinedly she worked away, refusing to succumb to disgust. The distress of the rest of the class to the obvious act of intolerance--assignment to a rotting cadaver--was so strong that the cadaver was eventually taken away from the women students.

Hittner grew up in a close-knit family that was forever urging a male cousin to go to medical school.

> Why is it so important for him to be a doctor and not for me? I began telling people that was what I wanted to do. In school, teachers would respond, "Be a nurse." Sometimes people smiled or laughed, so I stopped telling them I was going to be a doctor, but I watched my cousin go to Rice and I followed his example, and when it came time to decide on a major, I took all the science courses.

Although Baylor College of Medicine had not exactly pounced on her application, Hittner graduated with honors. Her internship was in pediatrics, and she went to Harvard Medical School for studies in ophthalmology and then did a residency at Baylor-affiliated hospitals. She comes from a family of pediatricians, so she feels comfortable among her role models. With another Houston ophthalmologist, Dr. Alice R. McPherson, she has studied premature infants with retinal detachments. (She notes that McPherson, president of the Retina Society of America, was one of the first doctors to help her.) Dr. Hittner has an impressive list of publications, and says smilingly that she enjoys writing and makes a hobby of reflecting on her research and recording it.

Her patients are infants and children from all classes of society, and she believes that patient acceptance of a woman doctor in ophthalmology is excellent because of greater hand dexterity and the concept of a mother-figure. Hittner is a warm and generous woman; speaking of the mother of a blind child, she recalls that she talked to her for an hour while the waiting room was full of patients. "She cried, I cried, and then when I had offered what help I could, she left, and I told my secretary, 'Don't charge her anything.'"

Dr. Helen Hittner, Houston ophthalmologist, with husband
and her "treasures"

The neonatal ophthalmologist sees many premature
infants who have severe problems. A baby who weighs only
three pounds after four months and has a detached retina is
not an uncommon challenge in her work. "Catching an eye
defect in a baby early enough to do successful surgery is my
real role," says Hittner.

Her husband David speaks of her with respect and
esteem, and her children are proud of their mother. "They
tell me when their friends for whom I've written a prescription are wearing their glasses." She recalls that she was
doing surgery when contractions began for the birth of her
first daughter, and she conscientiously completed the surgery
and then went to obstetrics to be delivered.

Functionaries in the medical school called her after
the baby was born, not to congratulate her, but to ask if she
were entitled to the vacation she was taking! Hittner laughs
without bitterness when she tells these stories.

Dr. Barbara Monstavicius has no children; her husband is a pathologist. Being an eye surgeon was a dream

she had from her girlhood. She was encouraged by the nuns who taught her in high school, but "I never expected the dream to become reality," she admits. Now practicing in San Francisco, Dr. Monstavicius, a specialist in the use of the laser beam in eye surgery, wishes more women would become surgeons. She scoffs at the idea of women swooning at the sight of blood. "In my experience it's the men who faint."

In the '70s she was one of about 300 women surgeons in the United States. Ophthalmology is a microcosm, a window opening on the world, she claims, a specialty that demands meticulous attention to detail, ideally suited for women. "I love surgery. I like working with my hands."

Dr. Monstavicius received her medical training at the University of Illinois and served her residency at the University of Iowa and has been a practicing surgeon since. "Every time you walk into a room to see a patient, or to operate, you never know exactly what the next few minutes will produce--chaos and the unexpected or reassurance. "It's a challenge which never ends."

Following morning surgery, she shuttles between two offices at opposite ends of the city. When a cornea shows up late in the evening, she rushes back to the hospital for a cornea transplant. "When the cornea is available, you operate."

Dr. Monstavicius is not enthusiastic about women electing pediatrics as their specialty. "Pediatrics, which attracts many women doctors, is a very demanding specialty. I've known women doctors whose marriages cracked up, especially if the husband wasn't in medicine. The men can't understand why wives have to get up and race out in the middle of a dinner party. Pediatricians can be overworked and overwhelmed. Many have told me this."

"It's an interesting comment on our culture," observes Estelle Ramey, that

pediatrics accounts for one-third of those with specialty certification. Other interests of women are psychiatry, internal medicine, obstetrics and gynecology, and anesthesiology. But women are beginning to seek out less traditional "women's specialties. " More are going into surgery, for example. Surgery has always been a male specialty, along with internal medicine, pediatrics, and obstetrics.

In medicine, as in other fields, a woman often has to be better at her job in order to get the same recognition as her male counterpart. For example, despite the relatively large proportion of women on medical school faculties, practically no women are called to deanships or chairmanships of major departments. This is, incidentally, just as true in countries like the Soviet Union, which have up to 75 percent women doctors. There is a strong bias against women at the top even among men who happily entertain the notion of a woman assistant professor. The excuses are clichés, "Women are too prone to emotion, verbosity, pettiness, and pregnancy." Even when they try to act like men, they just aren't gentlemen.

Yet academic or institutional medicine is a more adaptable arrangement for a woman, and the reasons for such occupation choices are obvious. Full-time private practice is the most demanding of all social uses of a medical training. Most women doctors are married and have children. All the world continues to assume that this necessarily is a primary responsibility of the woman whatever her professional activities. Under these circumstances she seeks out areas of medical service more amenable to pre-scheduling and a flexible time input.

The income of women doctors tends to be lower, and women doctors spend more time with each patient, seeing fewer per day. The differences are significant, in that a woman in full-time private practice of internal medicine, according to surveys, sees an average of 56 patients per week; a man averages 100 ("Hello, how are you? Well, I want you to have all these tests taken").

"Very few women graduates of medical school drop out of the profession entirely, " according to Dr. Ramey. "Of all physicians receiving the M. D. between 1931 and 1956, only 1. 7 percent of the women never practiced medicine at all. Yet this is appreciably higher than the comparable fig-

ure of 0. 1 percent for men. " Any medical school graduate
who doesn't practice medicine constitutes a serious social
loss.

Furthermore, far more women than men use their
skills only part-time during their child-rearing
years. After the age of 45, however, these wom-
en become increasingly active in the delivery of
medical services, and since they tend to outlive
men by about seven to ten years, they stay in
practice relatively longer. (Overall, women physicians have not contributed as many physician hours
as their male colleagues.) The reasons are not
mental, physical, or emotional. They are social
and economic. Many of these problems can be resolved by better social engineering (Ramey, a).

In 1968 Dr. Alice D. Chenoweth, in her talk as re-
tiring president of the American Medical Women's Association, challenged her colleagues: "Has society's expectation
of women gradually changed so that now talented women may
be expected to aspire to a professional career and at the
same time pursue their feminine roles of wife and mother?
Self-fulfillment and a substantial contribution to society are
worthy goals for women. "

The question of what happens to children during a
professional woman's child-bearing and child-rearing years
is important in career determination. Many women manage
well to have careers that enrich the lives of their own, and
often of other's, children.

Professional women have begun to promote day-care
centers, not only for their own children, but for the children of all working mothers. The tradition that even professional women should stay home to care for the children
is an American idea. In other developed countries first-
rate day-care centers free mothers for work.

Furthermore, in order for women to become doctors
or scientists, husbands must assume a share in child-rearing
and housekeeping. "I have every confidence, " observes Dr.
Ramey, "in the innate ability of men to do as good a job
with household drudgery as women do. But the first major
step in freeing women to increase their services to society
must come from the establishment of sophisticated day-care
centers for their children. "

Dr. Susan Daum, a resident in internal medicine in New York's Mt. Sinai Hospital in 1970, declared that child care must be the responsibility of society, as health and medical treatment should be. "If the tax money that now goes into war and war industry could be diverted to human needs," said Dr. Daum, "then we could have all the schools and medical centers and day-care units we want."

An example of a woman with a large family is Marie Valdes-Dapena, formerly professor of pathology at Temple University in Philadelphia and now with the University of Miami school of medicine. When she examines the body of an infant claimed by crib death her concern is more than professional; it is involved and personal. An authority on sudden infant death, Dr. Valdes-Dapena is the mother of 11 children and the wife of Dr. Antonio Valdes-Dapena. Formerly chief pathologist at the Graduate Hospital of the University of Pennsylvania, she began her study of crib deaths when she was assistant at autopsies in the medical examiner's office. Between 1956 and 1963 she performed about 50 autopsies each year on infants who died suddenly. Two groups of parents who lost children to crib death--the National Foundation for Sudden Infant Death and the Philadelphia Guild for Infant Survival--elected her to their board.

With each of her six children born since 1956, she has, she admits, worried about crib death as an unsolved medical mystery that might affect her own family. The cause of crib death is unknown. A red substance found in the baby's brain has been implicated by one scientist-investigator. Death may result from parathyroid pathology, smothering, or shock, say some doctors, while others believe a top-heavy head might cause fatal cervical injury. Some point to honey, which may cause infant botulism.

Dr. Valdes-Dapena came to believe that the cause might be a power failure in the baby's vital mechanism, which controls such functions as respiration and heart action. Admitting that many questions remain unanswered, she holds that low birth weight may be related to crib death. The majority of infants who die suddenly and inexplicably exhibit an infection of the upper respiratory tract, made visible by light microscopy. Some doctors believe that the baby is asphyxiated because infants do not readily breathe through their mouths, and the respiratory infection may have caused nasal obstruction.

"Approximately one out of every 350 infants dies

Marie Valdes-Dapena

suddenly and unexpectedly--a victim of crib death, one of
medicine's more frustrating unsolved mysteries," observes
Valdes-Dapena.

Dr. Valdes-Dapena, now in private practice in Miami,
Fla., is compassionate and careful when telling a mother
there is no visible explanation for the death of her child.
"I try to put myself in the mother's place, but it is impossible to imagine such a shock." She traces her interest in
crib death to her medical school days, when she met her
future husband, then a resident in pathology.

"I had my mind set on becoming a radiologist after
graduation from Temple. One day Antonio suggested that I
apply for a residency in pathology and that we get married
(not necessarily in that order)." In 1945 she accepted both
proposals. Her husband was consistently supportive of her
career.

Finding time for a profession and 11 children "takes
some doing." Fortunately, being a pathologist allows Valdes-
Dapena to leave the office behind at the end of the work day,

and the doctor stresses how close the family remains. An important time of the day is supper, served at a ten-foot-long table. "We all eat together."

Women doctors agree that the life situation is less complex if the husband is also a doctor. Women physicians are not as likely to promote the God-image. When Dr. Philip A. Baratta, Jr., discovered that many of his women patients (one-fourth) were married to doctors, the psychiatrist created a class called "Physician's Wife--No Bed of Roses" at the University of California/San Diego. The course was so successful that Baratta introduced two more: "Doctor as Spouse and Parent--So Little Time" and "Balancing the Demands of Family Life and Medical Practice."

Social life, revolving around professional contacts, may be stultifying to the husband of a woman physician, just as it may be for the wife of a male doctor. A geophysicist remarked, "You don't know how deadly a party can be until you've spent hours with pediatricians. You can almost hear the sick kids wailing!"

Sometimes a couple cooperate in research, as in the case of Dr. Lida Holmes Mattman, associate professor of microbiology at Wayne State University in Detroit, who with her husband has investigated the role of L-variants in the failure of conventional treatment of septicemia or blood poisoning. Both doctors Mattman discovered in their research numerous L-variants of the pathogen in the blood of two patients whose septicemia became increasingly severe during treatment. These studies have launched new attacks on chronic infections.

In recent years the Army and Navy have made greater opportunities for young couples wanting to become physician teams. Drs. Roger and Theresa Crenshaw, seeking summer work when they were sophomores in the Medical School at the University of California/San Diego, investigated the Navy's clinical clerkship and program. Single at the time, the medical students were highly motivated to join. "We got our first raw exposure to clinical medicine. It was a fun summer; we could be together and do what we wanted to do." Navy funds paid their medical schooling during their senior year. Roger Crenshaw says, "I was able to live like a human being for the first time."

A military wedding followed graduation from medical

school. After their honeymoon the couple interned at Balboa Naval Hospital in San Diego and found they were doing useful work in the military, including research, which they find rewarding. "I've seen diseases here at the naval hospital I'd probably never see in 20 years of civilian practice," Roger Crenshaw says. "I've seen 30 cases of malaria, which I might never have seen in a civilian hospital."

Another couple, the Joneses, are Army doctors. Two months after they were married they faced separation, for Frank Jones was called for military service. What could his wife, Dr. Carole Jones, do to keep them together?

She did not find the decision easy, but she volunteered to go with her husband to Vietnam, carrying with them brand-new commissions as captains in the Army. For almost six months they were in the dispensary at Long Binh. "One of us was on call every night," Frank Jones recalls. "We never got off together all the time we were there." The husband-and-wife team rounded out their year in Southeast Asia at Can Tho, where conditions were a little better. "We worked closely with the Vietnamese, and my wife, whose main interest is pediatrics, gained valuable experience." Completing their enlistment service at Walson Army Hospital, Fort Dix, N. J., they were awarded Bronze Stars for meritorious service.

Progress is being made in the armed services. By 1977 women were receiving commissions to study medicine and to serve as doctors with the Army and Navy Air Forces. A consulting physician at Veterans Administration Hospital in Manhattan, Dr. Anne Logan Davis was elected 1975-76 president of the New York Lung Association. She held an associate professorship of clinical medicine at New York University School of Medicine and directed respiratory therapy and the emphysema clinic at Bellevue Hospital.

In the 1960s medical schools began making adjustments for physician-mothers. Instead of being bound to the usual non-stop 36-month residency, women at New York Medical College, for instance, might divide their training into four nine-month periods. Such a program permitted women to spend evenings and most weekends and holidays with their families. In seven years, in a practical, productive schedule, not one of the 48 women enrolled dropped out.

The Women's Equity Action League, an organization seeking equal opportunity for women, had filed sex-discrimination charges against all U. S. medical schools in the fall of 1970. Filed with the Department of Health, Education and Welfare, the charges focused attention on a dozen universities, which were required to show evidence that they were encouraging applications from women.

"What women in medicine ought to say is, 'Now look, make it possible for us to have our families and our jobs too,'" insists Dr. Leona Baumgartner, former New York City Commissioner of Health and professor of social medicine at Harvard ("Women M. D.'s Join the Fight"). As New York's first woman Commissioner of Health, she was concerned with the health and welfare of some eight million people in the 1950s, and it was plain that she was thriving "at the cutting edge of social progress" (Modern Medicine). As a pediatrician, she had become director of the maternal and child health program in New York City in 1940.

Data on women physicians collected since 1931 reveal that about 75 percent have married, and the proportion of married women doctors is rising. Some 60 percent of the women married other doctors or other medical scientists.

"Propinquity," Estelle Ramey points out, "is a powerful matchmaker, and love blooms happily even in the anatomy lab." Dr. Ramey holds that women doctors are entitled to a normal home life. Most women refuse to abandon their children entirely to the care of others, and once the doctors have completed residency, they manage to do a neat juggling act between balancing home and career. Dr. Nancy Hendrie of Concord, Mass., virtually abandoned her family to the costly care of a housekeeper so she could complete her residency in pediatrics at Children's Medical Center in Boston. Since then the center has finally yielded to a dozen petitions from Dr. Hendrie to operate a part-time residency in pediatrics, women's prime specialty.

No one expects men to deny themselves the pleasures of a home and the joys of parenthood in order to have a satisfactory career. Yet some medical schools regard maternity as a misdemeanor and require new mothers to return to class within two or three weeks after childbirth. Because of such attitudes, medicine is a career only for women who are stubbornly determined. Dr. Edith Shapiro, a psychiatrist at Manhattan's Beth Israel Medical Center,

was forced to delay her entrance into medical school by a
year when faculty members learned of her pregnancy. She
avoided another delay only by concealing her second pregnancy and managed to have the baby during a summer vacation, stoically returning to classes two weeks later. That's
the kind of determination required for a woman to succeed
in medicine.

In the '60s women accounted for about 6 percent of
the nation's 260,000 doctors. By 1972 they accounted for
7.6 percent out of 345,000. Despite continuing resistance
to women in medical schools, the number of women studying
for medical careers increased in 1973-74 to 19.7 percent of
first-year enrollments (Dube). By 1979 of the 408,000 medical doctors in the United States, some 34,000 were women,
and about 35.6 percent of these were specialists, in every
medical area from psychiatry to pediatrics. One of every
four medical students in 1979 is female.

Roberta Fenlon

In 1971 Dr. Roberta
Fenlon was the first woman
ever elected president of a
state medical society, the
25,000-member California
Medical Association. Then
around 60 years of age, Dr.
Fenlon, a specialist in internal medicine in San Francisco was a faculty member
at the University of California. She recalls the dis-
crimination she had to fight.
Her doctor father, thinking
that medical school would be
too strenuous for a woman,
had said, "No daughter of
mine is going to medical
school." Her mother kept
saying, be a mother, a

teacher, a nurse. "There's nothing finer than a good
schoolteacher," she insisted.

In Clinton, Iowa, in the 1930s, Fenlon helped her
father in his medical office, and, ignoring her parents' advice, worked her way through college. Asked if she has
encountered discrimination as a woman in her practice, she

insists, absolutely not. "My colleagues have been wonderful, all of them."

And what about in medical school? "Oh, I could say
that maybe there was some discrimination in medical school.
But I can also say I saw some of my professors discriminate against some of my male colleagues. Teachers, after
all, are only human."

Dr. Fenlon, who never married, agrees with the
goals of women's liberationists, but she objects to some of
their extremist methods. "I can see what women's lib is
saying and trying to do in terms of jobs and equal rights,"
says Dr. Fenlon, "but any changes in our place in this
world must come through evolution and not revolution."

Nevertheless, women in the liberation movement have
raised the consciousness of medical schools, such as the
Albert Einstein College of Medicine in New York. Take
Judy Blitman, a 1961 graduate of Radcliffe. In 1970 she
went to Einstein to apply and was told she "didn't look like
a doctor." To discourage her further, the school informed
her that the preceding applicant already had a Ph.D. in
molecular biology. Blitman had hated science as an undergraduate, and her grades reflected that hatred. But she
was encouraged by the "premed coach," Sylvia Bassoff, to
enroll anyway in the Einstein general studies courses offered
at night for working students. She blossomed in the postgraduate premed training program, among other women dis-
satisfied with their status and pay in other professions.

Vassar graduate Barbara Geiger, who had been told
medicine was only for super-duper students, at 26 decided to
get out of Newsweek offices, where she had specialized, she
says, in "sharpening some guy's pencil." With straight A's
in premed, she was accepted by Cornell Medical College.
English major Barbara Nash, whose brother was already a
doctor, decided to switch to medicine, enrolling at the
Columbia College of Physicians and Surgeons.

By 1978 the mass infusion of women into medicine
prompted speculation on where this might lead: Dr. Naomi
Bluestone of Montefiore Hospital in New York, warned that
male doctors might feel threatened and try to reassert authority and regain control of medical-school enrollment. At
the turn of the century 20 percent of the physicians in Boston were women, and the early 1900s saw many male doctors

fighting to wipe out female advances. When women first entered medicine most opted for pediatrics, child psychiatry, or public-health positions. Women were satisfied, as we shall see later, with lower pay and slower career advancement and recognition, and some dropped out of the profession early in their child-bearing years.

Now women are entering specialties that have long been regarded as the masculine arena, and today's women physicians demand equal pay and equal respect. Vocal in protecting themselves from the slurs of prejudice against women, Dr. Bluestone says, "They rebuke their professors when subjected to sexist remarks. They are establishing mutual support networks to countervail the 'old boy' clubbiness of the locker room."

Nor are women flattered to be "one of the boys." We know that in the '60s only 6 percent of freshman medical students were women. By 1979, due to federal legislation prohibiting discrimination in educational opportunities, female enrollment had passed the 25-percent mark. In the next decade half the nation's graduating physicians may be women. The dinosaur is twitching!

"THE DINOSAUR IS TWITCHING"

3. Women and Medicine Abroad

Was there less discrimination abroad against women in medicine? A century ago Sir William Jenner, Queen Victoria's doctor, lecturing at the University of London, commented that he had "but one dear daughter, and would rather follow her bier to the grave than allow her to go through such a course of study" as medicine. His daughter, refusing gallantly to die an early death, became an ardent suffragist.

The opposition of the father to the careers of Sophia Jex-Blake, Karen Horney, and other famous women doctors seemed more to spur them on than to deter them.

When Mary Cassatt, the American artist who went to Paris and became a member of the French Impressionist group, was 20, she confided to her father her determination to be a professional painter. His reply was: "I would almost rather see you dead."

Anecdotal evidence supports the view that most countries have sex-bias built in, both in the way women are treated as individuals, as potential scholars, and as patients, and in their efforts to reach top-level positions in medicine and science. Women seem to have the least disadvantage in Turkey, where they may hold as many as 25 percent of the Ph. D.'s, high academic positions, and M. D.'s; and there appears to be little bias in the social sciences. Women have been emancipated only in recent years, and low-paid servants free women to seek fulfillment in scholarship, science and medicine.

In the '70s the United States--of all free-world countries--was closest to the bottom in numbers of women physicians. Seventeen western countries had upward of 20 percent women physicians. Three countries, Finland, the Philippines, and Thailand, had more than 25 percent. In

33

this decade the Iron Curtain countries had the highest percentage of women health scientists.

Switzerland was the first country to open its doors of
higher education to women. The University of Zurich offered
complete educational equality to women in 1854. In the first
years the number of women studying medicine ranged between
one and eight, and climbed to 88 in 1872-73. Most of the
women studying medicine in Zurich (and later in Bern) were
Russian, and mostly Jewish. The main problem that women
faced was that their undergraduate preparation was unequal
to the men's, but the medical faculty reported few problems
resulting from mixed classes and no concessions were made
for women. Ten women passed the M. D. examination in the
early years of the school, and three Russian women achieved
the degree in three years instead of the normal four and a
half (Böhmert, pp. 1-12).

In 1897 American women studying medicine at Zurich
University issued a guide to prospective students, full of
helpful information on costs, behavior, course offerings, and
suggestions on learning German. As we shall see, two
British women, Sophia Jex-Blake and Edith Pechey, unable
to get degrees in Britain, went to Bern and fulfilled the requirements of education and hospital work and took examinations to qualify them to become doctors.

In 1863 and 1864 a university charter prohibited
Russian women from studying science or medicine, and
Russian women, learning that the University of Zurich was
admitting women, went to Switzerland. The first Russian
women to graduate from the University of Zurich as physicians were M. A. Bokova and Nadya Prokofievna Suslova.
Dr. Suslova graduated within two years of her acceptance to
Zurich! Both women successfully defended their doctoral
theses. Suslova wrote on the "Lymphatic Heart."

The Russian women were extraordinary, and not only
brilliant in their studies; they also took courses in Western
revolutionary movements and history, socialism, and political economy. Russia may have been willing to have the
women become doctors (particularly at the expense of another
country), but the Russian government wasn't happy about the
women becoming activists. [In 1874 the women were called
home, but some medical students turned a deaf ear to the
call. Those who returned tended to join the revolutionary
movement, and of them many became leaders in the propaganda of the revolution (Dionesov, pp. 68-72).

Having jerked the women mid-stream from their medical education in Switzerland, the government found a severe doctor shortage in Russia on their hands in 1869. As a result the doors to medical schools were opened to women, and in 1872, the Czarist government opened the Women's Medical Courses in Petersburg. In St. Petersburg the Medico-Surgical Academy conferred its first degree on a woman, Varvara Alexandra Kashevarova-Rudneva. She had studied at the Institute for Midwives in St. Petersburg in 1861, graduated in 1862, and, after a year of delivering babies, decided to apply to the academy, from which she graduated in December 1868 with a gold medal for excellence. When her name was called, the graduating class gave an ovation that seemed to rise to the ceiling, sending shock waves through the assembly. Her insignia was presented to her, and her fellow students lifted her on a chair as though she were a bride. She was carried with triumphant songs through the hall, while applause thundered in waves around her.

In 1879 Edmund Rose wrote an article, "Zurich Female Students," for the Boston Medical and Surgical Journal in which he said that at first only earnest, hard-working, determined women entered the university, "but later many coquettish and hysterical ones." But at the time he was writing, he approved of the caliber of the woman student who proved industrious and did "not cause any great excitement." Women composed about a fourth of the total medical student population of Zurich.

When Faculties of Medicine were opened in Paris, dozens of Russian Jewish women went there with the idea of becoming doctors.

The great number of women doctors in Russia in the 1970s, from 65 to 85 percent of all physicians, resulted from the terrible need for doctors during the Second World War. With men at the battlefront, women had to take over hospitals and other services. Women had already proven themselves in medicine.

National Soviet policy encourages women to enter medicine and health sciences. Medicine in Russia seems to be held in less esteem than it is in other countries, and the best and brightest male students choose other professions.

Despite the great number of Russian women doctors, Soviet women do not regard themselves as living in the best of all possible worlds. They complain that they find it impossible to hire a baby-sitter or a maid because factories and stores offer higher pay for unskilled help. Women physicians are expected to come home from the hospital or office and do household chores, marketing and cooking, sometimes to the point of exhaustion. Public attitudes in Russia are a paradox. Women do heavy manual work, such as ditch digging, street paving, garbage collecting, and bus driving, but men bluntly refuse to share housework. Even where women have more gratifying positions, such as in medicine, teaching, and engineering, men are usually supervisors or "the boss. "

Despite raises in the early '70s, Russian physicians and teachers still have lower-than-average per capita incomes. Beginning doctors expect to earn less than $150 a month; after some ten years they are earning about $216 per month working for the state. Extra income is possible if they are willing to take extra patients.

Because doctors are so poorly paid they try to earn extra money. "This is illegal, " said one doctor who recently emigrated from Moscow, "and there is a certain amount of blackmarketing in operations. Say you need an operation. To go through regular channels, it may be a three-week affair, tests, surgery, recuperation. But you want to get it over with quickly. You make an appointment with a doctor you trust. Then doctor and patient work things out, but they don't feel honest about it. "

One Russian doctor has said, "Money isn't everything. We complain. True. But women patients are grateful to women doctors, who are sympathetic to their problems of pregnancy, birth control, childbirth, child-rearing. When it comes to menopause, the women patients particularly appreciate a sympathetic ear. "

In 1979 in Shanghai, China, there was a "Democracy Wall, " where citizens air their complaints. One doctor who felt he should be promoted covered 50 yards of the wall with testimonials from his patients!

In 1975 fully 90 percent of the obstetricians and gynecologists at the Anti-Imperialist Hospital in Peking were women. Visiting mainland China in 1971, American writer Edgar Snow reported interviewing his old friend, Dr. Lin

Ch'iao-chih, the first Chinese woman gynecologist to graduate from an English medical school. The leading gynecologist in the country, the 70-year-old Dr. Lin began her career as a pediatrician. "But I could not stand to see babies die. So I switched to bringing them to life" (Snow).

Long past retirement age, Dr. Lin practiced in the former Peking Union Medicine Center, founded and financed by the Rockefeller Foundation in 1912. Here many Chinese doctors practice the age-old art of acupuncture, an Oriental practice using needles to treat illness. Mysterious to Westerners, this method has been dismissed in the West--out of hand--as folklore or superstition, and only recently have Westerners acknowledge that this treatment frequently works.

Chinese doctors, however, do not make many claims for acupuncture for inducing abortion. Such experiments have had only poor results. Dr. Lin hoped that the need for abortions would be reduced through the teaching of birth control in family-planning clinics. Women in China are encouraged to use contraceptives. Should a mother become pregnant with a third child, abortion is available on request. A few first-pregnancy mothers ask for abortion, but doctors persuade them to have their babies, unless the mother's health is endangered. Abortion, like birth-control pills, is free of charge in China. Since 1968 the 22-day pill, which was developed in China, has increasingly replaced other contraceptive devices. All medical organizations, mobile units, "barefoot doctors" and army medical teams distribute control propaganda and pills (Falto).

"Women want to be free to work for their nation," said Dr. Lin. Infant mortality was running more than 100 per 1,000 people at the time the Communists came to power in 1949. That figure dropped to nine per 1,000 by the '70s. By the end of 1978 China's birthrate was down to 15.5 per 1,000 and the death rate to six per 1,000. By comparison, the U.S. figures were 15 per 1,000 birthrate, and nine per 1,000 death rate, causing a yearly population increase of 6 percent. *

Dr. Lin said that natural childbirth is common in China. About 90 percent of deliveries are done without anesthetics, but in difficult deliveries anesthesia and other modern methods benefit the patient.

_____

*Chicago Sun-Times, December 13, 1978.

Unquestionably, China's family-planning campaign is more effective in cities than in the country, where 85 percent of the population resides. On farms enforcement appears to be lax. Many couples have children to help with the work. In the city couples may have a first child at any time, but if they desire another child, they have to get on a four-to-six-year waiting list. The population bureaucracy tells them whether or not a wife may have a baby. A woman who has an abortion gets two weeks off with pay, one who gets sterilized, three weeks; male sterilization allows for one week off. Birth control is socially desirable: overproductive parents are publicly chastised, and they may have their rice ration cut or pay increases denied, or they may be passed over for promotion at work.

Swedish women with aspirations to be doctors attend tuition-free medical schools. Speaking about medicine in Sweden, Dr. Anne Lavall Sundstrom, visiting in Florida, said that Sweden has high taxes, but citizens are entitled to free hospital care. Women are cared for throughout their pregnancy and lying-in period. The government provides a subsistence allowance for every child born, and education through university graduation is entirely free.

Dr. Sundstrom, a graduate of the Karolinska Institute in Stockholm (the college that awards the Nobel prizes and is the largest medical school in Sweden), said that a general shortage of doctors and psychiatrists in Sweden requires newly graduated doctors to spend three months in psychiatric practice. She herself spent six months in general practice and the three required months in psychiatry in a remote village, making three or four house calls per day and sometimes as many as ten per day during an influenza epidemic. At the end of a long day she enjoyed having coffee with her patient in some cottage kitchen.

As a small girl, Sundstrom was a gymnast, but at 16 she was stricken with polio. She was able to come to America to be treated in Florida's Hope Haven Children's Hospital, and, fascinated by the dedication of the doctors and what they did for her recovery, she decided she had to be a doctor herself (Kent).

In Israel a woman doctor is considered an asset to family stability. At Hadassah-Hebrew University Medical

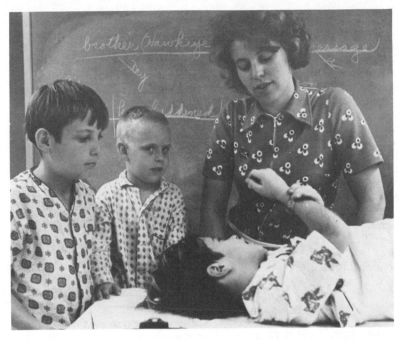

Dr. Anne Lavall Sundstrom, a Swedish physician, visits Hope Haven Children's Hospital in Florida. (Photo courtesy Florida Times-Union.)

Center women doctors Chloe Tal and Alaine R. Berman are engaged in separate research that has attracted international attention and respect.

Dr. Tal, an immunologist and a graduate of the Hebrew University-Hadassah Medical School, is developing a test for the early detection of cancer. She reported in 1971 that she had discovered a certain protein, which she called "T-globulin," in the blood of persons with cancer and--surprisingly--in pregnant women. T-globulin couldn't be found in the blood of patients with a wide vareity of other diseases.

Testing 520 patients in different departments of her hospital, Dr. Tal found T-globulin in the blood of 356 of them. Subsequently, it was determined that 350 of the 356 patients with T-globulin had verified cases of cancer, three were suspected but nonverified cancer patients and three were pregnant.

Thirteen patients who showed positive for T-globulin had not been diagnosed as having cancer, but within a year, the diagnosis of cancer was confirmed, Dr. Tal reported. Dr. Tal believes that cancer causes the formation in the body of a specific antigen--a protein ordinarily not found in the body. The antigen causes the formation of an antibody, in this case, Dr. Tal's T-globulin. Pregnant women show the presence of T-globulin, she believes, because the primitive cells in the placenta, from which the fetus derives nourishment, stimulate the production of T-globulin just as tumor cells do.

Professor Alaine Berman has for years engaged in research on hereditary childhood diseases, such as mental retardation, dwarfism, skeletal dyspiasias, and eye problems. She hopes to develop some simple diagnostic test for a reliable screening procedure to detect these disorders. Dr. Berman is one of many women in Israel's medical research facilities.

In Czechoslovakia Dr. Jara Moser is as well known as a sculptor as she is as a doctor. She came to the United States in 1975 as a senior research fellow at the Galveston Shrine Institute for Burned Children to learn what America had to teach her in treating burns. Dr. Moser, a surgeon in the Clinic of Plastic Surgery, King Charles University, specializes in plastic surgery. She regarded the Texas burn hospital as the seventh level of hell; there she had seen children without noses, men without features, women who without help from a plastic surgeon would be condemned to a life of horror, ugliness, and pain.

As a sculptor whose art reveals beauty, grace, and form, she resolved to make life more beautiful for her patients. She was not going to make a lot of money fixing noses or doing face lifts for "vain women," she says. "I believed that compared with some romantic areas of medicine, plastic surgery in burn cases was neglected. There were too few specialists, too few burn hospitals."

Dr. Moser observed research on stretching the unaffected skin in burn victims around the burn to cover the affected area. Artificial skin has been developed that may temporarily do the work of real skin to cover a burned or healed area.

"This would not be much better than a homograft--

grafting skin from another
donor. A homograft will
stay only 20 days or so,
and artificial skin about the
same length of time." The
challenge is in managing
heterografts," said Dr.
Moser. Until then, the
basic treatment of burn
patients must be fluid-
replacement therapy. In a
burn case, there is not only
skin loss, but the disruption
of body organs.

"The burn upsets the
hemodynamics of the body,
the whole metabolism. The
heart, the blood, the liver,
even the kidneys are af-
fected. Most important to
survival of the patient is
the percentage of body surface affected by the burn."

Dr. Chloe Tal

Dr. Moser continues:
"There's no quick way to save a burn victim. The burn is
dirty and smelly. The patient may be deeply depressed,
incontinent, half out of his mind in shock and pain. The
energy of the patient must be preserved because the body
organs are faced with an overwhelming number of problems:
healing wounds, fighting infection, restoring metabolism,
combating searing pain.

"Scarring, especially facial scars, may be horrible.
When the patient leaves the hospital where he has been surrounded by similarly scarred people, he begins to realize
how terrible he looked. The shock may be more than he
can bear.

"Burn hospitals require psychologists to work with
burn victims," claims Moser.

Conservative attitudes and respect for historical
precedence delayed the admission of women medical students
to German universities until 1904. Franziska Tiburtius
(1843-1927), in her autobiography Memories of an Octogen-

arian, describes her experiences as a medical student in Zurich, where in 1870 she was among the first women admitted to the medical school, and the joys of sharing with fellow students the friendship and encouragement of sympathetic professors. In 1876, in Berlin, she opened a free women's clinic with Emilie Lehmus, a fellow student, and she ran a private practice. She lived to a great old age, active to the end; the practice of medicine for women seems to be life-sustaining.

Dr. Jara Moser

Tiburtius recorded that the idea of women's medical colleges was fought by women physicians who were afraid that a graduate of a woman's institution might be regarded as a second-class doctor. Universities in Heidelberg and Freiburg were the first to accept women as medical students. In 1904, though women had won the right to attend medical school, a professor of anatomy in Berlin courteously escorted a woman from his anatomy class before demonstrating something he considered too delicate for feminine sensibilities.

In 1906 Karen Horney was the only woman in her Prussian university class of seven, as shown in a photograph taken to celebrate the successful passing of the pre-clinical examination.

Being the lone woman in that male-dominated school may have been hard, but the challenge and the atmosphere of freedom widened Horney's horizons. She relished the lectures and really loved medicine.

As we will see, Lise Meitner applied in 1907 to attend physics lectures and was allowed to do part-time work with Otto Hahn. But she had to creep around the laboratory to do her experiments when no men were around. Not until after World War I were women permitted to have academic careers in Germany.

There's some evidence that the first German woman physician may have been the long-lived Hildegard von Bingen, born around 1098 and living until 1179 as Abbess of Ruppertsberg Abbey, who published a number of theological and medical works, perhaps dictated in German and later translated into Latin. In Frankfurt in the fifteenth century, historians reported five women doctors, mostly surgeons and eye doctors. Many Jewish women, wives, widows, or daughters of physicians, practiced medicine in Germany.

Two women from Germany who have had successful medical careers in the United States are an eye doctor, Ingeborg Schmidt, and a psychiatrist, Dr. Hilde Bruch, one of the leading authorities in the world on emotional problems related to eating.

Dr. Schmidt, professor of optometry at Indiana University, teaches applied pathology of the eye and physiological optics. She says of herself:

> Baltic-German woman, born in Estonia in 1899, when it belonged to Czarist Russia. At home we spoke German. I am a descendant of German knights of a religious order who, in the twelfth century, with great cruelty, introduced Christianity to the Estonians, and also a descendant of German merchants who later settled in Estonia.
>
> At the University of Tartu (Dorpat), where I studied medicine, most of my fellow students were Estonians with whom I spoke Estonian. Lectures were given in Estonian, Russian, and German. In high school I studied Russian and French, but not English.
>
> I had a grant to work in Women's Hospital at the University of Tübingen, Germany, and in 1927 I wrote a thesis on "Binocular color vision" and obtained the degree of medical doctor. My professor was sent as director of the Physiological Institute to Berlin and he invited his assistants to go with him. I worked with him in Berlin until my contract expired in 1936, when the Nazis required women to leave the university. I found a position at the Institute of Aviation Medicine of the Air Ministry in Berlin as a specialist in color vision, and I also supervised their library.

In 1946, after the war, Americans assembled the scientists who had worked on aviation medicine, and we were asked to write reviews.

Later she was offered a contract as a color-vision specialist, and she was hired by the School of Aviation Medicine in Randolph Field, Texas.

She received a research grant from the department of ophthalmology at Columbia University in 1952. She joined Indiana University two years later; there she taught and did research. She has published over 80 papers, mostly on color vision, night vision, and astronautics, and she has contributed to four books on optics. She says the unhappiest time of her life was when she was regarded as a Nazi by New Yorkers, although she had never been a member of the Nazi party. Her happiest year was in Heidelberg, after the hardships of the war were over, and the years at Indiana University were also pleasant. She retired in 1970 but continued to do research and to write. Her most famous paper caused a member of the School of Optometry of the University of California/Berkeley to name a sign of color deficiency detectable in protan carriers "Schmidt's sign."

In January 1970 the Journal of the American Optometric Association published her paper on "Visual Problems When Walking on the Moon."

Clinical professor of psychiatry in Baylor University Medical College and an authority on the psychological aspects of obesity, Dr. Hilde Bruch believes that psychiatry is a particularly congenial profession for women. "It's very difficult for an American to get into medical school," observes Dr. Bruch. "I know some young men who study abroad and then come to America to take the necessary examinations, and they become qualified to practice. When I studied in Germany anyone who was qualified could get into medical school. A much higher percentage of women were accepted. Of course, if you ask me if there is prejudice where patients refuse to go to women doctors, I'm sure some men would never go see a woman physician. I wouldn't have had occasion to meet such men. Before I was a psychiatrist," she smiled, "I was a pediatrician, and I'm sure that women pediatricians treat as many baby boys as baby girls."

She continued, "Once a woman doctor is established, she has the same opportunities for consultation and other professional privileges as are available to men doctors."

"Is there a general feeling that women are afraid to go into medicine for fear of being discriminated against, or is that a fashionable question to ask because of Women's Lib?"

She paused thoughtfully, "There is a realistic problem, of course, that young women with children may have many conflicting obligations with their children. During these years when academic careers are built, women may be under a handicap. I would think that medicine is one of the professions in which women have as free a choice of field as men and probably meet less prejudice than in other professions."

Dr. Bruch graduated from the University of Freiburg and did her internship and specialized training in Germany. Her training was different from what young women today experience, because her very existence was threatened by the advent of the Hitler regime.

"We had to flee Germany. My family arrived in America in the midst of the Depression. You cannot imagine the situation. There were simply no positions available. Most German-Jewish refugees arrived with valuable professional training and experience."

The doctor was motivated to go into medicine because she had a love of learning and was very curious. "Yes, curiosity was strong. The motivation which led me to medicine was complex. I was a teenager when I first learned that girls could go to the university. I decided that was what I wanted to do. I was good in mathematics and wanted to major in math, but an uncle vetoed that idea. He said, 'You will get only second-rate high school teaching or boring jobs with no future. Why not study medicine?'"

She loves working with people and has never regretted her decision. "Higher mathematics would never have been as stimulating as I have found medicine. My uncle said that if I tried to go into higher mathematics I would run into prejudice because of my religion rather than because of being a woman," she adds. "This was the age of Hitler, and Jews had no future in Germany."

What does one know at 18? We cannot foresee what it means to live with a profession. There are so many exciting aspects of medicine from which to choose.   How did I decide to go to medical school?

I remember that I went ice-skating, and the medical students skimming around on the ice were wearing their class caps, the fellows wearing red caps and the girls wearing crimson berets.   I was envious of those crimson hats.   That may have been my prime motive--to have the right to wear one of those pretty crimson berets when I went ice-skating!   Anyway, in a few months I was wearing one!

In Europe, the university was a much more free-wheeling situation than it is here.   You had a great deal of freedom about choice of subjects and studying on your own and choosing courses you liked.   Of course, you had been through a rigid, structured, highly-disciplined high school, and you had learned to apply yourself and study.   You had fulfilled certain minimum requirements.   In medical school you could take your time, four, five, even six years to finish the work.   Your early upbringing and education and school experience had been rigid and demanding, and poor students simply did not graduate.   Only excellent students came to the university.

You had to take your lab work and you had to show up for ward assignments, naturally, but the responsibility for study, the testing of knowledge, was left up to you, and you did your reading on your own.   No one shadowed you to remind you to get your studies done.

Women were even more conscientious than the men.   American women medical students tend to be more conscientious and often more brilliant than men students.   Restricted admissions make the girls work harder.

After I came to this country in 1934 I went to New York Babies Hospital.   There were already three or four women on the staff there doing outstanding work.   Three were Johns Hopkins graduates, and there was an entirely different attitude toward women in medicine there--a more liberal

attitude, a more matter-of-fact attitude toward
women in medicine. I would say complete acceptance. Later I went to Johns Hopkins and there
again I met with respect.

In the half century since Dr. Bruch went to medical
school she continued to be grateful to the uncle who steered
her toward a profession. "He was absolutely right," she says.
"The great joy of my life is being a woman in medicine."

Part II

REACHING

FOR THE

STARS

REACHING FOR THE STARS

4. The President's Doctor

There is no telling how many capable doctors have been lost
to science because women were long discouraged from studying medicine.

"We are not without very grave objections to women
taking on themselves the heavy duties and responsibilities of
the practice of medicine.... Man, with his robust frame
and trained self-command, is often barely equal to the task,"
is the statement in a resolution issued in 1867 by the Philadelphia County Medical Society.

Willa Cather became a famous novelist, but she
might have been a famous doctor if she had had her wish.
Born in the home of her grandmother in Virginia, December
7, 1873, she had a young uncle who died not long after he
had become a doctor. His personal belongings remained in
the Cather home. Cather was fascinated by the instruments
and books, and she longed to become a doctor herself.
Her favorite subjects were the sciences, and she was especially interested in zoology. Chosen to give her high school
commencement address, she spoke on "Superstition versus
Investigations," saying, "It is the most sacred right of man
to investigate. We paid dearly for it in Eden...." She
was delighted when people nicknamed her "Dr. Will."

Cather's contribution to American literature is considerable, with brilliant short stories and fine novels, including Death Comes for the Archbishop, but no one knows
what contribution she might have made to the life sciences.
Within a century, however, other determined women earned
medical degrees, and two women received appointments to
the White House, Dr. Janet Travell and Dr. Anna Easton
Lake.

Dr. Lake's story comes to us mostly by word of
mouth. Born in 1849, she and her husband Albert, turning

51

a deaf ear to the protests of friends and relatives (who
scorned her profession and called her "that Damned Yankee
who married Albert"), she converted the first floor of their
Baltimore home into a free clinic for handicapped children.
Idealistic Albert eventually left the family firm to assist his
wife's work; together they made orthopedic appliances for
the crippled youngsters.   Through the notorious Dr. Mary
Walker (of whom we shall hear more soon), Dr. Lake was
appointed as a White House physician to minister to President Grover Cleveland's daughter, who suffered from cerebral
palsy.   However, Dr. Lake suffered a stroke before she ever
reported to the White House.

Dr. Janet Travell's phone rang in her office on
December 14, 1955.   Senator John F. Kennedy of Massachusetts was calling.   Would Dr. Travell fly down and spend
the weekend with him and his wife in Palm Beach?   Kennedy
had seen Dr. Travell in her New York office earlier in
December for a chronic back problem.   Travell had seen a
New York Times (September 22, 1955) photo of Kennedy
leaning on crutches at a private audience with Pope Pius
XIII.   Kennedy admitted to Travell, "I used the crutches
then only because I couldn't kneel gracefully."   Kennedy was
more uncomfortable than he admitted.   Dr. Travell checked
his shoes for the left heel lift she had earlier prescribed.
His beech sandals lacked that correction.   As he walked barefoot, his disparity in leg length created with each step an abnor-
mal seesaw motion in the sacroiliac and lumbosacral re-
gions.   That was a potential source of his back pain.

Dr. Travell suggested that he avoid going barefoot.
Walking on sand involved heavy muscular effort.   A special
kind of strain is put on the back when someone walks on a
surface sloped sideways, like a beach.   Such a slant makes
one leg function as if longer than the other, tilting the
sacrum and pelvis.   A curvature of the spine is produced,
and pain is likely to follow.   Dr. Travell assured Senator
Kennedy that he could swim in the ocean, as long as the
surf wasn't rough.   "It's more invigorating to swim in the
ocean than in a pool," she said.   "The water is alive and
it moves you.   It creates a helpful variety of both active
and passive motion in a way that still water never does.
It's like riding a horse."

Thereupon Kennedy and Dr. Travell went straight to
the beach and swam together in the ocean.   This became
one of Dr. Travell's most cherished memories.   Later
Kennedy questioned the uncomfortable chairs around him.

The rocker Dr. Travell had ordered for his Senate office was his only really comfortable chair. When she came to the White House with Kennedy in 1961 Dr. Travell had a chance to provide the President with consistently good seating that reduced muscular fatigue and strain, according to her autobiography, Office Hours: Day and Night.

"When I was a little girl, I decided to be a doctor like my father because he was a magician and whatever he did was wonderful. ... Through my father's eyes, every living creature became a challenging mystery. He led me to wonder, to observe, and to think about what I saw" (Travell, p. 75).

J. Willard Travell's example made it inevitable that his daughter should be concerned with nature; the "frogs and snakes that we caught served first as our pets, but if disaster overtook them we set about dissecting them and learning anatomy and physiology."

Travell and her sister Virginia followed their mother's example and graduated from Wellesley. Cornell University Medical College was the only medical school to which Janet applied. She knew the demands of the medical profession. "I had witnessed the tedious hours and hard work that my father gave to his medical practice, but his unfailing enthusiasm for it was contagious. He and I never discussed any special hardships or prejudices that the doctor who was a woman might encounter. I think that those were taken for granted. We also assumed that whatever the obstacles, Ginny and I would surmount them " (Travell, p. 116).

The Cornell Medical College class of 1926 graduated 63 students, nine of them women; Virginia's class, 1925, had contributed 58 doctors, 12 of them women. The competition to enter medical school was not as keen then as it is now.

To Travell, anatomy, the major course in first-year medical school, was anything but ghoulish. "I never had qualms about dissecting a cadaver. The techniques were not strange to me after my advanced course in comparative mammalian anatomy at Wellesley."

Internship appointments were the main event in the final year at medical school. Since Travell had substituted as an intern at New York Hospital when Evelyn Holt (Wellesley, 1919)--the hospital's first woman intern--took her vacation, Travell applied there and was accepted. At graduation, she received the Polk Memorial Prize for highest scholastic standing.

At 25 Janet Travell fell in love with Jack Powell, 29, at a dance. He sat with her between trips when she was on ambulance duty at New York Hospital.

In 1930 Dr. Travell did drug research and taught pharmacology at Cornell Medical College. Curiously, she discovered that what her medical students required most was a mathematical aptitude.

Dr. Travell admits that the tenor of her professional life changed when she became a part-time teacher at Cornell University medical school after the birth of her daughter Virginia in 1935. She was able to keep her time more flexible than under the restrictions of a full-time appointment in the pre-clinical science department, and in her spare time she had a small private practice in her father's office. This was an earth-shaking arrangement for the era; few women were able to find fulfilling part-time employment.

Her father's knowledge of electrotherapy brought to his office people in intense pain. His techniques were not taught in medical school: he used a static machine, which alerted his daughter to the crippling consequences of muscle spasm. While championing static electricity as therapy, Dr. Travell became a beneficiary of its effects, having developed a painful right shoulder and arm. Her father provided the "static surge," which gave her periodic relief from the steady, severe pain.

She began to study heart-attack patients who developed persistent pains in the shoulder region. "The Cardiac Consultation Service at Sea View, the city hospital for tuberculosis on Staten Island to which I was appointed in 1936, supplied the conditions that crystallized my emerging interest in muscular pain. Most patients there had life-threatening pulmonary disease, but some of them complained more about devastating pain in their shoulders and arms than about their major illness" (Travell, p. 252).

Dr. Travell initiated treatment of patients by local injection of the intramuscular trigger areas with procaine (Novocain). The outcome was "prompt and lasting pain relief, return of the normal range of motion at the shoulder joint, and some very grateful patients. "

Procaine is a versatile drug that has been used to reduce pain in childbirth and to treat heart patients. Like curare, a drug used to relax skeletal muscles during surgery under anesthesia, procaine interupts the flow of nerve impulses and may help a patient with chronic muscle spasm to find comfort. Travell was "surprised to learn that even the pain of classical myocardial infarction [i. e. , heart attack] ... might be relieved at once by local procaine infiltration. "

Dr. Travell discovered that the clinical trial of a therapeutic agent was subject to the influence of subconscious bias. One of her colleagues told her that she could not trust her own clinical observations because she had the primary requirement for a physician--"a therapeutic personality" (Travell, p. 262).

Assisted by her niece, Dr. Virginia Davidson Weeks, Travell prepared a scientific exhibit on "How to Give Painless Injections. " Fear of the needleprick is an old problem in medical care, and Dr. Travell quoted the limerick:

> There was a Faith Healer from Deal
> Who said, "Although pain isn't real,
>   When I sit on a pin
>   And it punctures the skin,
> I dislike what I fancy I feel. "

When her two little girls started school, her husband Jack Powell encouraged her to continue research in heart disease and the use of cardiac drugs at Beth Israel Hospital in New York. At the time she went to the White House, she was officially "on leave" from Beth Israel.

In the meantime Travell was speaking at medical symposiums around the world. In Galveston, Texas, on April 23, 1956, speaking on "The Management of Skeletal Muscle Pain, " she noted the dearth of women doctors in the audience. Looking at the program, she saw that Dr. Sara M. Jordan of the Lahey Clinic was also a speaker, and they met after the program to bring each other up-to-date on the medical reports on Senator Jack Kennedy. Dr. Jordan was from Boston, Dr. Travell from New York, yet it did not seem odd to discuss "our mutual patient from Washington in Texas" (Travell, p. 317).

When Kennedy was a candidate for the Presidency Dr. Travell agreed to serve on the National Committee of Doctors for Kennedy. She was sympathetic to his views on medical education, research, and care for the aged (Travell, p. 335).

On Saturday, January 21, 1961, President Kennedy made his first appointment in the White House. By choosing Dr. Janet Travell, he publicized a positive role model for young women who might be considering a medical career (Fay). The story of Dr. Travell's prescribing a rocking chair for the President became headline news. Now, people who had been putting out old rockers to be collected with the trash rushed to find them in attics and second-hand stores. For a quarter of a century Dr. Travell had been prescribing the old porch rocker with head-high support for the management of back pain. In every furniture store window in the country rockers were displayed. Overnight the rocker was transformed into an emblem of the Kennedy administration!

After Kennedy's tragic death Dr. Travell consulted with Luci Johnson, who years later related how she had grown up in a "can-do" family but was unable to do anything scholastically significant. Although tests revealed high intelligence, Luci kept failing. "At age sixteen, I was belligerent, angry, unhappy and frustrated ... I had severe headaches and nausea." About the time her father became President, Luci said the source of her problems was discovered by Dr. Janet Travell, who referred Luci to a Washington optometrist. Her problem was a common one, a near-point stress-induced visual defect. Whenever she concentrated hard on anything, such as school work, she really did not see what she was doing. Visual corrective procedures were instituted. Within a year, Luci said, she went from "a D-as-in-dog student to a B student."

Returning from a radiant trip to Europe with President Kennedy and the First Lady, Travell was invited to present the commencement address at Meharry Medical College in Nashville, Tenn., on June 5, 1961. She remarked that

No profession sets for itself such high standards of intellectual achievement and at the same time devotion to human welfare as do medicine and its partner professions.... In the medical sciences, our real uniqueness lies in the fact that we often hold in our hands the specific tools for alleviating pain and illness, immediately, personally, directly. This power to relieve suffering must be nurtured with humility, and never tarnished by jealousy, avarice, laziness or disinterest on our part....

It has been said that medicine is the only profession that consistently works to put itself out of business. If its goal, the conquest of disease, were achieved, what would be left for us to do?

The challenge of the future for medicine lies in the possibilities of modifying the behavioral patterns of the human race for the good of society.

REACHING FOR THE STARS

5. Elizabeth Blackwell

In 1767 the first American medical school was launched at the University of Pennsylvania. No one dreamed of admitting a woman. John B. Blake has noted that the only careers to which an educated woman might then aspire were writing (for the talented few) and teaching. School boards discovered that they could hire women for half the salary they had to pay men, and there was a rapid rise in the number of women teachers after 1820 (Blake, p. 107).

A generation of ambitious women who later became famous began careers as teachers. Among them was Elizabeth Blackwell, America's first woman doctor. In her autobiography, Pioneer Work in Opening the Medical Profession to Women, Dr. Blackwell documents her persistent fight against the prejudices that existed toward women who wanted a professional career. Her English father, a sugar refiner, was active in the anti-slavery struggle in England. Blackwell recalled that the children in the family voluntarily gave up the use of sugar as a "slave product." Of the nine children the two older girls, Elizabeth and Emily, were in their teens when the family came to New York. Governesses and masters had tutored the children and developed in them a passion for reading. Elizabeth was enrolled in an excellent New York school and early became ardently involved in the anti-slavery struggle.

When she was 17 the family moved to Cincinnati. There they joined the Unitarian Church and continued their activity in the anti-slavery movement. The girls were disciples of Harriet Beecher Stowe, author of Uncle Tom's Cabin, the book that was said to have ignited the Civil War.

Within a few months after the move to Cincinnati the heat of summer proved too much for the English constitution of the father. He died of fever, leaving a widow and nine children in poverty.

Elizabeth Blackwell, America's first woman doctor (photo courtesy of the New York Infirmary)

The three older sisters started a day school for girls and managed somehow to support the family, but Elizabeth was bored with teaching. (She considered becoming a midwife, because obstetrics was still a woman's profession.) Most pregnant women were painfully shy about submitting to an examination by a male doctor. Victorian women, trained to be excessively modest, suffered sickness for years rather than disrobe before a male doctor. Some extremely ill women were embarrassed to discuss their symptoms or pain. Until 1780 most American babies were delivered by midwives. If a midwife wanted the advice of a male doctor, he gave it to her through a closed door. Exceptions were made in the case of prostitutes, who were not supposed to have modesty. In the 1840s there were some lectures on diet and hygiene given by Sylvester Graham and Paulina Wright. Women who came to these lectures were so prudish that some of them actually fainted when Paulina Wright spoke about anatomy. (It was an era when it was fashionable to faint!)

In her autobiography Elizabeth Blackwell admits she was "ashamed of any form of illness." She considered sickness contemptible. As a girl she tried to harden her body by sleeping on the floor at night. One of her teachers had tried to enliven a lesson by passing around a bull's eye, and Elizabeth almost upchucked.

Yet after she decided to become a doctor she let nothing discourage her. She was repeatedly told she had chosen an unrealistic goal. She wrote, "The idea of winning a doctor's degree gradually assumed the aspect of a great moral struggle." She was furious that the term "woman physician" had come to mean an abortionist.

She took a job as a governess in the home of a North Carolina doctor and studied his books in her spare time, squirreling away money until 1847, when she applied to medical schools. She went to Philadelphia, then considered the seat of medical learning, and boarded with the family of Dr. William Elder. Doctors who interviewed her gave her no encouragement. Some frankly admitted a sense of being threatened by women entering their profession. "You can't expect us to furnish you with a stick to break our heads with," said one dean. Another professor wanted to enter into partnership with Elizabeth on the condition of sharing profits over $5,000 on her first year's practice. Another professor made the bizarre suggestion that she could be accepted to medical school if she disguised herself as a man.

The first English woman doctor, James (Miranda) Berry was discovered to be a woman only after her death in 1865. She had worked all her life in the guise of a man, and had become Inspector General of Hospitals for the British Army (Lovejoy, a).

While applying to medical school Blackwell wasted no time. She began anatomical studies in a private school. Her first lesson in practical anatomy involved the human wrist. "The beauty of the tendons and the exquisite arrangements of this part of the body" so appealed to her that she was never again repelled by anatomy (Blackwell, a, p. 59).

Finally, she was overjoyed to be accepted by the Geneva College of Medicine in New York on October 20, 1847. In the two years she was in Geneva her enthusiasm for medicine grew. At that time almost any man with an elementary education could take a course of lectures for a winter or two, pass an examination, and achieve the right to practice medicine. Doctors were turned out in less than a year. As late as 1900 there were medical schools that admitted students who could not get into a liberal arts college (Shyrock, p. 152). Certainly excellent medical schools existed, but a study made at Yale in 1850 indicated that the graduates preferred law and theology.

One of Blackwell's medical classmates recalled the amazement when the woman student walked into the lecture hall. "Her entrance into that bedlam of confusion acted like magic upon every student.... For the first time a lecture was given without the slightest interruption, and every word could be heard as distinctly as it would if there had been but a single person in the room. The sudden transformation of this class from a band of lawless desperadoes to gentlemen, by the mere presence of a lady, proved to be permanent in its effect" (Hume, p. 17).

Blackwell, asked to stay away from class during the lectures on the reproductive system, wrote a letter to the professor insisting that anatomy was a serious study and "reflected glory on the Creator." The professor could hardly refuse her, and when she entered the hall her fellow students gave her a standing ovation. A classmate recalled that thereafter the lectures on anatomy proceeded in much better taste than they had, for it was well known that the professor liked off-color jokes and wisecracks.

The disastrous potato famine of 1848 brought boat-

loads of starving Irish immigrants to America. Hundreds of
fever victims became patients of Elizabeth Blackwell. Her
paper on fever victims was hailed as a contribution to medicine and caused the National Medical Association to remove
the censure that had been leveled at Geneva College for having accepted her as a student. But discussion continued on
whether the college could actually confer the degree of Doctor of Medicine on a female.

On the morning that Elizabeth Blackwell dressed for
commencement some of her warmest supporters on the faculty were in their glory. All of the women of the town
turned out to see a woman receive a medical diploma.
Blackwell, elegant in a black silk brocaded gown, green
gloves, and black silk stockings, watched her fellow graduates, four at a time, ascend the steps to the platform and
ceremoniously receive diplomas. Left to the very last,
Blackwell was called up alone. The president removed his
hat and handed her the diploma.

Feminine and graceful, she decided to speak, and did
so with dignity: "It shall be the effort of my life to shed
honor on this diploma." The audience applauded its approval,
and, nodding gravely, the faculty joined in. The next an-
nouncement was that Blackwell had graduated at the head of
her class!

Determined to learn more about medicine, Blackwell
returned to England, which she had left as a teenager.
Curious about the English medical world, she worked at
Lying-in Hospital. She was a curiosity in England, and the
British humor magazine Punch published a long poem in
her honor. One of its verses:

> Young ladies all, of every clime,
> Especially of Britain,
> Who wholly occupy your time
> In novels or in knitting,
> Whose highest skill is but to play,
> Sing, dance, or French to clack well,
> Reflect on the example, pray,
> Of excellent Miss Blackwell!

Later Blackwell went to Paris and worked in an obstetrical hospital, La Maternité, where the 28-year-old
American medical graduate, without rancor, willingly led
the rigid life of an 18-year-old French student midwife.

Where, she questioned, could she improve her methods of delivering babies better than in a hospital where 3,000 babies were born annually?

A tragedy she suffered in November 1849 almost brought an end to her medical career. Washing the eye of a baby afflicted with ophthalmia, she caught a drop of infected water in her own eye. That night the eye was swollen shut. The senior intern, Dr. Hippolyte Blot, who had earlier taken a shine to Blackwell and was exchanging lessons in science with her for lessons in English, came to the infirmary to examine her eye. Asking to be relieved of his hospital duties entirely for a while, he confined her to bed in complete darkness and steadily applied compresses. The only methods known then were ineffective leechings, ointments, footbaths, and such compresses as Dr. Blot tried. No known medical care could save the sight of the eye and it had to be removed.

When she had recuperated Blackwell went to stay with her sister Anna, a newspaper correspondent in Paris. When her fellow students at La Maternité embraced her in farewell they admitted they had, at first, been disappointed that she was not black. They had been under the impression that all Americans were.

During the following months Blackwell had to adjust to using one eye. She had perhaps been in love with Blot, and he had given her special attention, warmth, and kindness. But now, with this handicap, she may have told him that their friendship (or if it was a courtship, we will never know) had to end. Blackwell, usually so frank about her life, leaves us no clue as to her real feelings about Dr. Blot.

She must have known that for her own mental health, she had to leave Paris. She went to visit Germany, and then she attended lectures and clinics at St. Bartholomew's Hospital in London. Two years of Europe in postgraduate studies led her to believe she was ready for practicing medicine in America. In July 1851 she sailed for home, only to face seven difficult years in New York.

Every previous challenge was dwarfed by these disappointing years. She could not find rooms for a clinic. Few patients came, and those who did seemed reluctant to trust her. She was lonely. The story of her first consultation would be funny if it were not so sad. An elderly patient had pneumonia, and Blackwell called in a doctor who had cared for her father in his final illness. In this generous act, she revealed a remarkable lack of prejudice. After seeing the patient the doctor went with Blackwell to her living room, pacing in agitation. "A most extraordinary case.... I really don't know what to do."

She was stunned. Clearly, pneumonia was not all that unusual. Why was the doctor making such a case of it? Finally the old doctor admitted his perplexity related to her and not to the patient. He couldn't figure out how to handle the "propriety of consulting a lady physician." Blackwell reassured the old doctor that he could just regard the consultation as a friendly conversation. He proceeded to give her his best advice, which she took. The patient recovered. Afterwards, having learned how to talk with a male doctor, Blackwell claimed she never had any further difficulty in obtaining consultations.

Blackwell made the rounds of every hospital and dispensary in New York, but not one would consider her application. To occupy the empty hours in her office she wrote a series of lectures on the physical education of girls. She hired a lecture hall. Tickets were sold, $2 for the six lectures. Among her small audience were some Quaker women who had long been talking about a medical college for women. A few of these women, impressed with Blackwell's ideas on room ventilation, exercise for girls, sensible nutrition, and comfortable clothes, became her patients. Her practice grew.

In 1854 Blackwell's younger sister Emily followed in her footsteps, graduating from the medical school at Western Reserve University in Cleveland. The two sisters were considering opening a hospital, when a tall, 26-year-old Polish woman, Marie Zakrzewska, made an appearance as if by magic to become the third pillar of the faculty to prepare women for study at an American medical school.

Blackwell had met the newly arrived immigrant in 1853 and was immediately impressed with Zakrzewska. When she first arrived in New York, German doctors had urged her to take up nursing and forget about her dreams of being a doctor. She was surprised that women physicians were regarded with little respect and considered inferior to nurses. Nursing was better than sewing, which was the way she earned her living when she first arrived.

Dr. Emily Blackwell, Elizabeth's younger sister (photo
courtesy of the New York Infirmary)

A big, rather unattractive woman with great energy,
Dr. Zak (called this from the time she despaired of teaching Americans to pronounce her name), was born in Berlin,
where her father, a Polish officer and patriot, lived in

exile. Her mother was a midwife, carrying on a long family tradition, but her father disapproved of Marie's ambition
to be a doctor. Stubbornly, Marie, by the time she was 22,
was the chief of the delivery room services at Berlin's Royal Hospital Charite. She taught a class of 100 women and
50 men. Envy and politics in the hospital forced her to
leave for America, where women could be real doctors. Of
Zakrzewska, Blackwell wrote Emily on May 12, 1853 "There
is true stuff in her, and I shall do my best to bring it out.
She must obtain a medical degree."

With Blackwell's help she learned what she needed to
know to be admitted to a college, the Cleveland medical
school, from which she received her M.D. in 1856 (one of
the first four women accepted in 1854).

In 1857 Elizabeth and Emily Blackwell, with Dr. Zak's
energetic support, opened the New York Infirmary for Women
and Children. Zak introduced record keeping on patients.
She had the revolutionary idea of recording sex, age, occupation, diagnosis, and treatment of each case. It is very true
that without Blackwell's help, Zakrzewska might never have
become a doctor. When she had first come to America,
Marie Zakrzewska knew only a little halting English, but
Blackwell had been able to speak fluent German and had welcomed her to the staff of the new dispensary. College instruction in medicine was available by this time to women,
but no hospital was willing to let them intern or pursue a
practice. The women's goal of establishing a New York
hospital where women would be interns and residents met
great opposition. But open it did on May 12, 1958, the
first of its kind in the world, at 64 Bleecker Street, and
Zakrzewska had proven the most able fund-raiser of them
all. And Dr. Zak repaid all of Dr. Blackwell's kindnesses
by dedicated service for two years in the infirmary without
salary.

At this time most medical schools for men had no
entrance requirements or examinations. From the first the
Blackwells required such examinations, a decade before they
were compulsory elsewhere. The medical course was for
three and a half years with a graded curriculum. Many
medical schools required only two years of five months instruction each year.

The newly created Chair of Hygiene was filled by
Elizabeth Blackwell. Under her firm hand a sanitary visiting

Elizabeth Blackwell teaching anatomy at the New York Infirmary for Women and Children (photo courtesy of the New York Infirmary)

service to city slums was started, headed by infirmary staff member Dr. Rebecca Cole, the second black woman to receive a medical degree. Cole was a graduate of Woman's Medical College of Pennsylvania (1867). *

Most of the women who became doctors during Elizabeth Blackwell's era went to "eclectic" or "homeopathic" schools, which were somewhat more liberal about accepting women. Questionable--even cockeyed--theories were taught in these schools. Students were idealistic and often learned as much about temperance, suffrage, and slavery as they did about community medicine and hygiene. Many of these women became leaders in the abolitionist movement.

*The first black woman to receive a medical degree may have been Rebecca Lee, who graduated from New England Female Medical College, Boston, in 1864.

In 1850, during Oliver Wendell Holmes's administration, Harvard University became coeducational. The faculty of Harvard Medical College accepted Harriet K. Hunt, who had practiced medicine without a license for a decade before applying to Harvard in 1847 and again in 1849. She and her sister Sarah were self-taught in medicine and had many devoted patients. In reply to Harriet's second application, which she was finally forced to withdraw, hot-headed Harvard students threatened to transfer to Yale if "female students" were admitted. When one woman and three blacks were accepted by Harvard over the men's opposition, the students rioted. Obviously Harvard students were not the liberals then that they seem to be today.

The Central Medical College in Syracuse, N. Y., was an eclectic school, the first to adopt coeducation, and in 1849-50, its first session enrolled 92 students. Of these, three were women.

Emily Blackwell wanted a merger of the Women's Medical College of New York Infirmary with Cornell Univer-

The Class of 1870, Women's Medical College of the New York Infirmary (photo courtesy of the New York Infirmary)

sity Medical College. At first Cornell flatly rejected the idea, but by 1899 Cornell was admitting women; it was then no longer necessary for the Women's Medical College to continue functioning, and it was closed.

By 1900 the only remaining women's medical college was that in Philadelphia. One university after another began accepting women. By 1941 only six out of the 77 medical schools in America remained exclusively male. By the '70s the idea of an all-male medical school was regarded as quaint.

But we've gotten ahead of our story. Back to the Civil War. In 1861 Dorothea Dix offered her services, proposing "to organize under the offical auspices of the War Department, an Army Nursing Corps made up of women volunteers. I am sure many would be glad to enlist, in fact will insist on doing so. They should not be prevented, but it is imperative that their services should be subject to regulation. I hope you will permit me to serve in this capacity" (Wilson, p. 266).

Responding to the desperate need for nurses for the front during the Civil War, Elizabeth Blackwell turned her great energies from getting women accepted to medical organizations to training nurses. Dix was appointed head of an Army Nursing Corps, but she was always more concerned with the morals of the nurses than with their training. In a letter to her friend Louisa Lee Schuyler she specified, "No woman under thirty need apply to serve in government hospitals. All nurses are required to be plain looking women. Their dresses must be brown or black, with no bows, no curls, no jewelry and no hoop-skirts."

Dr. Blackwell screened candidates for preparation at Bellevue or New York Hospital and lectured on ventilation, cleanliness, food, care of helpless patients, symptoms, surgical dressings, bandaging, and precautions for nurses. Blackwell was unimpressed by Dorothea Dix, who had courageously crusaded for reform in the treatment of the insane and the retarded. Blackwell found Dix overbearing and dictatorial, and disapproved of her methods.

After the Civil War Dr. Mary Edwards Walker, a feminist and a graduate of the Syracuse Medical College (the only woman in her class) received the Medal of Honor, the nation's highest military award, from President Andrew

Johnson on November 11, 1865, for her dedication as a surgeon. In 1855, at the age of 22, she graduated from medical school. Mary Walker's certificate from the short-lived college did not have the respect eventually given Elizabeth Blackwell's degree from Geneva Medical College. But Walker's qualifications were accepted by the Union Army for volunteer service in 1861, and three years later she was commissioned an Acting Assistant Surgeon and a first lieutenant (Woodward, pp. 282-84). She claimed to be the first woman to serve on the surgical staff of any modern army in wartime. Born November 26, 1832, she was educated by her parents on the family farm. Alvah Walker, a doctor, taught his daughter all he knew about medicine.

In a spiteful letter to the New York Medical Journal in May 1867 (pp. 167-70), a Captain Roberts Bartholow accused her of being a "spy and informer," and claimed "she had no more medical knowledge than any ordinary house-wife."

Proof exists in the War Department documents that Mary Walker was captured by the Confederates near Chattanooga and spent four months under cruel conditions in terrible prisons. Eventually she was traded with 24 other Union doctors for 17 Confederate surgeons. She was constantly harassed by her male colleagues, but she managed to make a lasting influence on the Confederate prison where she was incarcerated. As a result of her pressures, the prisoners now and then had wheat bread and vegetables instead of cornbread. Not only was she among the first women in the country to study medicine, she also studied law and used her legal knowledge to help the poverty-stricken and the veterans of the war and their dependents to secure pensions (Poynter). While in the Union Army, she organized an association to help women looking for relatives or friends among the soldiers in Washington, D. C., and prospective mothers who were homeless. Enormously innovative, she is credited with the return receipt for registered mail and the inscribing of return addresses on envelopes.

For her "untiring service on the field of duty," President Lincoln recommended the Medal of Honor.

She was made to appear crazy, for cutting off her hair to sell for a woman who was desperate for money. She liked to wear pants and wore them to her wedding ceremony with Albert Miller. She refused to take her husband's name and insisted that any vow to obey her husband would be omitted from the ceremony. The marriage was short-lived. She taught prevention of tuberculosis and ran a sanitarium and always had one foot on a soap box, lecturing on smoking, drinking, capital punishment, women's suffrage, and the right of women to dress as they pleased. Eventually she was reduced to a freak lecturing at dime museums for her living (Edwards, pp. 1296-98).

In 1917, two years before her death, the award of the Medal of Honor was reversed, when guidelines for receiving the award were revised so that only a man carrying a gun and engaged in combat could receive the Medal of Honor.

But Dr. Walker refused to return the medal to the government, even though she was stripped of the right to have it. In 1977 the issue of the Medal of Honor that had been revoked 60 years earlier again came up in Congress, and an Army review board recommended restoring the medal. Dr. Walker, a militant feminist, had fought for equal rights for women, taught, written books, and generally distressed conservative men and women with her outspoken views. She died at 87 on February 19, 1919, penniless and ostracized by her family. History has restored her honor.

After the Civil War Dr. Ann Preston, dean of Woman's Medical College of Pennsylvania, reopened the school. She took up the battle for women's admission to national medical conventions.

Elizabeth Blackwell, involved with women's rights, was invited by her English friends to return to her native land. In March 1859 she lectured at Marylebone Institute on medical education for women. During that London visit she was honored as the first recognized woman physician in Great Britain as well as in America.

In the nineteenth century there was no shortage of doctors, and male doctors may have feared the economic competition of the women working toward medical degrees. The Female Medical College of Pennsylvania was seen as a threat by the Pennsylvania State Medical Society, and resolutions were passed against its professors and graduates. Women were said to be unfit to practice medicine.

In addition to opposition from their male counterparts

women doctors sometimes faced a further obstacle--
opposition from other women. When Fanny Kemble, the
British actress, was touring America in benefit perform-
ances, Blackwell recalled that she had met Miss Kemble at
Lord Byron's London home, and had asked her to give a
performance for the benefit of the hospital. Kemble listened
graciously until it dawned on her that the hospital was not
only for women patients, but for women doctors! Her face
reflected her disgust, "Trust a woman as a doctor!"; her
voice rose dramatically, "Never! Never!"

Despite the discrimination with which she had to con-
tend, Elizabeth Blackwell never lost her sense of humor.
To appease her great loneliness, in October 1854 she adopted
a little 7-year-old orphan, Katherine Barrie (Bass). The
child brought pleasure to Blackwell. Kitty called her "Doctor" rather than "Mother," and during the visit of a consulting physician, the child seemed puzzled. After he left, she
said to Blackwell, "Doctor, how very odd it is to hear a
man called Doctor!"

Footnote: Dr. Marie Zakrzewska was resident physician of the New York Infirmary from 1857-59. In 1859 the
New England Female Medical College invited her to become
the first professor in obstetrics. When its hospital closed,
Dr. Zak helped organize a hospital for women and children,
which became known as the New England Hospital, the first
in America with a nursing school. Dr. Zak, brilliant and
creative, started the first hospital social service and became one of the leading doctors of Boston. Eventually, she
retired to a country home, which became a social center
for her German and American friends (Bass).

REACHING FOR THE STARS

6. Elizabeth Garrett Anderson

In 1859 Elizabeth Blackwell offered a series of well-attended
lectures in England. In the audience were two sisters,
Elizabeth and Emily Garrett. The press was sometimes in-
sulting to Dr. Blackwell. One columnist observed, "It is
impossible that a woman whose hands reek with gore can be
possessed of the same nature or feelings as the generality
of women" (in Cuttington, p. 144). This statement--or one
similar to it--was quoted by the father of Elizabeth Garrett
at home, and Elizabeth jumped to defend the woman doctor.

"How can you judge a woman of whom you know nothing? At least find out about Dr. Blackwell before you make
up your mind," insisted the woman who was to become England's first woman doctor (Anderson, p. 42).

The press was not always hostile, and (as noted in
the previous chapter) Punch had saluted Blackwell's arrival
in England with a long poem:

> For Doctrix Blackwell--that's the way
> To dub in rightful gender--
> In her profession, ever may
> Prosperity attend her!
> Punch a gold handled parasol
> Suggests for presentation
> To one so well deserving all
> Esteem and admiration.

The Garrett sisters were impressed by Blackwell's
simplicity and authority. Dr. Blackwell emphasized the
value of women doctors to their own sex in sickness, the
contribution they might make to the education of mothers in
nutrition and child-rearing, and the work they could do in
hospitals, schools, prisons, and other institutions. As an
example, she contrasted the useless life of a lady of leisure

73

Elizabeth Garrett, about 1860

with the well-organized service of nuns in continental countries, such as the religious orders working in French hospitals. The sense of belonging to the world and having a role in life appealed to Elizabeth Garrett.

Blackwell went on to speak of women in medicine, pointing out that medical practice involved women and children--obvious proof that "there is a great deal women could do for themselves." She insisted that women doctors must be fully qualified and make a full contribution to the profession.

When the two Elizabeths met face to face Dr. Blackwell assumed she was speaking to a future colleague. Elizabeth Garrett believed she "had no particular genius for medicine or anything else," but in the following weeks she and her good friend Emily Davies attended two more Blackwell lectures. Davies, obsessed with the need for women doctors, knew that Garrett was intelligent, ambitious, and from a wealthy family; she thought of her friend as the perfect medical pioneer.

Women had long held a low, though traditional, place in British medicine. "A doctor," observed Miss Mitford, surveying the scene in 1824, "is sometimes an old man, sometimes an old woman, but generally an oracle and always ... a quack" (in Manton, p. 53).

Women doctors appear in Roman literature from early on, especially in obstetrics. Household slaves often were involved in the magic ritual of caring for the sick with herbs, mandragora and mistletoe, massage, or other primitive methods. A woman was naturally expected to care for the sick in her house, and certain religious orders specialized in nursing. In medieval Britain the most famous hospital was the nunnery at Sion on the Thames. Male doctors were usually monks, Jews, or others barred from military service.

An eleventh-century woman doctor from Salerno, Trotula, had remedies for damaged maidenheads (which included putting a leech cautiously on the labia, allowing blood to trickle out and form a crust on the labia) (O'Faolain and Martines, p. 142).

In a license dated Naples, 10 September 1321, Charles, Duke of Calabria, named Francesca, the wife of

Matteo de Romana of Salerno, as "proficient in the art of surgery," through a certificate presented by the University of Salerno. Francesca had been examined and "found competent by our own royal physicians and surgeons, even though it be unusual and unseemly for women to appear among assemblies of men...."

Women practiced as surgeons in Paris and in other parts of France, although medieval surgeons were grouped with barbers and received training through apprenticeship rather than in universities. Charles VIII of France withdrew the right of women to practice medicine in 1485.

In England master surgeons were supposed to supervise the work of both men and women who practiced surgery. (Practice is the word to emphasize here!) In Yorkshire Isabell Warwicke developed the skill of "the science of surgery" and was licensed to practice the same as other surgeons in York in 1572 (O'Faolain and Martines, p. 166).

Though women doctors in Britain never attained the fame of the women professors of Salerno, they were respected enough that Edward I planned to send a team of women doctors with the Crusaders to the Holy Land, in order to win over the inhabitants (Lipinska, p. 21). The wife of Edward III, Queen Philipa, may have appointed a court surgeon, Cecilia of Oxford. By the end of the fourteenth century a few women were recognized surgeons, but within 100 years women were forbidden to practice surgery under pain of long imprisonment. An act of Henry V repealed the law of Edgar, which had allowed medical women to have legal rights in Britain.

From that time on English women were denied scientific study, and the medical advances were made by men alone. By 1860 there were few prospects for a woman who wanted to study medicine. "Vested interest, prejudice and custom, so potent in British society, were all against her," according to Jo Manton, biographer of Elizabeth Garrett Anderson (p. 66). "Nowhere in Europe was the woman who wished to study medicine so stubbornly opposed as in Britain, yet nowhere was her final victory so complete.... Among the reasons for victory may be found the character of Elizabeth Garrett, the first woman in this country to qualify as physician and surgeon" (Manton, p. 67).

In January 1860 Garrett, who had a special interest in

The Englishwoman's Journal because of its devotion to women's causes, read in that magazine a letter from Dr. Blackwell that described a four-year medical course. Garrett knew she could qualify for medicine in America or in Switzerland, where medical schools were now open to women, but this qualification would have no legal value in England. She had to gain admission to a British medical school and a British examining body. She was encouraged, if not pushed, by Emily Davies, who believed that women's status would be improved only through higher education.

Garrett plunged happily into studies with tutors; she waited until after her 24th birthday to tell her father, who had just recovered from some financial setbacks, that she wanted to be a doctor. He said the idea was disgusting.

This opposition stiffened Elizabeth's resolve. The Newson Garretts had four sons and six daughters. If one of the brothers had announced his intention of becoming a doctor, he would have had nothing but encouragement. "What is there to make doctoring more disgusting than nursing, which women are always doing and which ladies have done publicly in the Crimea?" Elizabeth countered.

Her father responded sympathetically to Elizabeth's insistence that she had to have medicine or some other kind of real work in the world. He pointed out that it would take seven years of hard study before she could practice; Elizabeth answered, "Six, not seven; and if it were seven years, I should be little more than thirty-one years old and able to work for twenty years probably."

Later, at a dinner party, Elizabeth heard her father say he would actually prefer a woman doctor for his wife and daughter, "if she was qualified." Elizabeth was able to overcome her father's opposition, but not her old-fashioned mother's. Mrs. Garrett had had ten children, and now, when life should have been easy and rewarding, her daughter's decision to be a doctor had unstrung her. If Elizabeth wanted to be useful, why didn't she stay home and take care of her younger siblings? This was as appealing to Elizabeth as cold mashed potatoes. But her mother simply could not understand Elizabeth's reluctance to spend the rest of her life at home.

She asked her father to take her to some of his doctor friends on Harley Street, London. The doctors received them but pointed out that the Medical Act of 1858 clearly stated that to be enrolled on the Medical Register required licensing by a qualified examining board--a British university--and no British examining board had ever admitted a woman. "My dear young lady," said one consultant, "why not be a nurse?"

Elizabeth replied emotionally, "Because, I prefer to earn a thousand rather than twenty pounds a year" (Anderson, L. G., p. 50).

Impressed with his daughter's spirit, her father, an attorney and a good businessman, became a firm supporter of Elizabeth's goals. But Elizabeth feared that he might become aware of the demand for women to be nurses; a new training school, endowed by the Nightingale Fund, was soon to open at St. Thomas's Hospital, and "lady pupils" were being encouraged to take hospital training. Elizabeth rejected the idea that women's nursing should complement men's medical careers.

Having won her father's support, Garrett, through friends of Elizabeth Blackwell's, the Russell Gurneys, met a director of Middlesex Hospital. Gurney suggested she might try a "trial marriage with the hospital, simply working as a nurse for half a year." Garrett began nursing at what was then London's greatest teaching hospital. Although many medical students have nightmares about anatomy and surgery, Garrett faced the ordeal of the surgical ward with calm resolve.

Garrett prudently kept her ambitions to herself. The long whitewashed walls, rows of curtained beds, and bare floors were dehumanizing enough, but the odors were nauseating. Middlesex surgeons wore old frock coats in dissecting and operating rooms until the coats, "stiffened with blood and pus ... stood upright" (Manton, p. 83). The operating assistants, like angels around a doomed crib, gathered round the wood table, bloody as a butcher's block, and contributed their germs to those of the student throng, pushing and jostling. Gangrene could be carried from patient to patient by the nurses. Garrett maintained a certain reasonable detachment working in the surgical wards, preparing poultices and ointments, rolling bandages, and dressing wounds. She accompanied the head nurse and observed closely. The house surgeon and physician were helpful to her after Dr. T. W. Nunn had made a point of explaining a ward operation. Nunn also pleased her by inviting her to his out-patient clinics.

By November 1860 Garrett completed her three-month probation at Middlesex Hospital, and all pretense of her being a nurse was abandoned. Unofficially, she became a medical student. Independently, she made rounds in wards, worked in the dispensary, helped with emergency patients, took private tutoring, and read and studied hard. In December her examinations covering the work of the past five months impressed her teachers; she had practically memorized two of her textbooks.

At Christmas she went home to Aldeburgh for a vacation. She had missed friends, music, reading that was not medical, and her family, but her life in the hospital had brought her satisfaction and fulfillment. She believed doctors were ready and willing to help her.

British universities had never accepted a woman; would Oxford or Cambridge change the rules to admit Garrett? Her father was familiar with the charter of the University of London: people of all classes and "denominations without distinction" were supposed to be admitted. But not women. Eventually, Garrett's struggles won her admission to the Society of Apothecaries in London. The society would be willing to examine her knowledge if she could fulfill its regulations, which included three years in a British medical school--not an easy regulation to fulfill. By this time she had a certificate from Dr. Joshua Plaskitt showing successful apprenticeship. Somewhere a university would accept her. She applied to St. Andrews in Scotland; at the time students only had to buy "matriculation tickets" for £1--about $5. When functionaries at St. Andrews discovered that Garrett had bought a ticket for a lecture series to which she'd been invited by a professor, the school refunded her money with a request that the ticket be returned. Garrett threatened to sue.

Failing to be accepted by St. Andrews, she decided to try Edinburgh. The university there would not hear of enrolling a woman. Again, Garrett turned to private tutoring, this time with one of the best-known doctors of his time, Sir James Young Simpson. He had previously tutored Elizabeth and Emily Blackwell.

Garrett, after her first flush of joy at being admitted

to the Society of Apothecaries and having their promise of
allowing her to take examinations, was appalled to receive a
letter from the school reneging at the last minute. The authorities told her to try again in five years, perhaps confident that such a lovely girl would be married in half a decade with a few children underfoot. Incensed, Newson Garrett issued an ultimatum, threatening a lawsuit if Elizabeth
were not admitted to the school's finals. The Society of
Apothecaries had a charter which did not exclude women.
She was told to appear for the examinations.

Garrett had over-fulfilled the modest requirements of
the Society of Apothecaries, and she sailed through the examinations, finding them ridiculously easy. No written papers or clinical trials were required, and the questions on
medicine, midwifery, and medical pathology were simple
for her. She was one of three candiates to receive a final
certificate.

She now held the degree of L. S. A. --Licentiate of the
Society of Apothecaries--and while not as prestigious as the
M. D. , it entitled her to be admitted to the Medical Register
and to practice in England.

Garrett had to turn to her father for financial help
to open a modest clinic. She called it St. Mary's Dispensary for Women, and within weeks of its opening in a slum,
she was examining and treating as many as 100 women. A
few years later the dispensary grew into the New Hospital
for Women.

Then, as now, community medicine for women and
children was a crying need. Garrett was not only physician
to the poor, she was pharmacist, surgeon, nurse, counselor,
and clerk. The tales told by her victimized, poverty-stricken
patients thrust her into the women's rights movement.

She felt sorely discriminated against because she had
so few doctors with whom she could consult. She wanted to
be on the consulting staff of a hospital, and she felt she be-
longed on the staff of the Shadwell Hospital for Children.
Should she use her feminine wiles for this objective?

Garrett could look in a mirror and see that she was
pretty. She wasn't dumb. She applied to the board of the
hospital, and at the meeting met a bachelor who confessed
that he strongly opposed admitting a woman to the consulting

staff. But he added he was taken with her beauty, and Garrett must have replied demurely and properly--she received the appointment.

Having achieved a long-delayed goal of her life, she decided she really wanted to be an M.D., something she could never achieve in England. She would go to France. She had spoken a little French as a young girl, but the language was long forgotten. The University of Paris was granting medical degrees to women. Would the British Ambassador arrange for her to take examinations in Paris? Lord Lyons agreed to try, and not long afterwards Garrett received permission to sit for the medical examinations required for the degree in Paris.

She had spent nine months in Scotland, for which she had received no credit toward a medical degree; she had, nevertheless, been exposed to brilliant teaching and had worked with Dr. David Murray, who reported 25 cases of successful vaccination of the newborn, a subject that engrossed Elizabeth for the rest of her life. And her first delivery had thrilled her: "I wonder if one will go on feeling an immediate affection for the little creatures that come first into your hands!... He weighs 8 lbs. and is 22 ins. long, so you see he is a good size. I did everything a doctor does usually, and found it very easy" (Manton, p. 143-44).

She had herself delivered a dozen babies and witnessed the delivery of over 100; but, more determined than ever to be a doctor, she knew that no matter how hardworking or capable she might be, no medical school or university in England was ever going to admit her on equal terms with men.

In Paris, at 32--self-assured, successful, respected, and the lone woman in her profession--Garrett awoke with the sun and at dawn studied French verbs and chemistry terms. She wanted that medical degree: the license from the Apothecary Hall was simply not enough. Mary Putnam, the American graduate of Woman's Medical College in Philadelphia, had been working in Paris hospitals since 1866. After 18 months of being refused admission to the medical faculty on the grounds that no woman had ever been accepted, she was at last admitted in 1868; all Garrett wanted was permission to take the six examinations required for a Paris M.D. Her name was familiar to the French because of the run-around she had had at St. Andrews, and her application for admission had the enthusiastic support of the dean of the faculty of medicine. Unfortunately, applications for admission came simultaneously from two other foreign women, and the faculty, fearing an influx of women, voted against accepting Elizabeth Garrett (Manton, p. 186).

However, Lord Lyons, who had promised to help Garrett's cause, was a diplomatic friend of France, and he prevailed upon the Empress Eugenie to intervene and authorize the admission of all the young women applicants. In February 1869 Lord Lyons received a letter informing him that Garrett could come to Paris for the first examination in a month.

She faced three examiners in black robes, and behind her were tiers of benches almost to the roof containing male students and lecturers. She responded to the questions so well that the gallery broke into applause.

In June 1869, for her second examination, she had to perform two operations before judges and students. For her thesis she decided to explore headaches--the pathology of migraine (Strachey, p. 172).

During the five difficult examinations she could not abandon her London clinic and the patients dependent on her, so she became a commuter. Such a program might make a modern woman blanch. Garrett, in 1869 and 1870, traveled back and forth across the rough English Channel as if the University of Paris were a mile from the dispensary. She had, during her examination ordeals, also served on the House Committee of the Cambridge College for Women, which opened in October 1869. She didn't forget her solitary student days in Middlesex Hospital, and she expressed warm interest in the college women.

On December 4 she had taken the third M. D. examination in Paris--chemistry, philosophy (physics), zoology, and botany, and she passed with "bien satisfait," the highest grade gained in these subjects. On December 24 she again faced three examiners, this time in medical jurisprudence, hygiene, and "materia medica." On January 4 she took her final and fifth examination in clinical medicine, midwifery, and surgery. Finally, in June, she had to read aloud her thesis and defend it to the questioners. She wore a long black wool gown with starched bands; when the reading was

over the candidate and spectators had to leave the room
while the judges deliberated. When she returned, she was
congratulated, the first woman M. D. of the Sorbonne!

Even the British Medical Journal, still hostile to wom-
en in medicine, admired the "perseverance and pluck which
Miss Garrett has shown." A headline in the Times, March
22, 1870, announced "Miss Garrett admitted on a Regular
Medical Staff."

When, during the cholera epidemic of 1866, Garrett
had opened St. Mary's Dispensary, she had had help from
Dr. Nathaniel Heckford. Now he wanted to open a children's hospital in East London, with Elizabeth Garrett as
medical officer for the hospital; after some opposition from
the board, including a hesitant James George Skelton Anderson, who was to become her husband, Garrett took up her
duties in March 1870.

The working men of the district where Garrett cared
for women and children approached her about running for
election to the school board, which was to be set up for the
first time for free compulsory education. She felt obliged
to campaign, and she enjoyed phenomenal success. When
James Anderson congratulated her on her victory, he added,
as if in afterthought, that he wished Elizabeth would marry
him.

Garrett's acceptance puzzled her father. After having
put out so much money, effort, and sheer gall into getting
her degree, why would Elizabeth throw over a career for
marriage? Garrett replied that she had no intention of giving up her medical practice. James Anderson may have
been surprised at first, but he became supportive of his
wife's desire to combine a successful medical career with
marriage.

Medical education for women became secured in the
years from 1874 to 1878. In 1874 the London School of
Medicine finally consented to enroll women. That year 14
were admitted. A quarter of a century had to pass before
women, in 1896, won the privilege of residency at Royal
Free Hospital. That year the Royal College of Physiology
in Ireland and London University admitted women to examinations to qualify for medicine. These women established
practices, but frequently they could not find a male doctor
willing to consult with them. Women were long prohibited
from joining medical societies.

The leadership of the movement passed from Elizabeth Garrett Anderson to Sophia Jex-Blake, whose tempestuous personality made headlines. She became the "pioneer doctor." Garrett preferred to be a private rather than a public person, and she looked with misgiving on the debates and difficulties in which Jex-Blake seemed to thrive. But Garrett did accept the post of lecturer at the London School of Medicine for Women, and she continued to work for the school all her life.

Elizabeth Garrett Anderson reared two children, who remembered her as a delightful, devoted mother. Her daughter Louisa, from the time she was a little girl, determined to be a doctor like her mother.

Until her death at the age of 81 Elizabeth Garrett actively served the community and her nation. The New Hospital for Women was recognized and respected throughout the medical world. After her death it was renamed in her honor the Elizabeth Garrett Anderson Hospital.

A distinguished graduate of the London School of Medicine for Women was Christine Murrell (1874-1933), who was born the year the school opened. Other women had established the right to become doctors; Christine Murrell was one of those who proved that women could be outstanding in their medical roles. Her tender care for babies and the sane approach to the rearing of children that she taught to mothers made her a first-line soldier in public health through preventive medicine.

Dr. Benjy F. Brooks, another, more recent, graduate and a pioneer in pediatric surgery, whose many honors include "Woman of the Year" in Scotland, where she served as lecturer in Children's Surgery at the University of Glasgow, moved to Houston, where she joined the staff of Texas Children's Hospital and became chief of Pediatric Surgery at Hermann Hospital.

Elizabeth Garrett was a standard-bearer for such women as Dr. Murrell and Dr. Brooks, but though she had proven to the Victorian society that women could behave with dignity as doctors, hers was a personal victory, gained through fighting a series of small wars on her own terms. But what about other women who wanted to go into medicine? The battle was only begun, and it was left to Sophia Jex-Blake to turn it into a full-scale war.

REACHING FOR THE STARS

7. Sophia Jex-Blake

Sophia Jex-Blake was the first woman physician in Scotland,
but getting that medical degree was not a piece of cake.
Her fierce crusade to convince the University of Edinburgh
to admit women reads like a battle history. Jex-Blake,
born at Hastings, Sussex, on January 21, 1840, studied at
Queen's College for Women in London and became a math
tutor there. There may be some correlation between a sour,
ultraconservative father and the achievements of a rebellious
daughter; perhaps in the girl's mind there springs a defiance
that stimulates her to do what her parent insists cannot be
done. Everything was done that could be done to make a
brilliant, energetic, innovative girl into a dutiful daughter;
all that was accomplished was to make Sophia hungry for
learning and determined to improve women's education,
which she considered stultifying. Many a young woman of
18 marries just to get away from a home where the parents
are constantly disapproving of her behavior and attitudes.
Sophia, at 18, learned that Queen's College of London had
just opened for women. She had to "go into hysterics" before her father would permit her to go.

Within a few months after winning the heady freedom
of being in Queen's College, she became a math tutor. Her
father was shocked that she would take money and urged her
to teach math as a volunteer. Sophia, excited about earning
her own money, paid as little attention to his opinions as she
always had in the past.

Jex-Blake was in Edinburgh in 1862 when Elizabeth
Garrett applied to the medical school there; her imagination
was fired by the wild idea of a woman applying for medical
school. She accompanied Garrett to see some of the faculty,
and the professors always assumed that the gentle, sweet
woman sitting beside the talkative, forceful, tall woman with
the flashing dark eyes was there to back up Sophia Jex-

85

Blake's application. At this time Sophia was interested only in reforming education for women; she had had a miserable year of teaching rambunctious girls in a German school in Mannheim. Disgruntled, she had the effrontery to sail for America to study colleges there.

A letter of introduction brought her to Dr. Lucy Sewall, a colleague of Marie Zakrzewska at the New England Hospital for Women.

A young woman, Florence Fenwick Miller, who was later to follow in Jex-Blake's footsteps and enter the University of Edinburgh in 1869, described Dr. Sewall's appearance as "quite alarming ... she wore terrible spectacles that magnified the entire eyeball, and she fixed this piercing gaze upon me...." She said she felt like an insect under a microscope.

Jex-Blake, thrilled by the companionship of women who had real roles in life--professions, no less--wrote home of the first female surgeon--much to the consternation of her parents. Dr. Sewall invited her to help in the dispensary, and Jex-Blake discovered a natural talent for administration.

In September 1866 she wrote asking Harvard to admit her; she received a form letter. There were no provisions for educating women at Harvard.

In 1866 Elizabeth and Emily Blackwell had opened a medical college for women, and Jex-Blake was the first student, working like a slave but still as high as a kite, her health and enthusiasm exuberant. She had been in America three years when her studies were cut short by her need to return to England because her father was dying. Now she was determined to study medicine in England, and she returned to Edinburgh, where she had supported Garrett's appeals for admission to the medical school.

Ironically, though most of Jex-Blake's friends encouraged her, Elizabeth Garrett did not, because Garrett had learned through tough experience that a doctor requires objectivity. Garrett saw Jex-Blake's temperament, her intense loves and hates and her sensitivity to criticism, as drawbacks; she told Jex-Blake to her face, "Frankly, I think you're not specially suited" (Todd, p. 186).

Of the three women who pioneered the medical women's movement, Elizabeth Blackwell, Elizabeth Garrett Anderson, and Sophia Jex-Blake, the evidence is that Jex-Blake was the most intelligent, perhaps a genius; but hers was a powerful, even brash, personality, so that she was as readily disliked as she was respected.

She heard that two influential men at Edinburgh might help her: David Masson of the English department and Sir James Simpson, who actually arranged a meeting with the dean of the medical school. He may have sympathized with this ambitious woman, but he was afraid she would not be able to dissect a cadaver. Jex-Blake assured him she had dissected several already. With this problem out of the way, and in view of her proven abilities as a scholar with a published book on higher education in the United States, the doctor said she was to be allowed to take botany and natural history during the summer session. Jex-Blake was thrilled to get into college, even sideways--"the edge of the wedge," she described it.

Although she had the approval of the marvelous Sir James Simpson, who had been so helpful to Elizabeth Garrett, a university faculty member vetoed Jex-Blake's permission to enroll for summer school on the grounds that her admission was a "temporary arrangement in the interests of only one lady."

Within two months Jex-Blake was back, sweetly admitting they were right, that it would not be worthwhile to change rules for only one woman. She had returned with five who would like to apply for university admission, and two more might apply the following year!

Jex-Blake had been sought out by these women, who volunteered to help her because they were incensed at her rebuff as a solitary applicant. Among these recruits was Isabel Thorne, a married woman who had spent years in China aware of terrible unsanitary conditions and the need to combat them. She had considered the study of medicine; and the publicity surrounding Jex-Blake had spurred her to apply to the university. Edith Pechey was 24 years old and hesitant about applying, but Jex-Blake encouraged her and Helen Evans and Matilda Chaplin, a "gallant little band." Jex-Blake proposed that the university permit her and these four women to take entrance examinations and to register to work toward a medical degree.

One mistake Jex-Blake made was to guarantee whatever

extra fees the university would charge for these separate
accommodations for teaching the women. After much legis-
lating, women, for the first time in history, were legally
and officially enrolled as students in a British university,
but they had to pay three times as much as other undergrad-
uates!

The honeymoon with the university was short. Although the women were taught in classes separate from the
men, they studied the same subjects. Publication of grades
caused keen embarrassment to a faculty that had long maintained that women had smaller and inferior brains. Of 140
men, 32 had taken honors in botany; five of the five women
also took honors. In chemistry, 31 of 226 men took honors;
four out of the five women also took honors. And one of
the women, Edith Pechey, who had come to the University
of Edinburgh sorely afraid that she could not compete with a
man, had won top class honors in chemistry and walked away
with the coveted Hope Scholarship! She would not have to
pay laboratory fees the following year.

Edinburgh had only admitted the five women to prove
they couldn't cope with the work. Now, the chemistry professor, Dr. Crum Brown (yes, Crum!) decided to give
Edith Pechey's prize to the male student just below her, because Pechey was not a regular class member and "was in-
eligible for the prize." When this tidbit hit the British
press, the Scots were up in arms. Until now the five wom-
en had been ignored or regarded as eccentric, but suddenly
all Edinburgh waxed indignant in letters-to-the-editor, and
the university faculty looked like a bunch of fools.

That summer, in "Surgeons' Hall," an extramural
school that offered anatomy and surgery among other courses,
the women were permitted to study in a peaceful atmosphere.
Now the time approached for the women to begin clinical
training in a hospital. The Royal Free Infirmary usually
accepted students for such training, and Jex-Blake optimistically, and unrealistically, anticipated no problems.

In November the women were to take the examinations in anatomy; Jex-Blake and her fellow women students
were mobbed when they tried to enter Surgeons' Hall. Not
a single police officer came to their aid. The gates were
slammed in their faces, and students, vagrants, and toughs
screamed insults at them in disgusting language. Finally a classmate proved himself a gentleman and ran down

to open the front door of the Hall and pull open the gates, ushering the women to their class. The exam was given amidst hooting, howling, cursing, and yelling from the mob.

The crowd, still waiting when the exam was over, pelted the women with mud and insults. The threat to the women aroused the chivalry of Edinburgh: a group of citizens formed a "Committee to Secure Complete Medical Education to Women in Edinburgh." At a mass meeting supporting the right of the women to study medicine, an elderly woman rose to ask, "If students studying in the Infirmary cannot accept women as fellow students, how can they have the scientific spirit or personal purity of mind to justify their presence in female wards during delicate operations or examinations of female patients?" The question was received with hoots, howls, and hisses from the balcony, but no one dignified the question with a reply. When Jex-Blake tried to speak, the horseplay was so noisy she couldn't be heard, and she was pelted with spitballs.

The women medical students managed to complete the classes that could be taken at Surgeons' Hall for credit toward a University of Edinburgh degree. The medical faculty, even those that had befriended the women, were now intimidated by Jex-Blake's enemies and refused to arrange for private tutoring for the few remaining courses the women needed for graduation. Not the smallest concession could be made toward helping the women get a medical degree. On the contrary, the university offered "certificates of proficiency" as an alternative. Jex-Blake insisted that the university had allowed the women to begin their medical studies and to continue them at great expense. She decided to turn to the courts. The courts found for Jex-Blake and her friends, and the women now hit their books to prepare for exams. Jex-Blake, still involved in litigation and committee work, was near exhaustion when she took her final examinations. What was to haunt her all the rest of her life was that all the women passed the exams except her. At the same time the lower court's decision finding in favor of the women medical students was reversed: the judges decided that the University of Edinburgh was not obligated to let the women graduate because the powers of the university had been exceeded by admitting women in the first place!

So four long years of fighting were for nothing; Jex-Blake was no nearer her goal than she had been before the battle of Edinburgh. She had become notorious in England.

The press had been brutal to the women. The Spectator for December 3, 1870, observed editorially, "The bitter and unprecedented malignity with which women who aspire to be doctors are pursued by the literary class is as hard to explain as it is to tolerate.... We can understand why doctors should be angry, for, after all, every profession in this country is more or less a trades-union...." But the writer wondered what possible reason the Saturday Review of the previous week had to publish an article "without a literary parallel in ... history ...," so brutal that a "costermonger quarrelling with a fishwife would be ashamed."

Jex-Blake later maintained that her finals had not been poor enough to justify failing grades, but that the faculty had failed her out of spite. An article in the Times commented that it was amusing that "one of the ladies who had rendered herself most conspicuous should after all have failed under the test of examinations."

Finally, Jex-Blake made up her mind to start her own hospital. She signed up a teaching staff and registered a dozen students, and on October 12, 1874, the London School of Medicine for Women opened its doors. She herself found a house, directed the builders, painters, and plumbers, and did all the organization.

Two years later she and Edith Pechey went to Bern to begin fulfilling the hours of hospital work required by Switzerland, and to take university examinations to qualify them to write M. D. after their names. Eight long years had passed since the time they should have had that right. The year 1876 remains a milestone, not only in the life of Sophia Jex-Blake, but in the history of education and medicine for women, for that year a bill was passed in England enabling all universities of the United Kingdom and Ireland to grant degrees to women--a bill that owes its origin to Jex-Blake's spunk and stamina.

Jex-Blake was 36 the year she studied at Bern to prepare for her medical examinations. She was not without qualms about failing again. But she passed, and that evening she wrote in her diary: "Now to see how much better an M. D. sleeps than other people!"

Jex-Blake and Edith Pechey still had to take the licensing examinations in Dublin. On May 6, 1877, two successful candidates were licensed to practice as members of the Irish College of Physicians. Their names, entered on the Medical Register of England, opened the way for all qualified woman doctors. They had won for women the right to a medical education, to hospital training, and to inclusion in the Medical Register. Jex-Blake observed that no monopolies were tolerated in the British Empire yet women were forcibly excluded from the legalized practice of medicine because of the Medical Act of 1858--which resulted from Elizabeth Garrett's being entered on the Medical Register.

Bursting with triumphant energy, Jex-Blake returned to the London School of Medicine she had founded. The Royal Free Hospital of London had agreed to admit women for clinical training--providing fees large enough to subsidize the hospital were paid. An executive secretary had to be appointed, and now that she was a doctor, she was qualified for the position of honor. However, while Jex-Blake was in Dublin, a group who opposed her nominated Elizabeth Garrett Anderson. Garrett must have recalled her opposition to Jex-Blake's becoming a physician, and both women were horrified. Garrett suggested Isabel Thorne as an alternative, and Thorne, who had at last come to the point in her life where her family responsibilities would allow her to complete the medical degree she had desired for so long, made the supreme sacrifice; she gave up further studies and accepted the position, in which she served for 30 years. There may have been a sweet irony in her heart the day her daughter graduated from the London School of Medicine, and we are indebted to Dr. May Thorne for recording the events and dates of importance about pioneer British medical women.

Isabel, who had wanted to study medicine because she believed the death of her first child was due to inadequate medical knowledge, proved a capable, tactful administrator. Jex-Blake respected her, but felt deprived by the fact that the school she had founded was being run by someone else. She decided to return to Edinburgh.

In 1885, Jex-Blake launched a hospital in Brompton Links, Edinburgh, for needy women and children. To this day, the hospital faithfully serves the city that was witness to one of the great crusades of women of all times. Her demands for justice won her the reputation of a battle-ax. Demands for justice usually come from angry, morally indignant people. To exclude anger from the human community, as Rousseau insisted, is to concentrate all the passions

in a "self-interest of the meanest sort." Such a universe
would offer no progress. Sophia Jex-Blake's book Medical
Women, published in 1886, was one of the first ever written
on a subject that has rocked the world.

REACHING FOR THE STARS

8. Susie O'Reilly

Sophia Jex-Blake's experiences were mirrored on the other
side of the world, in Sydney, Australia. Susannah Hennessy
O'Reilly, the oldest child of a physician, was educated at
Methodist Ladies' College and the University of Sydney, received her M. B. and M. Ch. in 1905, and applied for residency at Sydney Hospital. She was better qualified than
many of the men applicants, but she was told there was no
place to house her. Annually six doctors completed residency, and their places would be filled by incoming students
who had passed examinations in the university medical school.

The year that Dr. O'Reilly applied the directors had
selected only five men, and her name was considered. The
directors agreed that she had a "splendid record, " but felt
that it would not be in the best interests of the hospital to
appoint a woman doctor. Since Dr. O'Reilly would be an
officer, she would not be comfortable in the nurses' quarters, and her presence might be a restraint on the nurses
because her orders had to be obeyed. Dr. O'Reilly might
have been housed in a room outside the hospital, but residents had always conformed to strict discipline and had not
been allowed outside hospital premises without permission.
Each resident was assigned special cases, and if a patient
were suddenly taken ill during the night, it might be difficult to get a woman doctor to his or her bedside. And
would a woman not have a restraining influence on her male
colleagues in certain cases? Some members of the board
who had worked with women doctors in hospitals stated that
it had been their experience that nurses seemed to resent
the authority of a woman doctor. So the sixth residency
was given to a man.

One indignant volunteer for Sydney Hospital wrote the
newspaper that she would no longer collect money for charity, as "it seems we get all work and no honey, we women. "

93

Undaunted, Susie O'Reilly read the verses about her in the letters-to-the-editor columns of the Sydney papers: public opinion was aroused.

'Tis in the Sydney hospital which people speak of highly
The doctors hate the doctor gal
Whose name is Sue O'Reilly!
They know she is a gifted maid
And Truly skilful in the trade,
But, sooth to say,
They seem afraid
Of Doctor Sue O'Reilly!...

Susie O'Reilly was accepted by the Royal Adelaide Hospital and later by the Queen Victoria Hospital in Melbourne; eventually she joined the staff of the Royal Hospital for Women in Sydney. In 1908 she practiced with her father, taking charge of his patients after his death.

Having walked into the brick wall of prejudice against women in medicine, Dr. O'Reilly gave her enthusiastic support to the founding of the New Hospital for Women and Children in Sydney in 1921. That year Dr. Lucy Gullett had attended the jubilee celebrations of the Queen Victoria Hospital, which had been established in 1896 by medical women for the care of women and children. The hospital had offered some solutions for training and practice of women who had graduated from medical school and had not been able to get on the staff of a hospital. Dr. Gullett, who had graduated from the medical school of the University of Sydney and had been resident medical officer at the Children's Hospital in Brisbane, saw the need for a similar hospital in Sydney.

During World War I Dr. Gullett drove an ambulance in France and served with a French hospital at Lyons. In 1918 she returned to practice in Kirribilli and was honorary physician to the Renwick Hospital for Infants.

Gullett, O'Reilly, and Dr. Harriet Biffin, among others, raised £1,000 to buy a house in Sydney's slum area; the hospital opened in January 1921. The doctors themselves scrubbed floors and walls, painted, and took up hammers and nails to do the repairs. The building was so unstable that an overweight patient, for her own protection, was kept on the ground floor. The hospital had to be confined to out-patients, since there were no beds. The women physicians made house calls for seriously ill patients and did all the work of management as well. The greatest challenge was establishing a venereal-disease clinic, which still functions as the largest and most proficient in Australia.

In 1925 the hospital, having outgrown its rickety shack, was moved to larger, better-equipped premises in George Street, Redfern. The name was changed to the Rachel Forster Hospital for Women and Children, honoring the wife of the Governor-General who had enjoyed great popularity during his term of office (1920-25). The Forsters had had four children, but the two daughters had married and the two sons had been killed in the war. Since there would be no way of continuing the name, the women doctors wished to show appreciation for Lady Forster's strong support.

The hospital is a testimony to the efforts of the women of Sydney, who collected old bottles, newspapers, and bacon and meat drippings in tins, and held "egg appeals." The limitations on practice that the founders of the Rachel Forster Hospital were forced to accept are now ancient history. In recent years the baby-health centers serve the people of the area, and men as well as women patients are treated by both men and women doctors. Dr. Margery Scott-Young teaches surgery to male and female residents and as superintendent of the hospital supervises the medical care of over 50,000 patients per year.

As in America and England, Australian women doctors have deeply influenced the awareness of the kind of health care that should be available to everyone.

REACHING FOR THE STARS

9. Mary Putnam Jacobi

Mary Corinna Putnam, the oldest of ten children, was a
girl who did what girls were not supposed to do. First of
all, she loved science. Her father, publisher George Pal-
mer Putnam, was the founder of G. P. Putnam. Mary in-
herited his literary talent. Her first story, "Lost and
Found, " sold to the Atlantic Monthly when she was 17. Her
proud father got hold of the check and converted it into $5
gold pieces, which he dropped one by one into Mary's hand.
With each piece Mary squealed, sure it was the last. She
couldn't believe she had been paid $80! That was a lot of
money in those days.

Mary Putnam graduated from the New York College
of Pharmacy in 1862. She thought of her graduation as a
stepping stone toward a medical career. Her parents were
broad-minded, but they hated to see their oldest girl head
for heartbreak. She was 21 and considered herself old
enough to make her own decisions. She left New York to
enroll in the Female Medical College in Philadelphia. The
college, founded in 1850 by Quakers, was headed
by Dr. Ann Preston, a mild Quaker of considerable courage.
The school fought one crisis after another. Male doctors
had been threatened with reprisals if they consented to teach
women medical students. During the Civil War the college,
sharing the fate of others, closed for lack of money. After
the war, Dr. Preston reopened the college and took up the
fight to get the graduates accepted in medical organizations.
In 1876, the American Medical Association (the dinosaur's
tail was already twitching) seated its first woman delegate--
a doctor from Illinois.

When Mary Putnam looked over the two-year course
of study at the Woman's Medical College, she realized that
the same sets of lectures were offered each year, the second year being merely a repetition of the first. Determined

96

not to miss a lecture, Putnam, already holding a diploma in pharmacy, decided to finish in a year. She asked to take the examinations at the end of the year, and she passed with flying colors. She and six classmates graduated in a decrepit waiting room of the Woman's Hospital in March 1866. Putnam, now legally qualified to practice medicine, interned at New England Hospital for Women in Boston, founded two years earlier by Marie Zakrzewska--Dr. Zak.

Putnam felt that she had had a deprived education in medicine. American doctors, she thought, relied too much on observation and experiences rather than on "science." Microscopes and stethoscopes were scorned by many American doctors. What she longed to do was go to Europe, to Paris, to improve her medical skills. Her income from her medical practice was so minuscule that to raise money she had to tutor a young fellow trying to pass West Point entrance examinations. (In 1866 her pupil successfully passed the tests, and Putnam's brother observed wryly, "After a year of working with a slave driver like Mary, the young man may find West Point discipline a relief!")

Putnam didn't know a word of French. But she enrolled in the University of Paris anyway. Thanks to Elizabeth Blackwell, who was in France at the time, she was able to rent a room with a view so lovely she remembered it the rest of her life. Within months she was talking a blue streak in French, although her accent had her French listeners covering their ears in distress.

At the Ecole de Médecine Putnam, following doctors on hospital rounds, was soon respected for her quickness at diagnosis. But there was a method in it for her: before the physician's rounds she examined the patients and considered what they said about their pains and problems. One day at Beaujon a physician asked her if she agreed with a doctor's diagnosis of typhoid.

"No, Monsieur, it's mumps," Putnam replied confidently, and then offered corroboration for her diagnosis.

"Correct!" said the doctor, and, turning to the other students, said: "Gentlemen, good students are not afraid to offer a minor ailment as a diagnosis."

Putnam was as excited as a girl on a date with a handsome guy the first time she put her eye to a borrowed

microscope. Her heart beat so hard she could hear the
pounding in her ears.

Though she was making rounds and observing in the
hospital, she was still not allowed to apply to the Ecole de
Médecine as a medical student. She watched surgery in the
clinic and borrowed books from the medical library. Formal acceptance as a student was still denied her. The Minister of Public Instruction was a progressive who let it be
known he'd like to have women admitted to the medical
school. Dr. Putnam made a formal application to the
school, but no one in the office of admission had ever heard
of the progressive minister's views, obviously, for she was
promptly turned down.

Her disappointment however, was assuaged by a professor of histology, who told her she'd be welcome in his
lectures. Her presence in the amphitheater didn't destroy
the university. Students soon became accustomed to the at-
tractive woman taking fastidious notes. After 18 months of
studying in French hospitals, she was allowed to take the
crucial entrance examinations. In a new dress--for her
morale--and a brightly flowered hat Mary Putnam passed
both written and oral examinations, and for the first time
the Ecole de Médecine enrolled a fully accredited woman
student, an American! She graduated with highest honors
in her class.

Once the barriers to women were down, Putnam soon
had other women walking with her in the hallowed halls of
the Ecole de Médecine.

Returning to America, she entered private practice
at last. Her father himself proudly drove the nails that
fastened the shingle to the window frame of her new office.
Dr. Emily Blackwell, director of the Women's Medical College of the New York Infirmary, asked Putnam to teach.

In 1880 the august New York Academy of Medicine
welcomed Dr. Putnam to membership. The following year
she was invited to join the New York County Medical Society, and the occasion was a turning point in her life. At a
Society meeting she met Dr. Abraham Jacobi, a professor
of children's diseases at New York University.

Born in Westphalia, Prussia, in 1830, Jacobi had
been a sickly child, (which, in addition to the loss of his

own children, may have accounted for his interest in pediatrics) and his mother had considered no expense or effort too great to save his life. He had received his education thanks to his sacrificing mother, who managed to get him through the Gymnasium. He studied clinical medicine, anatomy, and chemistry in Göttingen, and from there went to Bonn for three semesters. Two years later he sailed for America and started a practice in New York, He received $5 for a confinement--when the patient could pay.

Jacobi, the father of American pediatrics, established the first special clinic for children in the country, which opened in New York in 1862. Traditionally the medical profession had regarded children as midget men and women. Children had been treated with the same medicine and methods as adults; one out of 25 infants failed to survive the first year of life--and thousands of death certificates of infants gave "teething" as the cause of death. Jacobi publicly expressed his view that city orphanages were graveyards, where infants, reared in a loveless environment, could not survive six months. He advocated placing children in foster homes. Because of his crusading this practice spread throughout America.

Dr. Jacobi, meeting Mary Putnam for the first time, recognized a great personal magnetism between them. They shared not only medical interests but liberal politics as well. She asked Dr. Jacobi why he had never married. He replied he was already twice a widower, his first wife having died in childbirth, his second wife with her fourth stillborn child.

Putnam could not hide her compassion for a man who had buried two wives and five infants. From sympathy and empathy her emotions turned quickly to love. She and Dr. Jacobi were married on July 22, 1883, in a City Hall ceremony.

Mary Putnam and Abraham Jacobi had another shared interest: medical writing. In his eighth year in America, in 1860, Dr. Jacobi with another physician had written a book on the disease of women and children. It cost them $800 to print. "We finally sold the edition for wastepaper," he remembered later, "and though that resulted in a profit of $68.00--it ended my career as a publisher."

The Jacobis disapproved of the tendency toward

specialization. They emphasized treating the whole patient, and kept drumming into their students that they were in medical school to become doctors.

Abraham Jacobi became the nineteenth-century Dr. Spock in response to the request of the Public Health Department to write a book on baby care for parents' guidance. Mary turned her literary talents to helping record her husband's observations and experience. Her father's firm, G. P. Putnam, published the book Infant Diet, on which generations of mothers came to rely with confidence.

Mary Jacobi founded The Association for the Advancement of Medical Education for Women, and continued to lecture at Female Medical College, although she was pregnant with her first child. Her pregnancy seemed normal, and she never complained. But the infant was born with defective lungs and did not survive. Dr. Jacobi had lost his sixth child. Mary shared his great grief.

Determined to see that her husband had the family he longed for, Mary Jacobi again became pregnant, and the second baby was born in August 1875, a blooming boy, named Ernst. Dr. Jacobi's cup of joy seemed to overflow as the months passed and the child flourished. Abraham Jacobi was elected president of the New York State Medical Society and became renowned as a doctor, but nothing gave him as much pleasure as his children, Ernst and Marjorie.

In 1875 Harvard University sponsored an essay contest, "Do women require mental and bodily rest during menstruation?" Mary Jacobi disapproved of the canard that a woman had to lose a week out of every month because she menstruated, and she found repulsive the idea that a woman could not compete in the professional world because of her natural functions, that she was unfit to be a doctor because a fourth of her life had to be spent under the influence "of a function in which neither mind nor body are in a condition to meet professional demands." (As old-fashioned as that argument sounds, it still comes up today, as it did in 1970, when Estelle Ramey made mincemeat out of Dr. Edgar Berman's arguments that women were not "hormonally suited to have highly responsible positions.") Mary was determined to do research on the subject. Since the Boylston Medical Prize entries would be submitted anonymously, the judges would have no way of knowing if the essay were written by a man or a woman.

Earlier she had written a paper encouraging girls to study and observe common-sense rules of good hygiene. Some doctors insisted that during "the temporary insanity of menstruation no mental activity can be carried out." Since Biblical times women had been considered unclean at certain times of the month. But in the hospital women doctors and nurses refused to be invalids for a week out of every month. Jacobi had certainly seen women suffer from menstrual misery. Using her wide acquaintance among women, rich and poor, educated and uneducated, married and single, she sent out 1,000 questionnaires. Among other questions, she asked "How far can you walk?" Such answers as "Five or six miles easily," to "Ten to fifteen if necessary," were common. In those days women walked.

Mary Jacobi was far ahead of her time when she observed the connection between celibacy and suffering. When marriage was regarded as the only life for a girl, failure to marry meant failure in life. Women who remained unmarried were frequently despairing. Jacobi saw that boredom could cause mental breakdowns. She came inevitably to the conclusion that mental and physical activity during menstruation was not only desirable but necessary.

With her data scientifically assembled, Jacobi wrote a paper so superior to any others submitted, she was the unquestioned winner of the contest.

In recent years a lecturer on women's health, Paula Weideger, wrote a book, Menstruation and Menopause, that carries forward Mary Jacobi's research. Weideger examined the physiology and psychology, the myths, legends, and reality of two of our last taboos. Even the words tend to be disguised, for women refer to their menses as "the period," or "the curse," or they're "unwell." Then they go through "the change of life." Or as one woman replied to another who had bragged about "going around the world"--"I've gone through the change." Millions of American women still harbor embarrassed shame about menstruation, and the most humiliating jokes aimed at women, next to mother-in-law stories, are those involving menopause, "the end of womanhood."

"Once women begin to consider the experiences of menstruation and menopause as legitimate parts of their lives and remove the moral judgments applied to those who have particular problems with these cycles," writes Weideger, "things will change." Like Mary Jacobi, Weideger urges women to seek meaningful medical care. Cramps are not illusions, she assures menstruating women, and very little is now known about either cause or cure. "This isn't surprising since the problem has only recently become a 'legitimate' medical issue." Yet in 1882, when Mary Putnam Jacobi was appointed to the faculty of the Post-Graduate Medical School of New York, she was already investigating such problems.

By 1883 Mary and Abraham Jacobi were known as "the first family of American medicine." Their home on 34th Street was a gathering place for young doctors. That year tragedy struck. Their eight-year-old son died of diphtheria. Abraham, the nation's leading authority on the disease, was plunged into depression. Mary developed splitting headaches and eventually put her diagnostic skills to study meningeal tumors compressing the cerebellum. She died on the 23rd anniversary of the death of her son, June 10, 1906.

Mary Jacobi's teaching reached not only women medical students but graduate physicians, male and female. Her love for and pride in her husband brought her great satisfaction, and she enjoyed telling of an invitation that came to her husband from the German Kaiser, offering to forgive Jacobi's trespasses (he had been a political prisoner in 1853-54) if only the good doctor would return to take care of the children of the royal nursery. Jacobi did not mull the matter over. He wrote back that since New York children needed him as much as the imperial court youngsters, he'd just stay where he was.

After his death someone found among Abraham Jacobi's papers, the scribbled lines: "If you asked an old man who had been through hard lifelong work and heartrending scenes, through success, maybe, and endless failures and disappointments, what he craved to be if he began life again, he would, I think, reply, 'Just a modern doctor.'"

Mary Putnam Jacobi was of the same mind.

REACHING FOR THE STARS

10. Rosalie Slaughter Morton

In 1937, when Rosalie Slaughter Morton published her autobiography, A Woman Surgeon, she assumed that discrimination against women in medicine was old hat. "Women doctors during the past fifty years have held a special place in
the field of Medicine," she wrote. She was already an officer in a section of the American Medical Association, the
first woman physician to receive such an appointment.
"Women have helped to humanize their profession as well as
to administer their scientific knowledge" (Morton, p. 7).

With a name like Slaughter, she might have eschewed
surgery, but she was determined. Before the turn of the
century, when Rosalie Slaughter began studying medicine, she
entered what was a man's profession. To her, "That it
should be exclusively his seemed ridiculous." In her town,
Lynchburg, Va., where she was born in 1876, she was a
minority of one, who believed minorities had rights. And
"then came what seems a miracle. The world speeded up
its revolutions, bringing changes overnight that ordinarily
would require a century." Thrilled to be part of the "ka-
leidoscope of evolution" from old forms to new, she saw
herself as a bridge between the pioneer women in medicine
and the college women "for whom everything is won and
done." Her optimism was premature. Yet she conquered
worlds, and her story is fascinating.

From the time her ancestors had come from England
to settle in Virginia in the eighteenth century, 17 of their
direct, and 52 of their collateral, descendants had become
doctors. This heritage captured the imagination of the little
girl. Her parents responded like the minister who when
calling on his congregation for volunteers to be missionaries,
saw his own daughter rise, and exclaimed, "Oh, Anna, I
didn't mean you!"

Nor did Rosalie expect her parent's wholehearted

approval. In 1893 wealthy families expected their daughters
to marry well and become "model mothers." "My entire
upbringing and education had been designed to make me a
capable wife--not to imbue me with a desire for a career"
(Morton, p. 13). "As I recall those years, I am sure my
choice caused my family as much anxiety as does ardent
youth of today."

Slaughter was born October 28, 1876, the same year
as Emily Dunning Barringer, who earned fame as New York's
First Woman Ambulance Surgeon.

"Long before my decision to study medicine, I developed resourcefulness in this two-fisted school of experience in a man's world." One day her older brother John
took her and her brother Will to the circus. Will bought
the tickets, exchanging three quarters for three pieces of
cardboard, but when they came to enter the big tent Will
had only two tickets. A look of dismay flitted across his
face. "Rose," he said, "it's too bad, but I lost your
ticket" (Morton, p. 21).

"No, you didn't!" said little Rose, "You lost yours!"
and, giving him a hearty shove, she walked in ahead of him.

"An emancipated woman," she heard John murmur to
the ticket man as he slipped him another quarter.

When Rosalie was 12 she went to Edge Hill, a private
school directed by a great-granddaughter of Thomas Jefferson.
Later, at a finishing school in Baltimore, she was called
"Johnny Reb" by other children until her Southern accent dis-
appeared. Back again in Lynchburg, she became "Yank" to
her playmates.

When Rosalie was 16 she told her mother that she
wanted to be a nurse, and she began to fill out and send applications to nursing schools. Meeting nothing but rejections,
Rosalie told her mother that she didn't really want to make
a life-work of nursing. ("What relief showed in her eyes!"
she recalled.) "That would be just to get started," Rosalie
added. "I really intend to be a doctor, like the boys."

With great reluctance Mrs. Slaughter spoke of how
the walls of Rosalie's sheltered life might crumble. When
Rosalie replied that Joan of Arc had become a soldier, her
distraught mother exclaimed, "She was a peasant! And she
was burned at the stake!"

However, her older brother Charles wrote from Duluth that if she graduated in medicine, she could come and practice with him. And Rosalie's Aunt Sue recalled that her Quaker grandmother had said, "If women had studied medicine when I was a girl, I would have done so." Rosalie became determined.

By the time of Rosalie's studies at Woman's Medical College in Philadelphia, successive classes of graduates had returned as members of the faculty, until two-thirds of the professors were women, many of them outstanding in their fields--Clara Marshall, dean of the college, was professor of therapeutics. But the year that Slaughter started medical school, 1893, there were only 133 women on civilian hospital staffs.

Slaughter was enchanted by her histology classes. Her pathology professor, Dr. Lydia Rabinovitch, had recently been associated with the great Dr. Koch in his discovery of the microorganism that causes tuberculosis. She treated her subject with dramatic flair. Morton was also excited by work with the microscope.

Rosalie's father had assumed that his daughters would marry and be cared for by dutiful husbands, and since one daughter was already happily married, he wrote a will that made no provisions for his girls. After providing for his wife, he left most of the money to his sons and grandchildren. Neither bitter nor resentful, Slaughter regarded her sudden financial independence as a newfound freedom. Her thin coat, warm enough for Virginia, proved inadequate for Pennsylvania winters, and she wore a jacket of newspapers with a hole torn for her head. She felt challenged to see how much she could go without.

Slaughter was spurred on by the thought that she was carrying a torch passed from hand to hand from the first American pioneer woman doctor. She read about the first person executed in Massachusetts Bay Colony, Margaret Jones, a physician accused of witchcraft--Joan of Arc was not the only heroine burned at the stake! And from the Connecticut blue laws, March 1638: "Jane Hawkins, the wife of Richard Hawkins, has liberty till the beginning of the third month called May, and the Magistrates (if she does not depart before) to dispose of her, and in the meantime she is not to meddle in surgery or phisick, drinks, plaisters, or oyles, nor to question matters of religion

except with the Elders for satisfaction." The town records
of Rehoboth, Mass., mention the arrival in July 1663 of Dr.
Sam Fuller and his mother, who began the practice of midwifery because the town's necessity "was great." In 1765
Marlboro, Vt., was served by Mrs. Thomas Whitemore,
"possessed of a vigorous constitution and frequently travelling through tne woods on snow-shoes ... to relieve the
distressed."

During her second summer vacation Slaughter worked
ten hours a day in Massachusetts State Hospital at Tewkes-
bury, assisting in the pharmacy, taking histories of patients,
recording physical examinations, and administering medicines
in the wards.

Her father had said he would not like to see his
daughter, reared as a lady, accept a salary. She told her
superintendent she was learning so much it did not seem
fair to be paid for it. She was told she had earned it, and
she must not upset the hospital's bookkeeping.

Slaughter's professional interest was quickly translated into personal concern: the patients were human beings
to her rather than "cases." Generally, hospital personnel
were detached and depersonalized; her youthful enthusiasm
endeared her to the patients, most of whom were paupers
and discards. She admired their courage and tried to make
friends among them. She gave them the understanding and
sympathy they needed as much as medicine. Here, too, she
had her first harrowing experiences with the insane.

Before her final examinations Slaughter had to attend,
deliver, and give after-care to ten obstetrical cases. Among
these was a pale little woman who lived in an alley and said,
"I hope the baby ain't living." Rosalie delivered a three-
and-a-half-pound baby, which was soon followed by a twin of
the same weight. The mother cried, "Lord, take it back!
I didn't want <u>any</u>, and now there are <u>two</u>. If I couldn't
take care of <u>six</u>, how can I take care of eight?"

Slaughter had to breathe life into the second baby.
But like other women doctors who went through the experience of delivering unwanted babies as part of their education,
the young intern worked just as hard at resuscitating the
scrawny little twins as though they were heirs to a fortune.
"The collapsed lungs gradually expanded, the spaces between
the fragile ribs filled out, and the rhythm of breathing began.

I hurried with the wrinkled, aged-looking babies to the Women's Hospital ..." (p. 46).

Concluding the grueling, practical obstetrical preparation for her medical degree Slaughter was lucky to be recommended to fill an emergency vacancy for an unexpired internship at the Philadelphia City Hospital. She still had to study evenings for final examinations, but the internship provided not only invaluable experience and chances to observe, but she could also save room-and-board expenses. She became familiar with diagnosis and treatment and internal medicine. She submitted a full case history of pernicious anaemia with lab reports and treatment records, and an essay that won the Alumnae Prize of $25 (which she "joyfully squandered on clothes") (p. 47).

On graduation day, an hour before Rosalie Slaughter was to receive her degree of Doctor of Medicine and Surgery, a telegram was delivered to her while she was on ward duty: "If you wish to see Mother alive, come home immediately." There was no train for Lynchburg for five hours; she received her degree in ice-cold hands and then took the Lynchburg train home.

She spent a month in her mother's room, and when Mary Slaughter died, her doctor daughter prayed that she would be worthy of such a mother.

Dean Clara Marshall wrote, asking Slaughter to become resident physician of the Alumnae Hospital and Dispensary of the Woman's Medical College in Philadelphia. Here, daily, from nine till five, six women physicians from the college came at scheduled hours to give unpaid care to the poor and ill.

Mornings were devoted to registering new patients and doing emergency work. Slaughter removed splinters, changed dressings, swabbed throats. Serious or chronic conditions were treated in special clinics upstairs.

Like many other American women physicians, Rosalie Slaughter went to Europe to do postgraduate study--Berlin for surgery, Vienna for internal diseases practice, and Paris for study of nervous ailments. She was primarily interested in gynecology. Graduates of European universities regarded their training as more thorough than that of Americans. European M. D. degrees required six years to four years in

America. The experience Slaughter had gained at Massachusetts General Hospital, Philadelphia City Hospital, and as a resident physician had given her, she believed, with her four-years' diploma, a little better training than most of the European graduates. She would not be intimidated.

Both her doctor brothers had studied in Vienna after their graduation from the University of Virginia medical school. "To be in the city of Mozart, Haydn and Beethoven, to walk in the Ring-strasse, to live in the most cosmopolitan place for education in the world, was a privilege indeed," she wrote in her autobiography (p. 67).

Classes of ten studied for two months with various professors. The professor of dermatology hesitated to have a young woman in class.

She admits she was shocked when a naked syphilitic man was brought before the class. The patient was probably as startled as the young doctor. For the first time Slaughter realized her father's worst fears for a lady, his daughter, studying medicine. Nevertheless, when she went to the professor and admitted her chagrin, he offered to take her on his rounds and give her special instruction. Elated, she accepted, for she would gain far more than if she continued in the class.

The charity hospital in Vienna was then the largest in the world, and Dr. Slaughter was allowed to observe operations and to study diagnosis in lung, heart, kidney, brain, and other conditions. What illustrations, textbooks, and lectures could not teach in a year, she later wrote, a professor of pathology could make clear in Vienna in a week. She remained five months in order to take courses (p. 71).

In Vienna she was disturbed by the unnecessary exposure of patients in the amphitheater when illness or operations were demonstrated to classes. She saw a poor woman in childbirth, lying uncovered on a revolving table, while students observed her agony for an hour and a half. Wealthy patients were handled with courtesy; the poor with unfeeling harshness.

Dr. Slaughter met Samuel Clemens and his wife, who were residing then in Vienna. Mark Twain did not think it ridiculous for her to be a physician. In her turn she admired the "deep human understanding" beneath his wit.

In 1899, the year she turned 23, she was invited to
spend Christmas in Russia. Amidst the men and women in
fur coats and caps, she wore a thin coat, but she insisted
she was warm enough. She was taken to the opera to hear
Alexander Borodin's Prince Igor. The composer, a professor of organic chemistry at the Military Academy, had been
among the first to demand that women be given the privilege
of studying medicine, and the Medical School of Women was
finally organized in 1878, with Borodin an important influence
in its founding.

From the opera she was whisked back to the hotel,
tucked into a horse-drawn troika and luxuriously wrapped in
rugs. Given some books that were to be delivered to Leo
Tolstoy, she was invited to visit with the great man himself.
The visit became three long conversations (which she records
at length in her autobiography), and when he walked with her
to the door, he said graciously, "I have enjoyed talking to
you as a comrade. We have crossed the thresholds of each
other's minds and found hospitality" (p. 84).

In Paris Dr. Slaughter began a thorough study of
nervous diseases and the relation of circulatory disturbances,
respiratory malfunction, and colon and other constitutional
conditions to what had until then been called "women's problems." She believed that with good hygiene many vague
feminine illnesses might disappear.

As a champion of women she wanted to study all
kinds of women "from charwomen to circus bare-back eques-
trians." She held that diagnoses made by men often were
cruel or, at least, unkind to women. Men found it easy to
dismiss a nervous woman as exaggerating her symptoms.
Dr. Slaughter believed many women actually had suffered
for years with an inflammatory or congestive condition, mis-
placed organs, tumors, or lacerations, but had neglected to
seek relief because of "modesty, poverty or the mistaken
idea that it is normal for women to have pain and endure
it" (p. 88). She insisted that no one in perfect health was
ever "irritable."

In Paris she followed celebrated specialists as they
made rounds of the Hôtel Dieu, the Hôtel des Invalides, the
Charité, and the Salpêtrière to observe methods of nursing.

Under Dr. Eugène Berillon, Slaughter studied hypnotism, although she was aware that a woman doctor practicing

hypnotism would add dynamite to the fire of existing prejudices.

During the summer of 1900 Dr. Slaughter sailed for Christiania, Norway, with a letter of introduction to the playwright Henrik Ibsen in her bag. Perhaps she was taken with Ibsen's views on the emancipation of women. She was told that Ibsen was so punctual in his habits that the town clock would be set by his crossing the lobby of the Grand Hotel. At precisely one o'clock Ibsen crossed the lobby and took a chair in the dining room. The shape of his head reminded Dr. Slaughter of her own father. She arranged to meet him, and they discussed his plays, her doctoring, and his early job as a clerk in an apothecary's shop.

Dr. Slaughter went to England intending to work in the laboratory of the celebrated brain surgeon Sir Victor Horsley. She helped the doctor experiment on monkeys, observing how pressure on various parts of the brain caused the monkey to move a finger, thumb, arm, foot, or other part of its body.

Slaughter was preparing to terminate three years of postgraduate studies when Sir Victor offered her a permanent position in his laboratory. Unprepared to do research rather than active practice, she was surprised to hear his next proposal. "Have you ever thought of returning to America by way of India?"

During the six months she spent in India fighting bubonic plague she wavered constantly between fascination and horror. "Fakirs along the roadside, with their grotesque physical disfigurations and self-imposed tortures, amazed me with their human endurance...." Dr. Slaughter found herself in charge of many native patients. In Calcutta she received a letter from Dr. Annie Young, who had graduated four years before from the Woman's Medical College of Pennsylvania and was now a missionary in northern Ceylon. Her hospital was at Inuvil, where she was associated with Dr. Isabell Carr. Dr. Slaughter was impressed again with the work of the missionaries (another active missionary, Dr. Bertha Caldwell, a college-mate of Dr. Slaughter's, worked in Allahabad).

In September 1905, she married George B. Morton, Jr., who died when they had been married only a short time. As a professional, Rosalie was able to support herself and avoid some of the indignities of being a dependent widow.

During the winter of 1915 she became determined to volunteer for war service. At the time she was not only teaching but also had her own clinic, with five assistants under her. But her friends, Dr. Hans Zinsser of Columbia Medical and Dr. Richard Strong, returning from helping to quell a typhus epidemic in Serbia, told her about conditions there. Her sympathies for Serbia were strong; she longed to go where help was most needed. She had neither parents nor children. She was made a special commissioner of the Red Cross.

In the spring of 1916, before America was drawn into the war, she sailed for England, where she saw the hospitals and supply methods. On the Salonica front, in Greece, two of the most interesting English-speaking hospitals were run by women: the American Unit of the Scottish Women's Hospitals in Macedonia, and another unit on the Bay of Salonica. She volunteered her surgical and medical services. "In our vast tent hospital and on the fields of Macedonia, we had three thousand men under canvas, and never an empty cot." The hospital, near the Bulgarian border, was not far from German troops and occupied area.

Returning to the United States to report on the work of the American Red Cross, Morton urged the idea of a woman's hospital to the Medical Women's National Association and proposed war service for women. The one-year-old association supported her proposals, and Dr. Morton herself designed the American Women's Hospitals insignia, the staff of Aesculapius, surrounded by sheltering wings. *

When the American Women's Medical Association organized the War Service Committee (later named the American Women's Hospitals), Rosalie Slaughter Morton was named chair and was commissioned in 1917 to take supplies to Serbia. Although women doctors made significant contributions to the military, they were not commissioned at the

---

*Esther P. Lovejoy, who was president of the National Association in 1932-33, weaves an exciting story of the experiences of women professionals in the service of the American Women's Hospitals in Certain Samaritans, published by Macmillan in 1933.

beginning of World War I.   They could only obtain appointments to serve as contract surgeons (Raven, pp. 105-11).

After the war she organized a program for Serbian
students to pursue higher education in the United States.
Her private practice, primarily in New York, made it possible for her to accept the honor of being the first woman
professor in the medical school of Columbia University
(1917-18).

Dr. Morton, in her autobiography, had expressed
interest in travelling to Iran to study social conditions there.
In 1940 she published A Doctor's Holiday in Iran (Funk and
Wagnalls) with perceptive observations of clinics, missions
and women physicians, and the rapid social advances of that
troubled nation.

In 1923 Rosalie Slaughter Morton presented a bas-
relief to the Woman's Medical College of Pennsylvania, an
interpretation of Dr. Morton's concept "of the maternal
spirit which especially animates women to lessen suffering
and heal the sick. ''*

A ten-foot statue of three heroic white limestone female figures--representing Kindliness, Vision, and Fortitude--
was presented by Dr. Morton to her birthplace, Lynchburg,
Virginia in 1944.

A photo of Dr. Rosalie S. Morton, taken during the
First World War, appears in Esther Pohl Lovejoy's' Certain
Samaritans, p. 9.   In a high-collared uniform and khaki
cap, only a little of her thick black hair showing, she is
a handsome woman, with a straight nose and fine eyes with
a straight look to them, an oval face and an intelligent expression.

Eventually, to escape the cold of New York, she
moved to Winter Park, Florida and continued in private
practice to a venerable age.   She died on May 5, 1968, aged 96.

At the turn of the century, as we have seen, Dr.
Slaughter Morton optimistically predicted the fight for equality would soon be won, that men and women released from

*Note in "The Woman Physician, " Medical Woman's Journal,
30 (March 1923), pp. 94-95.

guilt or blame or hate, could use the best of each other's qualities to understand life and love. But her optimism was premature.

The author Marya Mannes has said, "The beautiful difference of our biological selves will not diminish this mutual fusion. It should indeed flower, expand; blow the mind as well as the flesh" so that men and women "could both breathe free."

REACHING FOR THE STARS

11.　Those Remarkable Johns Hopkins Women

The Jacobis were convinced that women would be admitted
to men's medical schools when women who held the philan-
thropic purses would put strings on their endowments.　Maybe money would talk where ability, determination, and ambition were mute.

This theory was tested when the trustees of Johns
Hopkins University ran into a financial iceberg.　In 1890
the university's projected medical school could not get off
the ground, though Johns Hopkins (1794-1873) had donated
$7 million, to be divided between a university and a hospi-
tal.　The university--without a medical school--opened February 22, 1876.　Fourteen years later the medical school
was still in the talking stage, the trustees begging for money.　The money soon appeared, but the trustees didn't like
the looks of Santa Claus.　They had never heard of a Ms.
Claus!

Baltimore, the home of Johns Hopkins, was the center of a movement for higher education for women.　A trus-
tee's daughter, M. Carey Thomas, and Mary Garrett (no
relative of Elizabeth Garrett), heir to a fortune from the
Baltimore and Ohio Railroad, were among the organizers of
Bryn Mawr School.　To provide women with college preparation matching that of men's prep schools, Bryn Mawr established a curriculum based on the undergraduate and graduate departments of Johns Hopkins.　These women gloatingly
recognized that the financial problems of the Johns Hopkins
medical school might be an ill wind that would blow some
good.　Determined to get women into the most advanced
school in America, they offered $200,000 to the school on
the condition that women be admitted.　The Hopkins trustees
heard this news with no enthusiasm.　They were openly
skeptical of the women's ability to raise the $200,000.

Undaunted, Mary Garrett contributed $10,000 to start

114

the ball rolling, and a "Women's Fund for the Higher Medical Education of Women," was launched. In a short time, by October 1890, the trustees were offered $100,000 with the proviso that women be admitted to the school.

The trustees, in the Southern manner rigidly courteous toward women, were determined to prevent coeducation at the Hopkins. But the women, all of them marriageable and all of them unmarried, were equally determined: no admission for women--no money.

The women refused to be ingratiating; they recognized the bag of tricks that the trustees held. The trustees might have actually refused to money did not two of the women, Mamie Gwinn and Elizabeth King, have fathers on the board. The trustees finally made a hard bargain; if the women would raise the $500,000 needed by the medical school, women might be admitted, but they hedged insultingly, "This board is satisfied that in hospital practice among women, in penal institutions in which women are prisoners, in charitable institutions in which women are cared for, and in private life when women are to be attended, there is a need and place for learned and capable women physicians."

While the medical school trustees were refusing to accept the women because the professors might find it embarrassing to teach them "indelicate subjects," the faculty was being recruited by other universities. Both Harvard and the University of Pennsylvania were known to have fished in the troubled waters.

In December 1892 Mary Garrett decided to add a personal gift of $306,977, which would make up the $500,000 thought necessary to open the school. But again she set some conditions: that the students must meet the requirements for admission to the graduate school of Johns Hopkins (at least a Bachelor's degree) and that they should know French and German as well as pre-medical subjects. Many Hopkins leaders had hoped to establish these standards, but the prevailing attitude was, "It is one thing to build an educational castle in the air at your library table, and another to face its actual appearance under existing circumstances." Fathers almost broke down and wept when they asked Mary Garrett to relax her requirements and conditions for donating the money. Such high requirements caused one doctor-teacher to observe, "We are lucky to get in as professors, for I am sure we could never get in as students."

But the true thorn in the side of the trustees was that Garrett continued to insist that women had to be admitted on the same terms as men. And she wanted men and women to have a four-year, rather than a three-year, course leading to the degree of doctor of medicine. Lengthening the medical curriculum was not a new idea. Northwestern University had pioneered the three-year medical school in 1859. When the Hopkins medical school opened its doors in 1893--the Johns Hopkins Hospital had opened in 1889--Harvard, the University of Michigan, and the University of Pennsylvania had gone on the four-year plan, with an eight-month school year (Flexner and Flexner, pp. 215-24).

From the beginning Johns Hopkins women distinguished themselves in scholarship.

Among those who entered the fourth class to include women was Florence Sabin. Her anatomy professor, Dr. Franklin Mall, recognized the woman's unusual gifts. He suggested an independent research project for her: investigation of the origin of lymphatic vessels. Sabin's discoveries on lymph had an explosive impact on medical views. *

Florence Sabin's biography is an affirmation of convictions about the responsibilities of people living in a democracy, of citizens, scientists, and women in medicine. Her struggle for a place in the world was a reality. She was not joking when she christened her first car "Susan B. Anthony."

Here was a woman who respected scholarship and knowledge. She felt she was too unattractive for any man to want to marry her. Born in 1871, Sabin grew into a fuzzy-haired, awkward little girl who looked through thick glasses out of the shaky frame house on a mountain in Silver City, Colo. A bookish girl, she escaped from her mining hometown through reading. When she was five years old a baby brother was born who lived only a year. A year later, Sabin's seventh birthday, her mother died a few days after the birth of another baby. This baby, too, managed to survive only a year, and Florence and her sister Mary, seven and nine, were sent to boarding schools. Despite a number of moves, Florence, by the time she was ready for

---

*The material to follow is based on Bluemel, Kubie, Rossi, and Rossiter.

Dr. Florence Sabin (photo courtesy Johns Hopkins University)

college, was affectionate, warm, amazingly secure and
trusting.

The sharp differences and animosities that developed
between the sisters when they were both at Smith College
may have whetted Sabin's lifelong interest in psychiatry and
psychoanalysis. In their motherless childhood they were
close, as they moved from Denver to Vermont to Chicago
and to their Sabin farming grandparents back in Vermont.
In these moves Mary provided the only continuity in Florence
Sabin's life, and surely Florence depended on her older sister for emotional support. After Mary's graduation from
college Florence remained behind, feeling alone and abandoned. Later in life Doctor Sabin was to become something
of a mother-figure to Mary, and they exchanged, almost
daily, letters unmarred by any hostility or bitterness.

As mentioned above, Florence and her sister, despite
their poverty, managed to graduate from Smith College,
Florence in 1893. She had made up her mind that she would
go to medical school. After teaching for three years--to
save some money--she was accepted by the Johns Hopkins
medical school, which was one of the best in the nation and
one of the few that admitted women.

Dr. Franklin Mall arranged for Sabin to be appointed
to the faculty in 1902, shortly after she earned her degree.
With his support she rose through faculty ranks to become
in 1917 the first female full professor at Johns Hopkins (she
had been one of the first two women interns at Johns Hopkins Hospital, in 1900). Eventually she became head of
histology there, but the road was not always smooth. When
Dr. Mall died in 1917 she might have expected to fill his
position as head of the department, but instead a young man
who had been Dr. Sabin's student was promoted over her.
She had been a staunch defender of women's abilities but had
always denied that she had ever been discriminated against.
Now she faced the truth that women's achievements were
rarely recognized, and she herself began to encourage younger women of talent. Her efforts on behalf of the women's
movement in the 1920s may have affected the National Academy of Sciences. In 1921 Madame Marie Curie visited the
United States to receive a number of honorary degrees and
a gram of radium--a gift paid for by a fund drive organized
by a woman's magazine. The National Academy of Sciences
pondered electing her an honorary member; but Curie got only
official greetings from the academy, when Robert Millikan

delivered a speech in her honor at the Smithsonian. However, the pondering finally focused on the question of whether or not women should be elected to membership in the academy.

In 1923 the medical scientists in the academy nominated Florence Sabin for membership, though she was not elected. In 1924 the American Association of Anatomists elected her the first woman president of the association, and then renominated her for the National Academy in 1925. At last she was elected to this high honor.

She became, also in 1925, the first woman to be a full member of the staff of the Rockefeller Institute. She was regarded by the institute director, Dr. Simon Flexner, as "the greatest living woman scientist and one of the foremost scientists of all time."

Inspired by her willingness to help students in the laboratory, many young scholars at the Johns Hopkins medical school were led by Dr. Sabin to new ideas, problems, and techniques. She was generous with her time, and she would rarely allow her name to appear on first publications, even as a co-author. Such unselfishness endeared her to her students. When they were well launched on their careers, she would collaborate with them and lend her famous name as co-author of the published reports of research accomplished jointly.

Sabin may have chosen her Baltimore apartment on a hillside out of nostalgia for her first, Silver City home. In any case, students were welcome there, and her biographer, Lawrence S. Kubie (p. 314), says she would assign them tasks of setting the table, fixing fruit or vegetables, or sitting with a stop watch on the floor before the oven with orders to turn the steak at precisely three minutes. In her last years dignity lent her the beauty she had been denied in her youth.

When she retired from the Rockefeller Institute in 1938 Sabin returned to Colorado, expecting to lead a quiet life with her sister Mary in Denver, close to the mountains she loved. But she did not retire. Finding the public health service in Colorado enmeshed in politics, she launched a one-woman campaign for "a politically independent and scientifically sound state department of health," writes Kubie (pp. 306-14). Sabin's work in three areas proved valuable:

her research into the anatomy of the brain, her research
into the embryology of the lymphatic system, and at the end
of her life, her efforts to bring about a drop in the incidence
of tuberculosis and other communicable diseases in Colorado.

She died in 1953; Kubie says, "To the very end she
was asking questions, doubting, questioning, accepting nothing
on faith; a resolute non-believer, looking for facts and evidence. What greater legacy can a human being leave to us?"

Other Johns Hopkins graduates deserve special mention: Louise Pearce, who led a Rockefeller Institute research team to the Congo to study sleeping sickness, and
Helen Taussig, who with Dr. Alfred Blalock was responsible
for saving the lives of countless infants by devising an operation to correct congenital malformation of the heart in newborn "blue babies."

Pearce graduated from Stanford in 1907, and after
she received her medical degree from Johns Hopkins in 1912
was appointed to the house staff of Johns Hopkins Hospital.
One year later she became a member of the Rockefeller Institute, a position she held until her retirement in 1950.
In 1920, as a result of her discovery of a drug to conquer
African sleeping sickness in the Belgian Congo, she was
awarded the Order of the Crown of Belgium. Thirty years
later she was honored with the King Leopold II Prize and
the Royal Order of the Lion. Dr. Pearce also made considerable contributions in the area of tumor studies.

Best known as the co-developer of the operation for
blue babies, Dr. Helen Taussig may be one of the most
honored women physicians in the world. The French made
her a chevalier of the Legion of Honor. Lyndon B. Johnson gave her the Medal of Freedom, the highest civilian
award an American President can bestow. From Athens,
Greece, to Oxford, Ohio, 20 colleges presented honorary
degrees to Dr. Taussig.

With all these public honors she has never become
blasé about donning a sterile cap, mask, and operating gown
to observe a surgeon making a "blue baby turn pink."

As a young woman, Taussig had faced an almost in-
surmountable obstacle--having been born a girl. She said,
"I grew up in an atmosphere that greatly differs from that
of today. Fifty years ago, an error made by a woman was

Dr. Helen Taussig

held against her, whereas any error made by a man was
just a mistake!"

Born into a family of scholars in Cambridge, Mass.,
on May 24, 1898, Helen Brooke Taussig was the grandchild
of a Czechoslovakian physician who specialized in problems
of children with bad eyes. Helen's mother, Edith Thomas
Guild, was one of the first graduates of Radcliffe College.
Her father, Frank William Taussig, was a famous economist
at Harvard, an advisor to President Woodrow Wilson.

Taussig had no particular calling to medicine when
she enrolled at Radcliffe. She studied biology and physics
and majored in tennis. Although her mother may have tried
to dissuade her, Helen and two friends decided to leave
Radcliffe to study at the University of California in Berkeley.
Perhaps they just wanted to get away from the cold New
England winters.

After graduating from Berkeley in 1921, she considered a career in medicine, but her father suggested she
might do better in public health and urged her to apply to
the Harvard School of Public Health, which was to open in
the fall of 1922. However, President Lowell was strongly
against admitting women to the medical school. When she
was interviewed at the school of public health the dean said
women could indeed study there, but they would not be
awarded a degree.

Who would be such a fool as that--spending years to
study medicine, knowing all the while you'd never be able
to use your knowledge professionally?

Angrily the young Taussig went back to confront her
father with the resolve that she was going to study medicine.
Although Harvard did not admit women, she was allowed to
enroll in a few courses. She studied histology (the study of
tissues), and was permitted to attend lectures, provided she
sat in the far corner of the room by herself; when she examined the slides she was in a separate room, forbidden to
speak to the male students. The professor was courteous
and gave her some personal attention.

Since she was refused permission to study anatomy
at Harvard, Taussig went over to Boston University, where
she studied with Dr. Alexander Begg. One day he thrust a
calf heart into her hand. "It won't do you any harm to get

interested in one of the larger organs of the body as you go through medical school. "

Taussig dissected the heart: "I got into cardiology." She impressed Dr. Begg, dean of the medical school, and he suggested she apply to Johns Hopkins. Annoyed that the head of a university would urge a good student to apply to another school, she took his advice and was accepted at Johns Hopkins, where she did very well. When the time came for her to choose a medical specialty, however, she lost out on her first choice of internal medicine to another woman physician, Vivian Tappan. Undaunted, Taussig decided to become a pediatrician, and she won a fellowship in the adult cardiac clinic. With memories of the excitement of dissecting a calf heart, she began investigating congenital malformations of the heart.

By 1930 she had been appointed head of the cardiac clinic of the children's unit at the Harriet Lane Home. Here she launched her studies of rheumatic fever, a disease that causes inflammation of joints and frequent complications of heart damage in children.

At the time simple bed rest and aspirin was the only treatment for rheumatic fever, to keep the strain off the heart so it would not enlarge. In 1935 a baby with bluish skin was brought to Dr. Taussig. Examining the child with an electrocardiographic machine, she thought one of the baby's heart chambers was missing. Later, another baby's x-rays revealed a similar malformation. "Then and there," says Dr. Taussig, "I realized that malformations of the heart repeat themselves and that similar malformations cause familiar changes in the size and shape of the heart."

Obsessed by the idea, she was excited when Dr. Alfred Blalock came to Johns Hopkins in 1941, and his skill made surgery possible on the infants. After two years of operating on animals successfully, he felt the time had come to try three operations on human blue babies.

They conceived the idea that many cyanotic (oxygen deprived) infants and children might be helped by increased circulation to the lungs. Blalock and Taussig proposed surgery to change the cyanotic infant from blue to a normal peach color. The surgery gave stimulus to correction of congenital malformations of the heart. For this achievement Taussig and Blalock received the Passano Foundation

Award in 1948, the Lasker Award of the American Public
Health Association in 1954, and the Award of Merit of the
Gardner Foundation in 1959.

Of special significance is the contribution made by
Taussig and Blalock to modern heart surgery. By demonstrating that even the deeply cyanotic child could survive
heart surgery, said one surgeon, the Johns Hopkins team
showed that almost any other child might do so, as well as
adults. Surgeons were prompted to venture where they had
previously not dared to go.

The third operation was on a "small, utterly miserable, six year old boy" no longer able even to walk. When
Dr. Blalock located the leak in his heart, the anesthesiolo-
gist cried, "He's a lovely color now!" Dr. Taussig walked
around to the head of the operating table and was thrilled to
see the child's normal, pink lips. "From that moment,"
she recalls, "the child was healthy, happy and active." She
was involved with her child-patients, and she suffered when
a child did not survive the surgery (Clymer and Erlich,
pp. 91-98; Froslid, pp. 389ff).

When, in 1945, Blalock and Taussig published the results of their studies of blue-baby operations, Dr. Blalock
won instant recognition and was elected to the National Academy of Sciences. For Dr. Taussig recognition came more
slowly; she received her first honorary degree in 1948 from
Boston University, became full professor at Johns Hopkins
in 1959, and was elected by the American Heart Association
to be its first female president.

In addition to making diagnoses and selecting patients
who could tolerate the dramatic operation, Taussig trained
many doctors in diagnosing congenital malformations. In the
area of rheumatic fever she demonstrated that cardiac en-
largement occurring during periods of active infection could
be detected through the use of fluoroscopy, and x-rays.

She continued to study congenital heart disease, maintained a busy clinic schedule, and became a great teacher of
pediatrics. She frequently invited her students, "Taussig
fellows," for informal evenings in her home. Among these
students was a German, Dr. Alois Beuren. In 1962 Beuren
mentioned that a number of deformed babies had been born
in Germany and other European countries. Dr. Taussig
mulled over the conversation and decided to go to Germany

and find out about the sleeping pill that her student had mentioned as a possible cause of the malformations. In Germany and England she visited clinics, interviewed doctors, and examined the malformed children. She was convinced that the deformities had to be linked to the pill, thalidomide.

On her return to the United States she warned physicians of the danger of thalidomide and other similar drugs. Her experience with thalidomide intensified Taussig's interest in the cause of malformed infants.

Women researchers at Johns Hopkins Hospital continue to explore the cause of deformities in children. In 1979 research was being done into the possibility that drugs, vitamin deficiencies, or exposure to environmental gases might increase risks of mothers with cleft-lip children giving birth to another child with the same defect.

Dr. Jennifer Niebyl, director of the study, canvassed the country for mothers of a child with cleft lip. Those mothers planning to have another baby could provide a clue to the cause of the second-most-common birth defect in the United States.

"We know that there's a strong genetic tendency in the cleft-lip syndrome," claims Dr. Niebyl, " but the risk is one in 20 of cleft lip appearing in a subsequent pregnancy. What we're really looking for is what environmental or metabolic factors could influence the expression of the defect."

Is there something in the environment or in the mother's body which might influence her chances of having another defective child? Dr. Niebyl said such things as paint fumes, hair spray, drugs, and anesthetic gas possibly could cause recurrences of the condition. Tests on laboratory mice found that high dosages of vitamin A and a number of chemicals and drugs, including cortisone and dilantin, a drug taken by epileptics, produced offspring with cleft-lip defects.

Such research gives continuity to the high purpose for which Johns Hopkins was founded.

REACHING FOR THE STARS

12. Marie Curie and Lise Meitner

"The image of Madame Curie is overdone, " snaps Valentine
Telegdi of the University of Chicago. "If I'd have been
married to Pierre Curie, I would have been Madame Curie,
too. "

"Only a man would make such an observation, " said
a member of the panel of the American Physical Society.
"Pierre was a genius, but Madame Curie's persistence led
her to a brilliant discovery of radium--on her own. Pierre
Curie joined his wife's research, not the other way around.
After her husband died, Marie Curie carried on the work
and won a second Nobel Prize five years later!"

"When I was a youngster, " observes Gloria Lubkin,
a nuclear physicist and senior editor of Physics Today, "I
was inspired by Marie Curie. "

The careers of both Marie Curie and Lise Meitner
illustrate the obstacles set in the path of European women
who wanted to be scientists at the beginning of the twentieth
century.

In France the Napoleonic Code has long bound woman
in a cell of obedience to her husband. Article 1124 said the
"unfit persons according to law are minors, ex-convicts, and
married women. " Article 1428 gave the husband the right
to administer his wife's money. Women were legally children. A woman couldn't even give permission to a doctor
to operate on her child without the father's consent.

It was not until 1910 that French women were allowed to pass the baccalaureate examinations, a prerequisite
to university entrance. Madame Marie Curie, Polish born,
went to France to study and combine a scientific career with
a flourishing family life.

Two of the potentially greatest medical discoveries of this century were made by women. Neither was a doctor, both of these scientists were physicists. Marie Curie and Lise Meitner were among the most gifted scientists of all time. Madame Curie's discovery of radium, like Lise Meitner's of nuclear fission, came in a form which only incidentally had a medical application. But the work of both these women changed the whole picture of modern science.

Manya Sklodovska--Marie's birth name--the daughter of a Warsaw science teacher, grew up with two fierce passions, patriotism and education. Neither of these passions were to bring her happiness in Poland. The ideals of democracy had affected the young people of Poland, but the country itself had been swallowed by greedy neighbors, Germany, Austria, and Russia. Warsaw was in the Russian sector, and Manya dreaded the inspection days when Russian educators made surprise visits, for she was always the one called on to recite in Russian.

Manya had always been fascinated by physics apparatus. Graduating from high school with every possible medal and honor, the 16-year-old girl was up against a blank wall as far as future education in Warsaw was concerned. Higher education for Polish girls was out of the question. Manya and an older sister, Bronya, dreamed of studying medicine in Paris. In the City of Light Manya would find sympathy for her revolutionary attitudes. The sisters tutored daughters of rich families and tried to save money to get to Paris.

At 17 Manya urged her sister to go to Paris alone to start studying. Manya would be a governess and send her salary to Bronya, and "When you are a doctor and earn money, you can help me," Manya insisted.

Bronya objected, "You'd have to wait six years!" But Manya was determined, and she took a position in the home of a rather spoiled ten-year-old. An older sister, just Manya's age, became her close friend. Soon Manya and the rich girl were teaching classes in the Polish language and Polish history for peasant children. This activity was illegal and dangerous.

When Bronya became engaged to a young Polish doctor in Paris, she sent for Manya, who set out for Paris in October 1891. For six years she had longed for this hour when she could at last enroll in the Sorbonne, and she devoted herself to her studies. In the university register, she became for the first time, "Marie."

In the Polish colony Marie found the home of Bronya and her husband, Dr. Casimir Dluski, intensely social. At many parties, young Paderewski played the Dluskis' upright piano. But Marie needed to study, so she moved to a small attic room and lived on bread, tea, and radishes, and now and then an egg. In the freezing Parisian winter she banked the fire and piled all her clothing on top of her bed. Passing the Master's examination in physics at the head of her class, she decided to work for a second Master's in mathematics.

She told a Polish friend she required practical laboratory experience. He introduced her to Pierre Curie, a gifted young French scientist. Pierre was much taken with the beautiful, pale blond Polish woman, shy, reserved, and obviously brilliant. He urged her to renounce her revolutionary ideas: "You're knocking your head against a stone wall." He wanted her to put her energies into the world of science.

They were married in July 1895. Marie insisted that their wedding had to be different from all other weddings-- no white dress, no gold ring, no wedding breakfast, no religious ceremony. All they had in the world were two bicycles, bought the day before the wedding with money sent by a cousin. Their life was as radiant as the radium they were to discover. Marie, cooking, keeping house, and taking care of her first child, was determined to finish her doctorate.

She had become interested in x-rays, which could expose a photographic plate even though the plate was protected by thick, black, light-proof paper. Thinking only of writing her doctoral dissertation, she worked in a small glass-enclosed storeroom full of defunct machinery. She explored the property of radioactivity, not only in uranium but in all known elements. Quickly eliminating 76 of the 78 elements then known, she explored two for radioactivity--uranium and thorium.

Acquainting herself with Bohemian pitchblende (a convenient ore to work with, important in the production of glass), Marie calculated the amounts of uranium and thorium it contained. In the pitchblende she found something that she would not have predicted in her wildest dreams: a new element!

Through the good graces of an Austrian friend a ton of pitchblende was shipped from Bohemia. The Curies had to pay for it from their meagre funds. Marie Curie must have been thrilled when the substance extracted from pitchblende proved to be a hitherto unobserved metal. She decided to call it polonium, for the Poland that had aroused in her such passionate patriotism as a child.

The second unknown element the Curies extracted was the most radioactive substance in the world, and Marie called it radium.

The hard physical labor of stirring a boiling mass all day long with a heavy iron rod exhausted her. Some 48 months passed before she was able to isolate three-tenths of an ounce of pure radium salt from the ton of pitchblende.

When in 1905 Curie completed her dissertation on radioactivity, she was granted the degree of doctor of physical science by the University of Paris. As Pierre had predicted, the whole world of science was affected by her dissertation. While Marie Curie did not live to see the development of the full resources of atomic energy, the Curies early recognized that radium could be a weapon in the fight against cancer.

Had Marie Curie decided to patent the method of extracting radium from uranium ore, she might have become the world's wealthiest woman. But she insisted, "Radium is for everybody."

In 1906, when Pierre Curie was killed by two runaway horses, Marie became a widow with small children to rear. In 1903 Pierre and Marie had been awarded the Nobel prize for physics with Henri Becquerel. In 1911, teaching at the University of Paris, she was again honored with the Nobel prize, this time for chemistry.

When war broke out in Europe in 1914 Marie Curie dedicated herself to French military medical service by equipping an automobile with a portable x-ray machine and a dynamo. At the battlefront, mutilated and wounded men were x-rayed. Madame Curie was able to show the doctors the exact location of bullets or shell fragments that might not have been found without painful searching.

In 1923 Curie, elected to the French Academy of Medicine, was honored "recognizing the role she took in the discovery of radium and of a new treatment in medicine, Curietherapy. " She died in 1934, a victim of the radioactive substances she had herself discovered.

The Encyclopaedia Britannica does not even have a separate entry for Marie Curie, but classifies her second to her husband, "CURIE, PIERRE (1859-1906), and MARIE (1867-1934), French physicists. "

Lise Meitner, another great woman physicist, also served her country as an x-ray technician in the first World War--but on the side that fought France. From July 1915 until the fall of 1917 Meitner was in Austrian field hospitals behind front lines. She had taken a course in roentgenology and human anatomy at City Hospital at Lichter-felde, a suburb of Berlin.

Meitner was one of those gifted women who earned a teaching degree to be sure of earning a living should she be denied a chance to do research. Fortunately for science, during her year of teaching at a high school for Viennese girls Meitner had the ambition and energy to continue her studies. With private tutors she prepared for an examina-tion to enter a university. She passed cum laude and in 1906 was the second woman ever to receive a doctorate in physics from the University of Vienna. In 1907 she went to Berlin to attend Max Planck's physics lectures. Meitner requested permission from the director of the Institute of Physics to do part-time work, and she was allowed to col-laborate with Otto Hahn. Hahn records in A Scientific Auto-biography that the two years she expected to be in Berlin "stretched to thirty years of collaboration and lasting friend-ship. "

At that time the director of the Chemical Institute, Emil Fischer, would not allow women to enter the labora-tory, and Meitner had to steal in when no men were around. Confined to the wood shop where she did her experiments, she was barred from other laboratories. But she studied with Max Planck and wrote elegant articles on physics. One article won the admiration of the editor of the Brockhause Encyclopedia (Hahn, p. 65), and he wrote "Herr Meitner" suggesting that "he" might want to write for him. Astonished to learn that Meitner was a woman, he turned down her ac-ceptance heatedly, saying he wouldn't dream of publishing anything written by a woman!

After World War I, when women were admitted to academic careers in Germany, Lise Meitner became a physics professor at the University of Berlin. Her first public lecture, "Problems of Cosmic Physics," was written up by a newspaper reporter as "Problems of Cosmetic Physics."

Eventually Meitner attained not only the dignified title of German professor, but also one of his proverbial attributes, absent-mindedness. Greeting a colleague who said, "We've already met," she replied, "You probably mistake me for Professor Otto Hahn."

Meitner was in on the discovery of uranium fission with her nephew; it was she who coined the phrase "nuclear fission." She never worked on the bomb itself, however, steadfastly refusing to lend her great genius and creativity to any project that might lead to destruction. Truly an international citizen, she was one of the great humanitarians of her time.

Before the turn of the century European universities that cultivated a spirit of freedom in scholarship were rare. Beside the University of Zurich in Switzerland, the first to open its doors to women, in 1873 Swedish universities began to admit women, and finally Germany in 1908. *

"Amusingly," Lise Meitner observed, "the main difficulty in Sweden--and in England, too--was that the regulations before 1873 referred specifically to men; the whole problem ultimately was to replace the word 'men' by the word 'persons,' in order to make the admission of women to high schools possible. This also gave women the possibility to acquire the right to lecture; in Germany, this did

---

*The English Medical Register of 1858 has the name of a single woman graduate of Geneva, and a second was examined and qualified in medicine in 1865. The first Swiss woman graduate was Marie Heim-Vogtlin (1845-1916). Swiss universities took the lead in admitting women medical students. At the University of Zurich the first woman to obtain a medical degree was a Russian, Nadya Suslova, in 1867. In 1874 the London School of Medicine was opened for women, with 14 students. In 1896 women acquired the privilege of resident posts at the Royal Free Hospital. The same year the Royal College of Physiology in Ireland and the London University admitted women to the privilege of examinations.

not happen until after the first World War. Even in 1918, when the great mathematician Hilbert, in Göttingen, tried to obtain the faculty's permission for his talented woman assistant--Dr. Emmy Nöther--to apply for the venia legendi which would have made her a faculty member, he met with such indignation that he snapped, 'But gentlemen, a faculty is not a swimming pool!' Nevertheless," Lise Meitner sadly recalled, "Dr. Emmy Nöther was not allowed to become a lecturer at that time."

Among Lise Meitner's friends were the world's eminent scientists. In 1908 she met New Zealand-born Ernest Rutherford, who had just been awarded the Nobel prize for chemistry. On being introduced to Dr. Meitner, he exclaimed, "I thought you were a man!"

Physics being considered a man's subject, Dr. Meitner was a constant curiosity. Working with Otto Hahn, she explored the mysteries of isotopes. On the edge of great discoveries, Dr. Meitner had to flee Germany because she was classified by the Nazis as "over fifty percent non-Aryan." The culmination of her life's work was snatched away. Through Niels Bohr, she was invited to the Nobel Institute for Physics in Stockholm; after two decades there she moved to Cambridge, England.

In April 1959, when she was over 80, as the guest of Bryn Mawr College, Meitner spoke to the physics students, reaffirming her convictions that women should be scientists, doctors, whatever their talents and abilities suggested, to bring their aspirations to fruition. "Undoubtedly," she said, "women can see no ideal solutions to their problem: profession and family. But for what human problems do ideal solutions exist?" She stressed that "we can no longer doubt the value and indeed the necessity of women's intellectual education for herself, her family and for mankind."

"Imagination and originality," were the two qualities that made her a great physicist. In 1966 Lise Meitner was honored with the Enrico Fermi Award, which she shared with Otto Hahn and Fritz Strassmann, chosen for their contributions to the discovery of nuclear fission.

She died two years later, at the age of 90.

REACHING FOR THE STARS

13. Rosalyn Yalow and Gerty Cori

Rosalyn Yalow graduated from Hunter College, an all-women's school in New York, as the first physics major; the only job she could get was as a secretary, sharpening pencils and taking other people's dictation.

Even as a little girl, the daughter of first-generation immigrants whose formal education had ended in elementary school, Rosalyn had her mind set on a career in medical research. With a college degree in physics, she was told she could forget about graduate school--she'd never be accepted in physics. But her secretarial job was at the College of Physicians and Surgeons, and she was permitted to take courses. Eventually, she won an assistantship in physics at the University of Illinois. She lost no time in tearing up her steno books!

While working for her doctorate at the University of Illinois she met her future husband, Dr. Aaron Yalow, now professor of physics at Cooper Union in New York City. Theirs was a two-career marriage. Even after her children were born Rosalyn Yalow had no feelings of guilt about working. She was an involved mother, and when her children's classes needed a chaperone, Yalow was always ready to volunteer, even when other mothers were available because they had no outside work.

Collaborating with the brilliant Solomon Berson until his death in 1972, Rosalyn Yalow used radioactive isotopes to detect and measure minute traces of hormones in blood and body tissue. Berson and Yalow together discovered that diabetics treated with insulin had developed antibodies to insulin. When they tried to publish this observation the work was rejected in the belief that insulin was incapable of inducing antibodies. Berson and Yalow then discovered that diabetes in adults results not from a shortage of insulin but from a blocking of insulin's sugar-metabolizing action. Dr.

133

Dr. Rosalyn Yalow

Yalow contends that these discoveries serve as a model for development of other measurement techniques in the study of infectious diseases (Meites).

Radioimmunoassay (R. I. A.), first discovered in 1959, measures peptide hormone insulin in the blood of diabetics. Unexpectedly researchers discovered that, unlike the juvenile diabetic, the adult diabetic has a higher-than-usual level of insulin in the blood. Radioimmunoassay revealed that the elevated blood sugar in adult diabetics is due to some unknown factor interfering with the action of insulin and not to insulin deficiency.

R. I. A. studies also help determine if the lack of growth in children is due to an inadequate amount of growth hormone; if excessive steroid production by the adrenal gland is due to a tumor of the gland or a message from an overactive pituitary; and if drugs like heroin, methadone, and L. S. D. have been abused or if lethal drugs have been administered. Radioimmunoassay is an extremely sensitive analytical technique now used routinely in hospitals for diagnosis of diabetes, thyroid diseases, growth disorders, hypertension, reproductive failures, hormone-secreting cancers, and other endocrine-related disorders.

In 1977, when Rosalyn Yalow won the Nobel prize for Medicine, the Veterans Administration Hospital in the Bronx where she worked exploded in hysterical joy; television crews descended on the hospital. Yalow was being interviewed by a half a dozen eager anchormen; and her husband was answering all the questions asked.

"Aaron! Aaron!" admonished the Nobel prize winner, "let me talk!" Yalow's was an award shared by three Americans for discoveries opening new vistas in biological and medical research far outside "the border of their own spheres of interests." The prize recognized the most valuable advance in basic research directly applicable to clinical medicine made in the past two decades, the development of the radioimmunoassay technique. Dr. Yalow, working at the Veterans Administration Hospital in the Bronx, N. Y., received half the prize; the other half was shared by Dr. Roger C. Fuillemin of the Salk Institute and Dr. Andrew V. Schally of the Veterans Administration Hospital in New Orleans. Radioimmunoassay uses radioactive isotopes to trace the body's immune reactions. This technique for identifying and measuring the concentration of hundreds of substances in

the blood and other tissues has grown rapidly; in 1974 perhaps 4,000 laboratories in the United States were using
R.I.A. in testing, and by 1979 the number rose to over
7,000. The technique helps prevent mental retardation and
blood-transfusion hepatitis and has brought new precision to
the use of antibiotics. Thousands of laboratories abroad
have adopted the technique.

Speaking in Moscow to a seminar for Soviet doctors,
Dr. Yalow urged development of a Russian R.I.A. program.
"Severe underactivity of the thyroid," she said, "if not
treated in the first three months, may lead to mental retardation. And it cannot be reversed after the first three
months. But if the baby gets treatment for the problem
within the first month or so, it will be equal to its siblings."*

"I love my work, and I do it at my own pace," says
Rosalyn Yalow. "Sometimes I work a hundred hours a week.
Sometimes I stop and read a detective story" (Yalow).

Dr. Yalow taught physics at Hunter College from
1946 to 1950. Her mother was in her 90s when Yalow received the Nobel prize. "I wish my father could have lived
to see this," she mused. "He died in 1959, just when I
started to win awards. He would have been so proud of
me."

Dr. Yalow holds the chair of Distinguished Professor
of Medicine at Mt. Sinai School of Medicine in New York.
She was the first woman to win the Albert Lasker Basic
Medical Research Award (in 1976) and the American Academy of Achievement Gold Plate Award (in 1977).

Yalow was the second woman ever to receive the
Nobel prize in medicine. She wrote of her predecessor
(Yalow),

> Consider the history of one woman who had an
> enormous impact on academic medicine. Gerty
> Radnitz was born in Prague in 1896, the eldest of
> three daughters. Graduating at sixteen from a
> girl's academy with the typical education appropr-
> ate to a woman, she decided on a career in medi-

---

*Houston Chronicle, June 10, 1979, Sec. 4, p. 4.

cine. To be accepted for medical school, she
needed eight years of Latin (she had none), five
more years of mathematics, plus physics and
chemistry. Vacationing in the Tyrol that summer
after graduation, she met a teacher in the gymnasium in Tetschen, who, hearing of her plans,
began her instruction in Latin. By the end of the
summer, Gerty Radnitz had mastered three years
of Latin. During the next year, she completed all
the course-work, including math through calculus,
passed the examinations and entered Medical School
at the University of Prague.

Gerty Radnitz met Carl F. Cori while they were doing
research in immunology. Shortly after they both received
M. D. degrees, they married, on August 5, 1920. Neither
ever practiced medicine, finding rather their fulfillment in
research. Before receiving her degree, Gerty Cori had
spent the years 1917 to 1919 as a student assistant in the
medical school. With her degree she was made an assistant in the Vienna Children's Hospital, where she worked
until 1922. That year the Coris left Austria to become,
five years later, citizens of the United States. Both Coris
worked at the New York State Institute for the Study of Malig-
nant Disease in Buffalo. He taught, as well, at the University of Buffalo. She worked as a biochemist.

In 1931 the two doctors, partners in parenthood and
research, were invited to Washington University in St.
Louis, Dr. Carl Cori as a professor and Dr. Gerty Cori
as a research associate, a lower position. In view of the
rules in those days, which prohibited hiring both husband
and wife, the university was doing her a favor. Gerty did
not attain full professorship until 16 years later, after she
and her husband jointly received the Nobel prize in 1947.
They became the third married couple to receive a Nobel
award in science (in 1903 the physics prize went to Pierre
and Marie Curie, who shared the award with a third French
scientist, and in 1935 the chemistry prize was awarded to
Frédéric and Irène Joliot-Curie, daughter of Madame Curie).
Like the Curies, the Coris also shared the 1947 Nobel prize
in physics and medicine with a third winner, Dr. Bernardo
Houssay of Argentina.

St. Louis had already had reason to be proud of the
Coris' achievements. A gold medallion was given them on
March 21, 1946, by the St. Louis Section of the American

Drs. Carl and Gerty Cori in their laboratory at Washington University, St. Louis

Chemical Society, and Dr. Arthur H. Compton, Nobel-prize winner and chancellor of Washington University, had said, "The fame of Carl and Gerty Cori is based upon the reliability of their careful measurements."

In the early years, Carl F. Cori alone received widespread recognition: the Isaac Adler Prize, the Lasker Award, the Sugar Foundation Prize in 1947 (for distinguished achievement in the field of human metabolism), two honorary doctorates and election to the National Association of Sciences in April, 1940. They worked closely together; so much so that it was difficult to tell where the work of one left off and the other began. Yet not until eight years after her husband had been elected to the National Academy of Sciences was Gerty Cori so honored. Not until after she was awarded the Nobel Prize in Medicine with her husband in 1947 did other honors come to her: in 1950, the Sugar Research Prize of the National Academy of

Sciences was granted her; she received honorary doctorates from Boston University in 1948; from Smith College ·in 1949, from Yale in 1951, and from Columbia in 1954. The work of the Coris in carbohydrate metabolism, especially the discovery of glucose-phosphate, which now bears the name "Cori ester" were of enormous value in understanding diabetes, and brought both Coris many honors.

A fellow scientist at Washington University, Edward A. Doisy, said, "Genius the Coris have ... no question about it. But their capacity for hard work has aided that genius to blossom and benefit mankind. "

Rosalyn Yalow admits good-naturedly, the coveted Nobel prize may be a mixed blessing, because the winner becomes a public personality besieged with requests to grant interviews, make speeches, and join committees--which leaves too little time for serious work. An awed public may take every statement with "oracular seriousness, " as Time suggested. At a scientific meeting in November 1978 Yalow described some recent work, using the radioimmunoassay techniques with lab animals, that found a possible link between obesity and the shortage of a certain chemical in the brain. Grossly fat mice seemed to have smaller amounts of the hormone cholecystokinin than their thinner litter-mates. As Rosalyn Yalow observed, the hormone may be suppressing rodent appetites. Yalow discussed these tentative findings with the press, and published accounts emphasized that any implications were only for the grossly obese. Yalow was inundated with letters asking for assistance that she could not provide. From now on, she said, she would be discreetly silent. *

As a lecturer and researcher, Dr. Yalow constantly encourages young women to become physicians. Our greatest concern, she believes, is to help medical students, college women, and girls still in high school who are now considering medicine and biomedical investigation as career choices....

"We like to believe that a young woman starting her professional career would find it easier today, but I am not certain how much easier it will be. The view of woman's

---

*Time, December 25, 1978, p. 61.

role in society which was prevalent in my generation is gradually changing. It is more acceptable now for women, even those with small children, to work. But it is unlikely that this will assure women of equal opportunity with men for professional success, especially in science and academic medicine" (Yalow).

Dr. Yalow, family cook, wife, mother of two, believes that the attack must be on "how society views women's aspirations and capabilities." She believes that we can't expect that

> in the foreseeable future women will achieve stature in academic medicine in proportion to their numbers. But if women are to start moving toward that goal we must believe in ourselves. For if we don't, no one else will. We must match our aspirations with the guts and determination to succeed. And those of us who have the good fortune to move upward, must feel a personal responsibility to serve as a role model and advisors to ease the path for those who come afterward. We should not ask for reverse discrimination but simply for equality of opportunity--so that those of us who wish to can reach for the stars.

Part III

MEDICAL

FACTS

AND

FANTASIES

MEDICAL FACTS AND FANTASIES

14.   Health Care in the Land of the Free

How would you feel about a country that in the past two
decades has dropped from seventh in the world to 16th in
prevention of infant deaths?

How about a country that has dropped from sixth to
eighth in female life expectancy?   From tenth to 24th in male
life expectancy?

In this country more of the gross national product is
spent for medical care--one dollar out of every 14--than in
any other country in the world.

What country am I talking about?   Shouldn't a medical ship like HOPE be sent there?   How about sending a
medical Peace Corps?   How about some foreign aid to help
them out?

The country I'm talking about is the United States,
the land of the free and the home of the brave.   This is the
country rejecting 50 percent of medical school applicants,
most of them fully qualified to study medicine.

The shortage of doctors in America is a national dis-
grace and is expected to get even worse.   The shortage exists more sharply in community medicine and family practice, and in rural areas.

Abuses in health care have cost the nation dearly.
The Medicare and Medicaid programs have caused patients
to be "ping-ponged" from one specialist to another for un-
needed tests and treatments.   Dr. Nancy Kurke, who in
1976 worked in what she called a "Medicaid mill," said she
was appalled by what she saw as a doctor in two clinics,
one in East Harlem, the other in the Bedford-Stuyvesant
section of Brooklyn.   "It is the worst medical care I have

143

ever seen, " she claimed, though she had worked in emergency rooms and city hospitals in New York and was already in her middle 40s. Kurke reported that the owner of the clinics was annoyed with her for seeing only 20 patients per day, while he was seeing 50. Programs for health care of the needy are essential, but so are rigorously supervised programs to avoid abuse by doctors, by druggists, welfare clients, and medical laboratories.

Since 1950 high infant mortality rates in the United States have been linked largely with the rural South and Southwest, and mostly with non-white mothers. Why are so many American babies born dead? Poverty is one reason, accompanied by bad nutrition, poor parental education, teenage pregnancies, illegitimacy, and premature births. In our densely populated areas the campaign against infant mortality must be waged. Teenaged mothers, even when married, are a high-risk group: when the girls are without a husband they are reluctant to go to a doctor. Good diet, proper medical care, and good hygiene would combine to produce healthy adults who have healthy babies.

Dr. Margaret Williams, chief of Philadelphia General Hospital's pediatric nursery services, has noted that the premature birth rate there is 18 to 20 percent, compared with 8 to 12 percent in private hospitals (in which women must pay their way). Women from poor homes also have a high rate of respiratory illnesses. Charity hospitals report that many young women show up for the first time at the social agency or hospital when labor pains have already started. Teenaged mothers leave the hospital a few nights later with their babies only to reappear some other night a year or so later in a similar condition.

Social caseworkers and doctors could and should reach these women early in their pregnancies. If care could be provided for the children, and psychiatric counseling for both the unmarried mothers and fathers, some kind of sense of kinship might be established for the potential families. Family-planning centers might be the answer to the problem of women whose infants are delivered at charity hospitals. Too many of these women had no medical care at all during the pregnancy. The center must assure a better pregnancy and fewer, healthier babies. Smaller families may afford better health care.

Moreover, attention must be paid to humanizing

clinics: doctors must be aware that a woman lying on an examination table, feet in stirrups, draped with a sheet so that she can't see what's happening, and the most personal part of her anatomy exposed, is hardly likely to feel dignified and cooperative. Dr. Joni Magee, a gynecologist at Philadelphia's Jefferson School of Medicine, suggests that doctors are going to have to talk to their patients more, work slowly, and watch for the patient's pain, which is likely to show up in her expression. "A pelvic exam does hurt ... at least it's damned uncomfortable," she says. "Should a patient tense up during an examination, the doctor's order to relax doesn't help. What the doctor must tell the patient is that the abdomen should go soft."

Young doctors express disapproval of the rapid technical advances that threaten to dehumanize medical practice; more and more attention must be paid to the patient as a person.

In the lower Rio Grande Valley of south Texas there are many specialists, neurosurgeons, endocrinologists, psychiatrists, cardiologists, and so on, but a real shortage exists of primary-care physicians, internists, family practitioners, obstetrician-gynecologists, and pediatricians. Students from the Baylor medical school are drawn to this area by special programs designed to convince them to practice in south Texas. Infant mortality in this region is 20 per 1,000 births, compared to the national average of 15 per 1,000. More than 6,000 south Texas women bear children every year without benefit of a physician's care.

Medical student Nancy Cain, 27, finished her undergraduate degree and began medical school only after her husband Bill got his degree. She looks forward to a small-town practice in south Texas where she and her patients might "trade services." "I don't expect all my patients to pay with money. If I know they can't afford treatment, I won't send a bill." Nancy recalls her family's struggles to pay medical bills, and the small regular payment sent to the family physician. "If a patient can pay only $1 a week, that's fine. I'll try to make them understand that's fine."

The problem in the Valley is similar to that in other places in the Deep South where people tend to put trust in folk medicine rather than in medical specialists. "To me," said one medical student, "the problem is educating the people--as well as the doctors, so they may help the patient

effectively. " Many Mexican-American medical students come
from the barrio and return as family practitioners--physicians
specializing in total care for the patient.

Residents of the inner city want doctors who not only
share their language but their customs and traditions, and
now Puerto Ricans, Filipinos, Vietnamese, and Chicanos
as well as blacks expect to find doctors not only with sympathy but with empathy. Spanish is an elective at New York
University medical school and at South Texas medical school
in San Antonio. Curriculum planning in these schools is
more flexible and emphasizes community service.

The New Jersey College of Medicine and Dentistry,
sheltered in one-story prefabs in the heart of Newark's black
slums, plays a major role in rescuing the crumbling city's
health facilities. Dr. Robert R. Cadmus, president of the
college, focuses on training physicians rather than research
scientists. Cadmus sees Newark's agony as a help rather
than a hindrance in recruiting a fine faculty from nearby
colleges.

Founded in 1965, the community college's main goal
is to lift Newark's rotting old Martland Hospital out of the
eighteenth century. Its founders, through sheer grit, managed to get the college moved into new $5-million quarters
in 11 steel temporary buildings across from the hospital.

A Family Health Care Center, opened in May 1970,
consolidates all Martland's old out-patient clinics and contains admitting rooms, a dozen fully-equipped treatment rooms,
and six dental units.

"Under the old system," said administrator Frank W.
Scott, "They'd count off the first 60, say, of 100 patients
waiting, and tell the rest to go home. We're trying to get
our community used to appointments so they can come in,
be examined and treated in an hour instead of waiting three
or four hours."

The curse of charity medicine has always been the
long wait to see the doctor. Patients in pain or even bleeding often had to wait hours on hard benches. Hospitalized
patients might be cured of a disease and then be sent home
to such an intolerable situation that they might have been
better off dying of the illness.

Such community clinics as the new Martland wing

not only serve the walking ill, but consult with families on all aspects of preventive medicine. Word of mouth is the most potent medium for informing the poor of the availability of medical care. The whole family will be seen by a doctor, and the detection of such ailments as early diabetes, veneral diseases, tuberculosis, drug addiction, and bad teeth may prevent major problems later. Nutritionists are important in these clinics. In the summer of 1970 the Newark community health program involved three first-year medical students, who conducted a lead-poisoning detection unit. In a storefront office they attracted patients, from whom they drew 30,000 samples of blood for analysis. Lead pica, a serious hazard among black children in Newark, could be detected to prevent the death of exposed youngsters. Such programs change the health picture in blighted urban areas.

From 1960 to 1975, responding to a 1959 U.S. Public Health Service report estimating a need for 20 to 24 new medical schools, 27 medical schools opened in the United States, while federal funds enabled other schools to expand. The number of places for incoming students has doubled since 1966.

Why are thousands of well-qualified, motivated American students unable to get into medical school? Many, failing to survive the fierce competition among United States applicants, turn to schools abroad. Many apply to Mexico (where all courses are taught in Spanish). Tuition is low, and quick acceptance means an end to making applications to schools that merely turn down the applicant. Reliable estimates reveal that roughly half the students applying for medical schools are rejected. In 1971 no fewer than 1,945 American women and men enrolled in the medical school at Guadalajara Autonomous University. A member of the faculty observed, "Mexico is simply the back door to medicine in the United States."

An American medical student added, "It's the back door only because the front door has been artificially barred."

The Autonomous University receives loans and grants from the United States government and foundations. One argument used to justify the channeling of National Institute of Health funds to foreign schools is the large number of Americans who receive their medical education in Mexican and European schools: more United States citizens study medicine in Guadalajara than in any school in the United States. How graduates of the medical school in Guadalajara fit into American medicine has become a political hot potato. One member of the New York legislature proposed a bill, aimed at helping Guadalajara graduates, that would guarantee foreign-educated state residents admission to clinical training programs at state medical schools. Of course, an M.D. acquired abroad does not qualify the student to practice medicine in the United States. The record of Guadalajara graduates has not impressed United States medical officials. Only 65 of 1,066, or 6 percent, of Guadalajara graduates passed the key examination in 1975 that would have qualified them to practice in this country. By contrast, 188 of 245, or 77 percent, of the graduates of Dutch medical schools passed the same examination.

There are simply not enough places to seat all premedical students whom the Association of American Medical Colleges in Washington, on the basis of a standardized test, considers qualified for admission. Serious obstacles exist to further expansion of enrollment, the most serious of which is economics. New medical schools to accommodate all qualified students who have been rejected from American schools would cost billions--and the money is not available.

Financial grants to qualified students who are accepted are few. "It is prohibitively expensive to be a medical student in this country," says Dr. Estelle Ramey.

> Relative to most other countries, we have a very small base of scholarship support. Even for men students, family resources must be considerable. Families make great financial sacrifices for sons. Everybody recognizes that a man's "success" in life depends on his training. The family sees little reason to go into endless debt for a daughter. They know that in our society all that a woman has to do to be admired, envied, and feted is to marry a successful man. If, in addition to this achievement, she manages to field a few non-criminal children, she is universally regarded as a "success fou." As a family symbol, one such daughter is worth a gaggle of unmarried daughter doctors.

Although there was an influx of women doctors to medical school in the early part of the century, by 1940 the percentage of women in medicine had fallen to 5.1. In view of the high cost of educating doctors, medical schools were loath to accept women, who might drop out before completing their education, either for marriage, child-bearing, or child-rearing. This fear was largely unfounded.

Gradually, women have come to make up more and more of the medical-school classes. Downstate Medical Center in Brooklyn, for example, in 1973 admitted a class of which 21.8 percent were women. An obstetrician, Dr. Joseph E. Renshaw, studied 325,000 physicians in the United States and found that 73 percent of all actively engaged women doctors work in seven specialties. Not surprisingly, more are in pediatrics than in any other field. The second largest group is in psychiatry, and the third largest group is in family practice. Women, as we have seen, are also in internal medicine, anesthesiology and obstetrics and there is no specialty in which there are no women.

(Back in 1881, Rachel Bodley, professor of chemistry and third Dean of the Woman's Medical College of Pennsylvania, sent questionnaires to the 244 living graduates of the college, asking them what kind of work they were doing, their social and financial status, and the influence of the "study and practice of medicine upon woman's holiest relations, as wife and mother." Of the 189 who responded Dean Bodley discovered 166 engaged in active medical practice, mostly in areas dealing with women: 35 in gynecology with medicine of surgery; 32 in gynecology; 23 in gynecology with obstetrics; ten in obstetrics; nine in obstetrics with general medicine; ten in internal medicine; seven in internal medicine and surgery; three in surgery; and 37 in "general practice without discrimination.")

Women have been willing to pioneer in areas where men have hesitated to tread. For example, Dr. Barbara Brown, neurophysiologist of the Veterans Administration Hospital in Sepulveda, Calif., is studying "biofeedback training," an exciting new way of teaching people to control the kind of waves their brains emit.

Dr. Brown explains that the brain's constant electrical activity produces wave patterns, which are measured with an electroencephalograph attached to the scalp. On ribbons of paper, the recorded patterns are tracings that come in four main wavelengths: delta, occurring in sleep; theta, linked to creativity; beta, identified with mental concentration; and the relaxed alpha.

Dr. Brown demonstrates that a tone or light activated by the E. E. G. tells the persons being trained when they are producing alpha. Requested to keep the feedback (the tone of light) steady, most trainees can comply simply by relaxing effectively. She is convinced that this will prove a boon for psychology, psychiatry, education, and industry. Introspective, intuitive, and creative people tend to produce more alpha when they are meditating than when they are not. Such persons may learn to switch alpha on and off. Psychiatrists see the tension-relieving control of alpha as potentially useful to patients. Claustrophobics, for example, may be trained to produce alpha and find themselves suddenly relaxed in an elevator or a windowless bathroom.

Well-educated specialists in parapsychology include many women who support unorthodox methods of healing. At a four-day symposium held in October 1972 at Stanford University, healing was viewed from the point of view of those who learn "to awaken those sensory systems which permit us to perceive different dimensions of the universe."

Some mysterious form of "energy" may flow from one person to another. People who can transfer such energy can be healers. The possibility that a healer who lacks self-confidence might drain a sick person, instead of injecting new energy, was proposed by Dr. Thelma S. Moss, assistant professor in the psychiatry department of the University of California/Los Angeles. Using a photographic method that allegedly records an aura of energy in and around living material, she places the object to be photographed over a film plate in a dark room. A high-frequency electrical current is generated around the plate. When the film is developed, objects of all kinds seem to radiate a form of luminescence, which is taken to manifest a mysterious form of energy.

A leaf photographed in this manner appears, in its live normal state, to be full of a myriad of tiny white bubbles that literally seem to burst with energy. A wounded leaf quickly develops gaping holes in this dynamic bubble pattern. A person with healing powers or with a "green thumb," says Dr. Moss, can restore the vitality of the leaf by simply laying a hand over it for a few minutes. Such treatment hastens the return of the energy bubbles within the leaf. Conversely, a person with a "brown thumb" who treats a wounded leaf in the same way hastens the death of the leaf. The energy drains out of the leaf, evidence of an energy transfer in the "laying on of hands," according to Moss. "After a healing session the fingertips' auras are unusually smaller, while the auras of the person being healed increase," she claims.

Sister Justa Smith of Rosary Hill College in Buffalo, N. Y., a Franciscan nun who holds a doctorate in biochemistry, has studied the laying on of hands. She believes a single energy or force is probably responsible for all parapsychological phenomena.

"We can measure all energies in the known electromagnetic spectrum directly," claims Sister Smith. "But we cannot directly measure psychic energy. Or is it another whole spectrum of energy? Is it really an energy? Is it really at one end or the other of the electromagnetic spectrum as we know it but we just can't measure it?"

A number of women are studying something as mysterious as "the laying on of hands," and that is cancer virus. In the Texas Medical Complex, Janet Butel of the Baylor College of Medicine department of virology has kept up a meaningful relationship with the same virus for a dozen years. A framed electromicrograph of what she terms "dear old SV40, magnified about 50, 000 times" hangs on her office wall.

Butel likes to come to work, and she continues to find fun in studying the same virus. "We're old friends," she says of the virus, which, magnified, looks like black splotches of bread mold. The tiny virus causes tumors in hamsters. "If we can understand how this virus works, perhaps we can take what we've learned and apply it to other systems," claims Dr. Butel. "Cell transformation refers to a change in cells growing in tissue culture.... Using temperature-sensitive mutants, we have determined which viral gene is involved in cell transformation."

Dr. Butel, wife of Baylor College gastroenterologist David Graham and a mother of two, packs her homework in a pink briefcase. She has manuscripts to work on, journals she has to catch up on, grant applications to prepare. She says, "In science, it's important to build a reputation. Before I married, I had already published a number of papers."*

---

*From an interview by Shirley Pfister, Houston Chronicle, April 20, 1975, Sec. 8, p. 2.

She kept her maiden name, as many professional women prefer to do. She admits that there are problems, handling home, family, and office. A full-time maid stays with the children and does the housework.

Working in the same Texas Medical Complex is Dr. Elizabeth Priori, who with Dr. Leon Dmochowski of the University of Texas M. D. Anderson Hospital and Tumor Institute created excitement by isolating a human cancer virus. The virus was extracted from the cells of a five-year-old boy who died of Burkitt's lymphoma, a lymph-gland cancer. The doctors then succeeded in growing the virus in human lymph cells in the laboratory. Identifying the virus--in electron microscope photos magnified perhaps 90,000 times--and pinpointing it was accomplished by Drs. Priori, Dmochowski, and colleagues with the virus that had affected the face and knee bones.

Having this virus provides a tool of great potential for investigating the role of viruses in human cancer and perhaps for vaccination, claimed Dr. Priori. She worked for more than three years on the virology project. Before taking on this position she had been interested in a musical career, and piano and violin remain great loves in her life. Her parents died when she was in college, both of cancer, but she says that was not the reason she went into cancer research: "No, it was more the challenge."

In July 1971, speaking of her research breakthrough, she said,

> We call this virus Type C, but really it looks like a pizza. Flat, sort of squashed. But it is a very broad statement in cancer virology to say that you have a human virus. It has been so difficult to find in the past. Difficult to find and almost impossible to grow. It is easy to grow mouse cultures, for example; you get a lot of virus from a mouse culture. So the first thing when you say, "Look, I have a culture that is producing virus," the response is that somehow you've gotten mouse culture in there. You have to prove this is a human culture (Smith).

The custom of naming the first culture of an experiment for the experimenter prompted Dr. Priori's colleagues jokingly to label it E.S.P.-1, "Because we were working in the dark."

"Fortunately," jokes the friendly Dr. Priori, "E. S. P. are also my initials so we were able to keep the name and still be dignified about it."

The chapters that follow will explore some of the issues in medicine that have a particular impact on women, both as doctors and as patients.

MEDICAL FACTS AND FANTASIES

15. The Second-Greatest Joy

The Swedish people have a proverb, "The greatest joy is to become a mother; the second greatest is to be a midwife." A young woman thinking of medicine as a career could do worse than consider the possibility of going into midwifery.

In 1979 the World Health Organization urged developing countries to revive the arts of traditional village healers. A severe shortage of doctors trained in Western medicine (a ratio of auxiliary personnel to population was less than one to 10,000) made it vital that traditional birth attendants, healers, and herbalists resort to the ancient healing practices, including the use of herbs, plants, and medicinal oils.

The W. H. O. report cited proven traditional medicines, such as Ammi visnaga, a plant found in the Mediterranean region that contains properties effective in treating angina pectoris. Certain roots from tropical plants were discovered to be successful in combating guinea-worm in Ghana. An Egyptian plant used as a diuretic, Cymbopogon proximus, helps to remove small stones from the urinary tract. For birth control or fertility regulation in Tibet a substance found in peaches, which are a major source of dietary protein, M-xylohydroquinone, was shown to be 60 percent effective.

For millions of people in remote areas such care is essential. Traditionally women have provided the attentions needed during birthing and illness.

In New York, in an effort to offset the high rate of infant mortality in ghettos and the shortage of maternity services in the United States, a program to expand the training of midwives was conducted by the Maternity Center Association of New York with a large grant from the Commonwealth Fund, a foundation working in medical education and community health.

In Colorado, Barbara Seifert, the mother of two children, was a biological researcher at the University of Colorado Medical Center who wanted to work with people; when Dr. Henry K. Silver of Colorado's Department of Pediatrics conceived of "child health associates" to give diagnostic, preventive, and therapeutic services to children, Seifert was enthusiastic.

To train a pediatrician takes 11 years, but to train an associate only five--two years of modified premed curriculum, two years of scientific and clinic training, and one year of internship. The promise of such a program for alleviating the chronic shortage of medical care is enticing. Physicians may be overqualified to perform many duties that midwives and associates can do. A doctor may be bored with a task in which there is no challenge. Examining a baby in good health may not thrill a pediatrician whose training was concentrated on finding serious illness.

Treating a simple fracture, a cut finger, or a black eye doesn't always call for a doctor's expertise. Physician's assistants, such as Seifert, may concentrate on what they are qualified to handle.

In May of 1972, when the state of Georgia decided to declare midwifery (by the way, it rhymes with "sniffery") illegal, Hattie Miller, 70, of West Point shrugged and declared she would practice in Alabama. In Alabama, one of 462 women (mostly black) who were still delivering babies in the '70s, mostly in rural or poor areas of cities, Miller is known as a "granny midwife." These women have delivered thousands of children. In the '70s Alabama, with one of the highest infant-mortality rates in the nation, set up a pilot program similar to China's barefoot doctors--to offer safe infant delivery in rural areas and provide information for family planning and prenatal and postnatal care. It launched an active nurse-midwife training program, teaching registered nurses to handle normal deliveries. Ultimately, when enough are trained, granny midwives will no longer be given permits.

One-third of Alabama mothers are simply too poor to pay the cost of adequate maternal or health care. Midwives frequently help these mothers deliver, but in complicated cases a doctor is needed. Home deliveries obviously cannot deal well with complications.

The new role of nurse-midwives is no longer confined

to backwoods America. In many cities young women, wishing to have their family or husband close by, are having home deliveries with the help of trained midwives.

Back in 1848 Dr. Samuel Gregory of Boston tried to revive the training of midwives. Women at that time had decided they preferred to have fully trained doctors. Doctors themselves opposed midwives because of economic competition, and Dr. Gregory accused the men of wanting a male monopoly of the baby business (Gregory, p. 18ff).

Nurse-midwives are highly trained women who relieve overworked doctors in delivery rooms around the United States; there were approximately 1, 500 practicing in the United States in 1977; several thousand foreign-trained nurse-midwives practice here as well.

"Most nurse-midwives' patients are awake and aware, " reported Brenda Doyle, who has delivered more than 1, 000 infants. "My patients walk right off the delivery table. " She--with other nurse-midwives--work at Lincoln Hospital in the Bronx, N. Y.

America might improve its poor rating in worldwide infant mortality if more nurse-midwives were to work in American clinics. When Sara Mata, who is now a physician's assistant in Alief, a suburb of Houston, was a midwife in Rafael, Argentina, she sometimes got paid with chickens, eggs, or fruit, but she didn't mind; she loved what she was doing. "Taking part in a birth is a beautiful experience. The father hugs you after it's over. The mother is all smiles and the grandmother usually cries. I was lucky because I never lost a patient in the 75 deliveries I performed. " The education she received at the College of Medical Sciences at the University of Cordoba, Argentina, was accepted in Houston as the equivalent of a registered nurse's degree, and Mata attended nursing school for two years before specializing in midwifery. Applying for the physician's assistant program at Baylor, she was turned down, but she talked them into changing their minds.

Midwifery was organized in New York in 1931 by the Maternity Center Association. Training is offered in ten medical colleges and nursing schools in the United States. The training involves eight to 24 months, depending on whether or not the nurse already has the R. N. , Bachelor's, or Master's degree. Each nurse must be certified by the

Dr. Dorothy Brown, the first black woman surgeon in the
South, teaches a medical class at Meharry in 1958. Dr.
Brown is still on the faculty of the Department of Surgery.

American College of Nurse-Midwives, and an additional
license is sometimes required by the state.

At most hospitals nurse-midwives attend women whose
babies are expected to be delivered without complication.
Women who might need forceps, special care, or operative
deliveries are assigned to specialists. "What we do is free
the doctor from vanilla-type deliveries," says one nurse-
midwife.

At Meharry Medical College in Nashville, Tenn., an
expanded nurse-training program under the direction of Mrs.
Evelyn Kennedy Tomes offers a nine-month program that
trains nurses for service in rural or densely populated urban
areas where available health services are inadequate.

"We don't train them to be nurses," says Mrs.
Tomes, "we add to their skills so they can go into areas
formerly reserved for physicians" (Meeker). The nurse-
midwife has more time to give than a doctor; a pregnant
woman is seen as soon as she realizes she is having a baby
and is given care until a month after the child is born.

Trainees are drawn to Meharry Medical College from

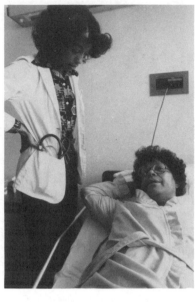

A medical student counsels
her patient.

all over the nation.   Beside
the Meharry nurse-midwife
program there is one other
training institution in the
Southeast, at the University
of Mississippi.

Midwifery was outlawed
in California in 1949, but a
number of midwives practice
in Santa Cruz, about 100
miles south of San Francisco.
They believe home births
create a sounder and more
loving bond between the child
and the family.   Founder of
the birth center in Santa
Cruz is Raven Lang, who
commits a misdemeanor every time she helps deliver a baby.

Midwifery is moving more and more into hospital
rooms, because some midwives are unenthusiastic about
home births.   Hospitals have equipment and facilities to
save mother and child in an obstetrical emergency, and
sometimes a surgeon or specialist is needed on the double.
But one day there may be some kind of mobile unit, a kind
of capsule, perhaps, that could be called in such an emergency to take care of blood transfusions or oxygen.

Doctors reject home deliveries because they find
them altogether too time-consuming: several patients in
labor can be attended simultaneously in a hospital.   But
many mothers are coming to believe that having a baby in
a hospital is too expensive and too dehumanizing an experience.   Natural childbirth has become one of the great adventures of a woman's life.   The chance that the mother
might be put to sleep at the most exciting moment of a
great achievement makes many a pregnant woman try to have
her baby at home.   The attention of a midwife in the home
may make a delivery memorable and happy.

In Phoenix and in San Francisco, and in Houston's
Women's Hospital of Texas, apartment settings with stereo

music and potted plants have been created only seconds away
from hospital operating rooms, but women are being delivered in the "birthing room," by obstetricians. The entire
family, children included, may be present at the delivery.
The baby remains with the mother from the moment of birth.
If there are no complications, mother, baby, and family go
home six hours later. A nurse from the hospital's nursery
and another from labor and delivery will make home visits
to mother and baby on the first and third days after baby's
birth.

A study conducted at Evanston Hospital, Illinois,
proved that women who used the Lamaze natural childbirth
method had far fewer problems in pregnancy than women
who did not. Results reported in Obstetrics and Gynecology*
reveal that 500 Lamaze-trained women benefited in nearly
every obstetrical area: they had one-fourth as many Cesar-
ean sections and one fifth the fetal distress as the 500 in the
control group who did not take training. The death rate for
fetuses and newborns was one-fourth that of the control group.
The control group had almost three times as much toxemia
of pregnancy and twice as many premature infants.

I myself used the Lamaze method in its pioneering
days, and look back on my experiences as great adventures,
joyous and exciting.

In recent years an innovative child-bearing center has
opened in New York as an alternative to rigid hospital procedures. Offering safeguards against the hazards of home
deliveries, the Maternity Center Association, a 60-year-old
organization, opened a six-story town house to demonstrate
that low-risk pregnancies and deliveries need not require a
traditional hospital setting. The center eliminates the rot-
ten, but now routine, procedures of strapping mothers to
tables, immobilizing legs in stirrups, and administering
enemas, pubic area shaves, and episiotomies.

Parents and new babies may be together the entire
time in the delivery room. Within a day of birth the babies
may go home. Couples now have more control over the delivery of their child. While this is not seen as the right
way for every child-bearing woman, the center is dedicated
to offering the alternative.

---

*J. W. Greene, Jr., 51 (June 1978), pp. 723-24.

The center will not accept anyone who is giving birth for the first time and is older than 35, or who has had more than four children, or who has had three or more miscarriages. Should anything go wrong while the patient is in the center, an ambulance would whisk the child-bearing woman immediately to the backup facility, Lennox Hill Hospital, only a short distance away.

The center offers classes in child-bearing and the physiological and emotional reactions of parents; these are obligatory for those who wish to have their children delivered within the center.

In 1972 a young medical student tore out some pages from the August 18 Life magazine to show me. The story was about Dr. Beatrice Tucker, the 75-year-old director of the Chicago Maternity Center who had been delivering babies in homes for 40 years. Dr. Tucker's picture showed her playing with a month-old baby in the family's apartment.

Under Dr. Tucker's administration the Chicago Maternity Center stays open 24 hours a day. She has trudged ghetto streets in freezing cold Chicago winters, climbed stairs of dangerous, dirty apartment projects where elevators wouldn't work, and often gone sleepless for 30 hours so that women in Chicago's poverty area had a doctor in attendance when the baby arrived.

In 1929, in the days when few women aspired to be doctors, Beatrice Tucker argued herself into becoming the first woman obstetrics resident at Chicago Lying-in Hospital. In 1932 she took charge of the Maternity Center, at the time called the Maxwell Street Dispensary. She ushered into the harsh world over 100,000 babies. She lived in a tiny room in the three-story brick building that housed the center in a depressing slum. "Bullet holes were all over the place when I first came down here 40 years ago," she told a Life correspondent. "Conditions have improved in the homes we visit over the years. In the 1930s, we'd deliver babies in rooms with dirt floors, no toilets and no electricity. We'd work by candlelight. Today 90 percent of the homes are adequate." But housing in the '70s presented other problems. "I dread--really dread--going into the high-rises alone. People so crowded together lose their individuality. In fact, the Cabrini-Green project is the only place in the city I won't send our crews. They were stoned there one night and that did it. Every place else in Chicago, people respect the Center."

Dr. Tucker, so tender, so grave, so heavy with compassion, believed that husbands were helpful at birth. A psychotic husband, however, once threatened to kill her if anything went wrong. "It was an interesting case and I wanted to see it through, so three plainclothes policemen watched me deliver the baby." Another husband insisted on helping her up the stairs of a high-rise apartment house. "I didn't want his help. He had been drinking a bit. He put his arm around my waist and every once in a while gave me a pinch. All the way up those stairs to the tenth floor, I kept telling myself that at age 75, a pinch doesn't matter."

"I am committed to home deliveries," she claimed. "At home, of course, deliveries are by natural childbirth. We have more pain. But in a hospital, the isolation is devastating. Both results are good. I believe a patient has a right to choose where she wants to have her baby." On her part, Dr. Tucker finds home deliveries "more fun. I never tire of delivering a baby at home. I really get a charge out of it."

My friend, the medical student, beamed at me and said, "That's what I hope to do ... be like Beatrice Tucker!"

Although midwives delivered more than three out of five babies born in Brownsville, Texas, in 1974, they worked in the shadows, unlicensed, unregulated, and untrained. Ironically, just across the border in Mexico midwives are regulated and given formal training by the national health service, and are accepted by the populace as traditional attendants at births. In 1975, with $15,000 provided by the Texas Department of Community Affairs, Brownsville hired a midwife educator, launched a training course, and passed a city ordinance requiring annual certification for midwives. A system of cooperation with doctors and hospitals was established. By 1978 the city had certified 16 midwives, and evaluators reveal early indications that infant-death rate may be dropping rapidly.

Studies of child-rearing practices show that a good environment with love and security may blot out the poorest intellectual effects of low birth weight due to prematurity. A responsive mother compensates a child for the bad effects of a complicated delivery.

Dr. Niles Newton, a psychologist on the faculty of Northwestern University's medical school, and a grandmother, challenges some American childbirth practices, insisting that they probably contribute to the nation's high infant-mortality rate. "These practices," she claims, "are so deeply imbedded in the culture that they will be difficult to change."

She would allow newborn babies to sleep with their mothers, so that breast feeding on demand rather than on schedule would ease the way for normal suckling, which is best for mother and infant. Dr. Newton says the predominence of male professionals who present theories about childbearing excludes the views of mothers. To Dr. Newton, the crucial questions are:

Why are expectant mothers still frequently hounded by the health team to keep their weight abnormally low in pregnancy when the evidence clearly shows that greater weight gain is associated with lower risk of prematurity?

Why isn't the childbearing experience used to strengthen the family instead of imposing rules that tend to weaken it?

Why aren't we more vigorous in telling women that drugs taken during pregnancy and labor do affect their babies?

Why do we ignore normal physiological needs in labor?

Why do we often give lip service to breast feeding, meanwhile giving directions to mothers that may help to cause nipple pain, breast pain, and too little milk?

Why do most of the hospitals in the United States have compulsory separation of mother and infant in the days after birth when the data suggest that this makes for poorer mother-child relations?

Dr. Niles Newton deplores the fact that the infant-mortality rate in the United States is higher than that of European and other countries. She stresses that physicians have an obligation to do more than hand an expectant mother a diet list and tell her not to gain more than 14 pounds during her pregnancy--when an average gain of no less than 24 pounds is best for the most favorable outcome of the pregnancy.

Women need to be taught certain exercises, not only for easier childbirth, but for more satisfactory sexual relations after childbirth. Today's young women do not grow up in large families where they can observe children being born at home, so they are ill prepared for what happens to their bodies during pregnancy, claims Dr. Newton. They may never have seen a baby breast fed and have no idea how to feed an infant.

Deploring the taboo against sexual intercourse during the late stages of pregnancy and after childbirth, Dr. Newton believes such strictures contribute to a mate's sexual infidelity.

Husbands ought to be included in the delivery room during childbirth, she insists. "When the husband is excluded from participation during labor and delivery, many women appear to form intense attachments to their obstetricians instead."

Dr. Newton does not favor the use of drugs during pregnancy. Many pain-killers and tranquilizers may affect the baby more than the mother. Many obstetricians have been trained to regard childbirth as a pathological condition, painful, messy, risky. They have come to rely heavily on hospital delivery, drugs, and mechanical and surgical interventions. Women in labor are refused anything to eat or drink. Doris Haire, president of the American Foundation for Maternal and Child Health, claims that government regulations in the past have permitted "massive unmonitored experimentation with human lives and mental potential." The overwhelming majority of pregnant women who are healthy may actually be in a more dangerous situation in the hospital at the time of giving birth than in their own homes.

An increasing number of the 3.5 million babies born each year in the United States are born of mothers receiving pain-killer drugs during labor and delivery. The doctors stress that there is a misconception abroad that the number of drugs given during labor and delivery is decreasing. In fact, it is increasing as are the number of drugs taken prenatally. What's more, often the mother isn't even asked if she wants drugs, nor is she informed of their possible dangers to her child.

A study released early in 1979 linked slower child development with anesthesia and pain-killing drugs administered during labor and delivery. Children of women given oxytocin and promethazine, commonly known as Phenergan, overcame the effects of the drugs as time passed, but the effects of inhalant anesthetics, such as ether, caused permanent, if slight, brain damage to children of women who were administered those general anesthetics during childbirth.

Results of the study, data gathered from 1959 to 1965, involved 3,528 full-term babies born to healthy mothers. Most of the mothers received some form of drugs, with 669, or 19 percent, taking the inhalant general anesthetic, 2,259 taking only local pain-killers, and 600 receiving both. This study was conducted by Dr. Sarah H. Broman and Dr. Yvonne Brackbill for the National Institute of Neurological and Communicative Disorders and Stroke. "Overall, there were highly significant associations between the infant's development through the first year and medication during labor and delivery," the doctors concluded. Children of women given pain-killer drugs were slower to sit up, stand, and walk than those babies whose mothers did not receive drugs.

Demerol, given to about half the women giving birth in this country, is usually described as a harmless drug that takes the edge off pain without knocking out the patient, like a strong alcoholic drink. Demerol may reduce tension in the birthing woman, but it may also add to her distress by slowing down or even stopping uterine contractions, and thus prolonging labor. Women who now work as trained birth attendants believe that it is better for mother and child to let the birth process--without chemical intervention--unfold at its own pace when possible.

Comparing the behavior of babies born to mothers who received at least one injection of Demerol during labor with the behavior of babies born to mothers who received no Demerol, Dr. Brackbill found small but disturbing differences. If you make a loud noise near a normal newborn baby, the infant reacts with a start, but will stop reacting if the noise is repeated again and again. This demonstration of an ability to get accustomed to strong but harmless stimuli is considered a sign of a healthy nervous system. In Dr. Brackbill's study the Demerol babies were significantly slower in adapting to a repeated loud noise, even when the tests were conducted two days after birth. This difference in behavior was evidently due to the continued presence of the Demerol drug in the infants; doctors once considered the placenta a kind of magic barrier preventing any foreign substance in the mother's blood from getting to the baby. Pharmacologists specializing in obstetrics now consider any drug given to the mother as winding up in the baby. This includes all kinds of opiates--tea, coffee, alcohol, tranquilizers, nicotine, and aspirin.

Researchers at the Boston University Medical Center drug epidemiology unit have conducted studies, involving 12 hospitals and about 51,000 women, that found no evidence that aspirin taken by pregnant women harms their unborn children. These studies, however, were funded by an aspirin manufacturer and the federal government. A year earlier two Australian doctors said that regular use of aspirin during pregnancy increased the chance of stillbirths and deaths in the first four weeks after birth. Gulping aspirins for every headache twinge or backache should certainly be discouraged in the pregnant mother.

To return to Dr. Newton's theories, she believes women could deliver more easily in a sitting or squatting position rather than flat on their backs. She insists that the routine practice of making surgical incisions to ease and hasten normal delivery is unjustified.

Many doctors around the country are now experimenting with placing low-risk birthing mothers in pleasant surroundings with a minimum of machinery and some supportive trained attendants who believe in a minimum of intervention. They are questioning the practice of tying a woman down on the delivery table or of delivering the baby under the harsh bright lights of the operating room. Dimmed lights, quiet voices, gentler handling, and placing the baby promptly to the mother's breast are new approaches that may give the infant a warmer welcome into the world.

MEDICAL FACTS AND FANTASIES

16. Thalidomide and Other Drugs*

Although it was Helen Taussig who first warned of the danger of thalidomide (see p. 124-5), it was Dr. Frances Oldham
Kelsey who became the eye of a storm that swept the Western world.

Thalidomide went on sale in Britain in 1958, and by
1962 there were some 400 deformed births; doctors estimated
twice that number died at birth from internal injury. Mar-
keted as a safe treatment for morning sickness and insomnia,
(though never sold commercially in the United States) thalidomide had been used experimentally in hospitals. How many
deformed babies were born, no one knows for sure. There
were as many as 8,000 victims of the drug, which left a
trail of deformed infants in 46 countries. In New York reports of many deformed infants born in the same block led
to a doctor who may have sold "drug samples" to nearby
pharmacists who resold them to pregnant women.

Infants were born with malformed limbs; some were
legless, armless, or earless. Many had congenital heart
problems, some had gastrointestinal malformations, some
had kidney trouble, others were just cocoons of flesh with
heads. Some infants were epileptic, some autistic, some
mentally retarded. In many cases the children had superior
intelligence. Newspapers published pictures of babies with
multiple malformations, fingers growing out of elbows,

---

*For material on Frances Kelsey I am indebted to: News-
week, 60 (June 24, 1963), p. 70; Saturday Review, 45 (September 1, 1962), pp. 36-37, and 46 (February 2, 1963),
p. 47; Science Digest, 53 (May 1963), p. 32; Time, 80 (August 10, 1962), p. 32; and U. S. News and World Report,
53 (August 13, 1962), pp. 54-55, and 53 (August 20, 1962),
p. 13. Life, 53 (August 10, 1962), pp. 28-29.

serious facial disfigurations. Years later Dr. Elizabeth Schwartshaupt, the West German minister of health, estimated that pregnant women who took thalidomide gave birth to dead babies in 50 percent of known cases.

Some parents committed suicide, many marriages were broken, and families lived in torment with thalidomide victims day by day. In Belgium a crowd cheered when a couple were freed of murder charges in the poisoning of their legless eight-day-old baby.

Some 2. 5 million thalidomide tablets were distributed free by the American branch of the Distillers Co. , and 1, 267 doctors had given the drug to about 20, 000 patients.

More than $100 million in compensation has been paid or put in trust for thalidomide victims in Germany-- where the drug was developed--in Britain, the United States, and Canada. The Distillers Co. , the British licensee, a marketer of alcoholic beverages, was persuaded by Ralph Nader, the consumer crusader, to increase dramatically its settlement on the threat of a possible boycott of their liquor.

In April 1979, two decades after the international thalidomide tragedy, Elaine Dale, who was born armless, gave birth to a normal baby in Grimsby Maternity Hospital in England. There were tears of joy throughout the hospital when Dale cuddled her baby with her feet and said, "The sheer joy of having her makes up for all the pain in the world. "

How did the name of Dr. Frances Oldham Kelsey become a household word? On July 15, 1962, the Washington Post, in an article implicating thalidomide in the birth of deformed babies, noted that the drug had been kept off the American market by Dr. Kelsey, then director of the Division of New Drugs of the United States Food and Drug Administration.

Holding a doctorate in pharmacology from the University of Chicago (1938), Dr. Kelsey was being urged to approve the tranquilizer thalidomide. Concerned about the drug's unproven side-effects, she refused to be hurried by the drug manufacturers into giving approval. She effectively blocked the sale of the drug in the United States.

Kelsey's predecessor in the F. D. A. post had been

Dr. Barbara Moulton, who in 1960 had resigned in disgust because of harassment. Dr. Moulton, a well-qualified bacteriologist before becoming a physician, had studied antibiotics long before they became applicable to clinical medicine. She had been an assistant director of the Municipal Contagious Disease Hospital in Chicago and had done research and taught in antibiotic medicine. Dr. Moulton heard foreign clinicians expressing shock over the obvious commercialism of the F.D.A. program. Instead of consumer protection the emphasis of the program was on approving drugs that the pharmaceutical industry wished to market. Drugs were approved for commercial sale before investigations were completed. Unable to change the situation, Dr. Moulton resigned.

In the F.D.A. Dr. Kelsey's view of her responsibility was protection of the drug consumer. She insisted on indisputable proof that thalidomide would be harmless to expectant mothers. As a result of her stubborn sense of duty, a fundamental human right was scrutinized: the right of patients to be free of taking medication without their informed consent.

Working in a rickety Washington, D.C., barracks, Kelsey reasoned, step by step, that the puzzling chemistry of thalidomide might cause paralysis of peripheral nerves. Two decades earlier she had studied quinine's effect on rabbit fetuses. In the laboratory she had learned how drugs which irritate adult nerves could wreak havoc on the nervous controls of embryos. She observed stunted growth, monsterism, and paralysis resulting from such drugs. Working with thalidomide, she saw that the drug had a harmful effect on animals. The poor beasts would not go to sleep! She poured over reports from England that the habitual use of the drug brought peripheral paralysis to some users. Finally there was the horrible evidence of the unfortunate babies born in Germany.

Dr. Kelsey and her husband had two children of their own. Her husband, pharmacologist Ellis Kelsey, followed his wife's research and confirmed her reasoning, and with his steady support she held fast to her refusal to approve the drug.

On August 7, 1962, President John F. Kennedy clasped about Dr. Frances Kelsey's neck a ribbon dangling the Distinguished Federal Civilian Service Medal in honor of her heroic resistance to pressure and her consistent refusal to approve thalidomide for commercial sale. Thousands of American women congratulated her. Some of those women had never opened a science book in their lives, but they cared about what happened to luckless unborn babies. Many read later, in December 1970, when the longest trial in West Germany's history came to a close, after two and a half years of court sessions, that thalidomide was indeed responsible for the epidemic of malformed infants born from 1957 to 1961, affecting 8,500 babies in 20 countries.

Federal regulation of medicine has come a far piece since the day President Kennedy honored Dr. Kelsey, but it still has some distance to go. In April 1975 the Senate approved a bill placing medical devices under the same kind of regulations that applied to drugs. The government had exercised regulation of one kind or another over drugs for seven decades, but there were only the most sketchy controls over such medical devices as cardiac pacemakers, heart valves, and artificial hip joints. While the F.D.A. had begun to require more careful scientific tests before a drug could be cleared for sale in the United States, the new Senate bill required pre-market proof of the safety and usefulness of such devices intended to sustain life or to be "implanted in human beings."

Of greatest interest to women was the usefulness and safety of the intrauterine contraceptive devices (I.U.D.). One I.U.D. manufacturer claimed that his device leached out copper after implantation in the uterus, and this "leaching" reinforced the contraceptive action of the I.U.D. The F.D.A. jumped with both feet on this claim, while in the case of another manufacturer, Dalkon Shield, the F.D.A. admitted it had no jurisdiction over a contraceptive that worked solely through mechanical action.

Much discretion remains the province of the doctors themselves. The government is reluctant to interfere in the practice of medicine, and there have been a number of cases in which the insertion of the intrauterine device was done so ineptly that the abdominal cavity was punctured. There's nothing in the world the F.D.A. or any other government agency could do about such ineptitude.

In two separate studies Dr. Anne Kimball with Dr. Fritz Fuchs and B. H. Kean at New York Hospital produced simultaneous evidence with researchers in Scotland pinpointing causes of toxoplasmosis. At New York Hospital some 4,000 obstetrical patients were given blood tests at their first visits to the obstetrician and again when they had their babies. Initially, about two-thirds of the group showed no antibodies for toxoplasmosis and were therefore susceptible. Of those women who were seen to have risk, six acquired toxoplasmosis while pregnant. In three of these women the parasites crossed the placental barrier and infected the baby.

"Among the mothers in this study who were susceptible, one in 1,000 gave birth to babies infected with toxoplasmosis. At New York Hospital, this was greater than the combined figure for babies born during the same period with defects from congenital syphilis, rubella, and phenylketonuria (P.K.U.)."

For over two decades doctors have been aware that raw or undercooked meat containing cysts caused toxoplasmosis, but the baffling mystery was the occurrence of cases in people who never ate meat. Now evidence from research in Scotland and the United States indicates there may well be another cause of toxoplasmosis: the common house pet-- the cat! Yes, the cat....

In the 1950s French children in St. Vincent de Paul Hospital were given barely seared meat daily as part of their tuberculosis therapy. These patients contracted toxoplasmosis five times as frequently as they did before coming to the sanitarium. Undercooked lamb and pork are the most common hosts for the toxoplasma parasites, but beef also is a source. Shortly after publication of the French proof of toxoplasmosis a Glasgow investigator found that toxoplasma parasites could be transmitted by live animals. At the University of Kansas research revealed that the intestinal tract of the cat provides not only a potential host for tiny organisms, but is also a virtual breeding ground as well. The cat's feces could contaminate the person who cleans up the litter boxes. Children playing in sandboxes or in garden dirt come in contact with cat offal and may be permanently infected with toxoplasmosis.

Now there is general recognition that every pregnant woman should be given a blood test for toxoplasmosis as a routine part of her prenatal examination. Until such tests become routine doctors inform pregnant women never to eat raw meat, and if there is a household cat, the pet should be sent away for nine months.

Most women are well informed about the danger of exposure to measles during pregnancy and know that an expectant mother who contracts the disease could deliver a malformed child. Measles used to be taken lightly, and often when a neighbor child had measles, a mother would take her child to be exposed "and get it over with. " The child had a one-in-ten chance of developing a serious complication, such as pneumonia, bronchitis, middle-ear infection, or even brain fever. Before the development of vaccines for measles, 400 or 500 victims died each year of the disease. Mass immunization programs have been waged on this children's disease, often by mother-doctors who had had to nurse their own children through it.

Dr. Kelsey's heroism did not serve as an example to the F. D. A. when "feminine sprays" came on the market, selling to the tune of an estimated yearly $53 million. It's not enough to spray under your dainty arms, television viewers were told, and many women suffered serious genital irritations from the sprays.

About this time, in August 1972, the French Health Ministry revealed that a French-made talcum powder, accidently laced with a double dose of a popular germ-fighter, hexachlorophene, had caused the death of several infants. The 6-percent H. C. P. content resulted in severe brain inflammation in the babies. The United States sent two F. D. A. experts to investigate the French tragedy, and shortly thereafter, the Food and Drug Administration announced permanent curbs on hexachlorophene, which had been used in vaginal and aerosol deodorants, soaps, toothpaste, baby lotion, and hair spray.

Two Houston doctors, Reba Hill and Marjorie Horning (mentioned earlier--see p. 2), conducted a study pinpointing commonly-used medications taken during pregnancy to determine if pills or drugs ordered by doctors for headache, backache, or discomfort would cause birth defects or later behavior or learning problems in the offspring. The mothers were examined in the hospital after giving birth, and the babies were checked from 1969 to 1974. Research revealed that the average baby in the study of middle- and upperclass women had been exposed to seven or more (up to 12!) drugs before birth. One mother took 69! The Baylor College of Medicine program further revealed that a baby born to an impoverished family may be in less danger from medications taken by the mother before the baby's birth than an infant from middle-class or rich families.

Babies whose mothers took aspirin before delivery eliminate aspirin from their bodies for as long as six days after birth. Even coffee and tea affect the child. Caffeine from non-prescription drugs is found in the infant's urine after birth. Drugs usually do not reach the baby in the original state, but in products formed through body chemistry. One conclusion drawn from the study is that middle- and upper-class women want and demand immediate relief of pain and discomfort during pregnancy, but women in lower economic groups neither expect nor seek such relief. (Although poor women regard pain as a normal part of pregnancy, no women should be expected to accept suffering silently. Doctors need not be too hasty in handing out prescriptions when a word of comfort and encouragement could do as well.)

Scientists found that some women do not regard non-prescription medications as drugs. One mother remarked she would not have taken so much aspirin while pregnant had she realized it was a drug. Women who must take drugs for a chronic ailment are more cautious about using medications than those who do not, the Houston study revealed. Some interviewed women had been using illicit drugs such as heroin, amphetamines, or L.S.D. Most of these women stopped cold when they found out for certain they were pregnant.

Babies of some women were born with typical signs of withdrawal from a medication; they were irritable and slept fitfully during the first few months of life. Some 23 percent of the women were given antibiotics during pregnancy. Of these four were given tetracycline, which is known to cause staining of teeth. For years tetracycline was given to little children in the cycle of childhood diseases, including ear infections, and these youngsters grew up with ugly, darkened teeth. Babies of all four of the mothers who received tetracycline had teeth that came in stained.

Dr. Hill said that many women get medications from several doctors. "She may get antibiotics from her internist, something else from her skin specialist, and medications from the obstetrician."

The experiment of the two doctors did not include counting the drugs of other potentially harmful substances, such as x-rays or pesticides, but the mothers were interviewed about them. Alarmingly, 30 percent of the women were exposed to pesticides used in the home and 40 percent to x-rays. The majority of x-rays were routine chest examinations or dental x-rays that could easily have been postponed until after the baby's birth.

In another experiment Dr. Lucile K. Kuchera, a University of Michigan Health Service doctor, studied 1,000 women, mostly college students who had been given a synthetic female hormone, diethylstilbestrol (D. E. S.) within 72 hours after the possibility of conception. The pill, designed to prevent bleeding and hemorrhaging, has also been called the "morning after" pill--an afterthought for birth control for women who indulge in sex without using contraceptives.

Based on the calculated risk of pregnancy after a single sex act, from 20 to 40 women in Dr. Kuchera's study might have expected to be pregnant had no treatment been given. In fact, no pregnancies occurred, Dr. Kuchera said. Of the women in the group half the number reported no side-effects. Dr. Kuchera regarded the use of the drug as something to be reserved for emergencies, such as in protecting rape victims. But the F. D. A. , in November 1971, warned doctors not to prescribe D. E. S. under any circumstances, because medical experts said that D. E. S. given to pregnant women to prevent miscarriage may cause cancer in female offspring.

A note on what help was given to babies who were born deformed or crippled: Dr. Mary D. Ames, pediatrician at the Children's Hospital of Philadelphia, has helped crippled children and infants born without limbs to live a more normal life. The children are fitted with artificial limbs at an early age, sometimes before they are three years old, and are given continuous attention. Pediatricians, orthopedists, prosthetists, nurses, physical and occupational therapists, psychologists, and social workers lend support. One 14-month-old child without the use of both legs and one arm was fitted with roller skates to allow for movement. The child became an accepted member of the family and grew so used to his artificial limbs he hardly knew he was an amputee.

Still, much discussion in recent years is aroused by the hospital cost of saving premature and deformed children. "The outcome justifies this expense, " says the health-care team responsible for saving the lives of extremely premature babies at Cedars-Mount Sinai Medical Center in Los Angeles.

This study, conducted between January 1973 and June 1975, of 75 of these babies (20 of whom survived) showed that the average cost of saving their lives was $90,000. In evaluating medical care, however, Dr. Jeffrey Pomerance, who headed the team, and his colleagues said they no longer believe that the "no cost is too great" attitude is supportable. Now we have to choose how to spend limited dollars. "We must make an enlightened choice," they say.

Writing in The Atlantic of July 1979, Robert and Peggy Stinson, the parents of two children, record the anguish involved with their desperately premature baby, who weighed less than two pounds at birth. After months of "heroic" efforts in an intensive care facility, the baby died. The parents were pessimistic from the onset about the chances of the boy's survival, and were told repeatedly that "someone must be the child's advocate." They were treated in a manner guaranteed to create profound psychological upset and were categorized as "hostile," "emotionally fragile," and "under psychiatric care." Hospital costs alone for Andrew Stinson's treatment came to $104,403.20, a reminder, write the parents, "that through the six months of hospital experiments, failures, and arrogance, the meter was ticking--but someone else would pay." The hospital remained above the protests of the parents, the infliction of constant pain on the infant, and the sense of impending financial disaster (Stinson, pp. 64-72).

McCall's magazine surveyed 200 women gynecologists in October 1975, asking about estrogen therapy for post-menopausal women. Estrogen is the active element in birth-control pills, and new findings link estrogen and endometrial cancer. The evidence has been building for years, and while these women doctors do not believe that estrogen actually causes cancer, they hold that sustained use may stimulate dormant factors in the body that might lead to cancer. Of the doctors surveyed, 88 percent reported they would refuse hormone therapy to women who actually have, or have had, cancer. What these doctors maintain is that no woman should take estrogen unless she really needs it; if she has no symptoms of a shortage of deficiency--such as dryness during intercourse--she should depend on her own natural protective system and not take estrogen.

The controversy over the safety of birth-control pills raged throughout the '70s. The British medical review The Lancet claimed the complications of pituitary tumor growth "may equal or exceed that of other risks attributable to the pill."

"When is the F. D. A. going to draw the line and take the pill off the market?" asked Dr. Herbert Ratner of the Loyola University school of medicine in an address to the participants from Europe, the Far East, New Zealand, and America at an international symposium on natural family planning at the Human Life Center of St. John's University, Collegeville, Minn., June 18, 1979. "The pill," Ratner said, "was originally promoted as physiologically natural, which was a medical fantasy." Liver tumors among pill users were reported in medical literature as early as 1973, as well as other complications, such as obstructions of blood vessels. "Pituitary tumors are now being reported," Ranter says. "These tumors have no clinical significance unless they enlarge--which would necessitate a cranial operation. What enlarges these harmless micro-tumors is the stimulation of estrogen, and the major contributor to this stimulation is the birth-control pill." Ratner said that another medical study showed "pituitary adenomas (tumors) have had a seven-fold increase in the 1970s--corresponding to the increase in the use of the pill."*

"The pill pushers originally said no contraceptives should be permitted if they disturbed the health of a woman. Now we have new complications reported weekly. There must be about 125 complications," Ratner said. "Many of them cause death and severe disability such as blindness." Yet doctors continue to prescribe birth-control pills.

Women patients at the end of the '70s were taking a hard look at the competence of the medical community, which was encouraging drug dependency by prescribing tranquilizers. Tranquilizers had become the most popular prescription drug in the nation--100 million prescriptions issued yearly, with Valium topping the list of abused prescription drugs and women the major abuser. To set the record straight, Barbara Gordon, whose psychiatrist had prescribed Valium to help her relax and had gradually increased the dosage until she had become completely dependent--so that she was up to 30 milligrams a day when she realized how ill she was and how addicted, wrote a book I'm Dancing as Fast as I Can warning others about the danger of taking drugs

---

*UPI report, Houston Chronicle, June 19, 1979, Sec. 7, p. 1.

to anesthetize emotions and avoiding facing real problems. She concludes that the "soft-core prescription-pad variety" of drug abuse is essentially a part of the picture.

The title of the book describes how she felt when she was suffering devastating effects on her body and an organic psychosis when she tried to withdraw from Valium. In her forties, Barbara Gordon says her favorite story is about the man and woman meeting at a Catskills resort for singles, and as they dance, he says, "I'm only here for the weekend." She replies: "I'm dancing as fast as I can."

In an age of terrible pressures, we are all dancing as fast as we can; we shouldn't be doing it under the influence of drugs.

MEDICAL FACTS AND FANTASIES

17. Cicely Williams and the Third World

The battles of medical women were not over when schools
began to graduate women doctors.   Not by a long shot!
There were still long fights to be waged for admission to
national medical conventions.   When at last women were admitted they received noteworthy recognition.   At the American Medical Association Convention in 1967 the A. M. A.
Council on Foods and Nutrition Award was presented to Dr.
Cicely D. Williams for identifying kwashiorkor as one of the
most widespread pediatric diseases of the tropics.   Associated with the Oxford Institute for Social Medicine in England,
the Jamaican-born Dr. Williams worked for two decades to
adapt Western medical techniques to care for mothers and
children in the underdeveloped areas of Africa and Asia.

She observes that she was lucky that her parents
were determined that she and her siblings would be educated.
Her father, James Rowland Williams, was director of education in Jamaica.   Born in 1893, Cicely Williams was educated at Bath High School for Girls and at Oxford (where she
was named an Honorary Fellow in 1977).   As a young girl,
Williams decided to be a nurse.   She was told she did not
have the physical stamina for nursing.

"I had some doubts about being a doctor during the
early purely scientific years at Oxford, but since I started
training at King's College Hospital in 1921, I don't think I
have really ever had a moment's boredom. "*

Because of a shortage of doctors during the First World
War forty-one women were admitted to Oxford, Cicely Williams
among them.   She was privileged to study with one of England's

---

*Material in this chapter is based on Williams's corres-
pondence with the author and on Ann Dally's Cicely: The
Story of a Doctor.

177

great teachers, Sir William Osler. He impressed her with his
priorities in medicine: "First, service to the patient. Second,
teaching of students, medical or nursing. Third, research. "

In 1923, when she passed her finals at Oxford, she sent
out seventy applications for an internship. The war was over
and so was the doctor shortage. No hospital would accept her.
Finally she was able to find a place at the South London Hospital
for Women and Children, where she assisted with gynecological
surgery. For two years she applied repeatedly for an overseas
position. At last she was sent to Africa, where she was told the
Colonial Office had been pleading for a decade for a woman doctor, but none had ever applied!

Her greatest test of courage came when she was transferred by the Colonial Office to Malaya. She hated to leave Africa, and she knew that a woman officer in Malaya had little chance
for promotion. Then came the war. In Singapore, bombs fell.
Williams transferred her hundreds of sick children from one
destroyed building to another. She was arrested and taken to the
Kempaitai, the Gestapo headquarters of the Japanese. Questioned time after time, fearful of torture, she had her glasses
taken from her, the hairpins pulled from her hair. She was the
only woman to lecture in the men's prisoner-of-war camp, and
this too the Japanese may have held against her. Forced to
crawl through a padlocked door two feet high into a cage with
nothing but a toilet, she vomited for hours. The lavatory was
the only source of water for washing or drinking, and was shared
with seven men. The prisoners were forced to sit along a bug-
infested wall, cross-legged, forbidden to lean back. A friend in
her cell was so badly beaten he looked like raw liver. The men
courteously turned their backs when Dr. Williams used the toilet.

When at last the war was over, her ordeal left her so
weak she couldn't walk. After a rest in England, she recovered
and returned to Malaya to take charge of Maternity and Child
Welfare, the highest Colonial Service position ever held by a
woman.

Williams's interest in nutrition led her to study
kwashiorkor, a form of protein malnutrition found in infants
and young children who have been fed on a diet low in protein. Such a diet, usually heavy in carbohydrates, has been
recognized in Africa, India, Indonesia, Southeast Asia, and
Central and Latin America. Children who have this disease
suffer from retarded growth, swollen stomachs, apathy,
skin lesions, changes in skin and hair pigmentation, and
distressing diarrhea. In areas where kwashiorkor is found,
animal protein may be difficult to provide in the diet, so

other sources of protein must be found, such as peanuts, soybeans, and legumes. "Health, in the words of W. H. O. [World Health Organization], means physical, mental, and social well being. My own interest is in children--pediatrics, but this includes mother and child health, nutrition, health education, mental health, cultural studies. In fact, the care of the child in his environment, and of course the environment is 'physical, mental, and social,'" says Dr. Williams. "It is the macro-environment of the country and community as well as the micro-environment of the home."

Cicely Williams discusses the evolving attitudes of young people:

> Some of the people with whom I have the greatest sympathy are the "revolting students," who tell me they dislike being coralled into institutions, wards, out-patients, laboratories. They want to get out and see how and where and why and when problems arise. And of course, they are perfectly right. The training of doctors, nurses, and midwives is all far too much institutionalized. The ornithologists have long recognized that you cannot study birds by studying birds in cages. But physicians have not yet realized this basic fact.

Dr. Cicely D. Williams

With the domination of institutions has come
the preponderance of "specialists" and "research. "
But to my mind it is the general practitioner who
is badly needed in medicine and in nursing--people
who will look after people, not just look after
diseases.

Medical care, health services are not just
methods of preventing and curing diseases; they
are methods of improving the progress of a community. They are peculiarly suitable for women
as the study is useful whether or not these women
have families of their own. Even if much of the
work involves getting "mud on your boots" and
"getting your hands dirty"--and much of it is infinitely distressing--it is infinitely worthwhile.
Here is a field of work that desperately needs
more recruits and more ideas.

Finally, to answer the question whether or not wom-
en run into strong prejudice in medicine, Williams wrote:
"In spite of all the protests and protestations, it is difficult
for women to get opportunities or promotions that are equivalent to those for men. But in medicine and nursing, this
does not matter very much. The lowlier jobs are generally
much more interesting than the more exalted--and they are
much more needed. "

It is only in the last 60 years, says Dr. Williams,
that doctors have come to specialize in pediatrics and child
welfare centers have come into being. "It was only after
the major epidemic diseases such as smallpox and cholera
were under control that pediatrics began to take a worthy
place. "

Dr. Williams deplores the fact that in the developing
countries major epidemic diseases still exist. Among poor
people sickness and death of the children is taken for granted. A farmer, claims Williams, will

readily go to a hospital with a broken arm. He
will go with an ulcer of long standing after he has
tried his own methods of treatment, or he will go
for an injection which he knows will cure his yaws.
But the sufferings of children are regarded as inevitable, and even as reasonable. Until his attitude
towards his children has been changed, as well as

his concept of what can be done for them, he will
not demand that they should get even the most
rudimentary attention.

Williams reports that a pediatrician went to Africa, where
he was told that they had never seen any disease resembling
kwashiorkor. Yet he concentrated on the care of children,
gained the confidence of the people, and soon had 400 cases
of kwashiorkor a year being brought to him!

Dr. Williams is convinced that a program that cares
for mothers and babies protects "the most vulnerable members of the population. Sir James Spence said, 'Look after
100 babies and you look after 100 families.'" She adds,
"This is absolutely true."

> In parts of Africa you cannot get children into the
> hospital unless you take in mothers as well. You
> cannot interest people in advice on "prevention"
> unless they have confidence in you. In any case,
> when children are dying of malnutrition and gastro-
> enteritis, it is useless to give lectures on boiling
> the water or opening the windows....

> In the past, medical programs have demanded
> acquiescence. People remained inactive while the
> rubbish was collected or the house sprayed for
> mosquitoes. They have gone to the hospital or
> passively permitted themselves to be vaccinated
> for one disease, injected for another or operated
> on for a third. These evolutions have often re-
> mained incomprehensible and mysterious. In this
> way, the people may become submissive to author-
> ity and irresponsible.... In parts of West Africa
> I know that the sanitary inspector was always known
> as the "Summons-Summons man."

Dr. Williams's foremost concern is that "in many
countries the population is ... increasing faster than the
food supply." She hopes to see the passing of the old tradition of women having 12 children in order to raise six.

"The countries," she observes, "which devote the
greatest attention to child care--Scandinavia, the United
Kingdom, New Zealand, and Australia--are not the countries
with an excessive birth rate. In these countries, the high
standard of child care is undoubtedly one of the factors con-
tributing toward prosperity" [Williams, C. D.].

In a special issue devoted to "Food and Nutrition,"
Science magazine of May 9, 1975, called attention to the
world's problems concerning food supplies and population
pressures and the distribution of the world's key cereal
grains and legumes to underdeveloped countries. However,
according to Derrick B. Jelliffe and E. F. Patrice Jelliffe
a key biological food and child-spacing system has received
too little attention. Human milk is rarely considered when
food is discussed, maybe because it is neither grown nor
bought. The Jelliffes maintain that the dramatic decline of
breast feeding has resulted from inappropriate training of
doctors and other medical personnel in maternity centers.
When the doula (the female assistant in childbirth in traditional societies) was respected, she would put the child to
the mother's breast soon after the birth. But mothers who
now are "modern" enough to go to a clinic or hospital for
the delivery of their children also equate modernness and
status with bottle feeding. Babies in poverty homes tend to
get a poor start on bottle feedings of overdiluted, occasion-
ally contaminated, formula. Protein-calorie malnutrition--
kwashiorkor, as we have learned from Dr. Williams--is a
world problem, but a study in ten countries in the Americas
under the auspices of the Pan-American Health Organization
in 1973 proved conclusively that breast feeding could protect
infants from both malnutrition and diarrhea. Mother's milk
has a biochemical composition that makes it not only nutri-
tious, but provides some immunity to illness, as well as
emotional closeness. The complexity of nutrients in human
milk has been underestimated in pediatrics textbooks.

Moreover, recent studies support the belief (sometimes laughed at by sophisticated obstetricians) that breast
feeding has a contraceptive influence on child-spacing. It
has been estimated that 5 million births per year in India
are prevented as a result of breast feeding.

According to the Jelliffes, "Human milk should be
recognized as a national resource in economic, agronomic,
and nutritional planning." The recorded decline in breast
feeding in Singapore in the 1950s and '60s required families
and agencies to spend almost $2 million to buy substitute
formulas. If all the women in India stopped breast feeding
and used cow's milk formula instead, an additional 114 million cows would be required! The energy used to process,
pack, distribute, prepare, and refrigerate cow's milk formulas must be considered. For example, a baby reared on
formula might use 150 cans in six months.

In Zambia baby bottles, rather than headstones, mark the graves of babies. The custom is for a mother to place on the child's grave the possessions thought to have been most valuable to the child's life. Now a teaching order of nuns from Dayton, Ohio, believes that bottle feeding may have actually contributed to the death of these children. The nuns compiled 1,000 pages of personal testimony from Third World countries that proves that bottle feeding contributes to the dramatic rise in malnutrition and mortality in the developing world among infants previously protected by the milk of their mother's breasts.

The "Baby Bottle Scandal" results from promotion of infant formulas, which has brought about a sharp decline in breast feeding in the developing world. In Chile, in the 1950s, most one-year-olds were breast fed. By the late '70s only 20 percent of infants were being breast fed at two months of age.

Advertising that critics view as unfair and unethical include posters, calendars, and billboards showing beautiful babies and such slogans as "The Very Best Milk for Your Baby" and "When Mother's Milk Fails." Many nurses in Third World countries are actually "health workers" who have been lured from low-paying jobs to propagandize for the milk manufacturers, who offer to equip whole nurseries and provide free samples and other gifts to clinics, hospitals, and the nurses to encourage use of their products.

Hoping to put an end to this propaganda, the Sisters of the Precious Blood in 1976 sued Bristol-Myers, one of many multinational companies pushing infant formula in the Third World. The nuns who owned 1,000 shares of Bristol-Myers stock, charged the manufacturers of OLAC and Enfamil with "false and misleading statements" in a company proxy statement to stockholders. In January 1978 the nuns won an out-of-court settlement, and publicized the marketing techniques of powdered baby milks.

Even in countries where mothers can afford bottled milk for infants, breast feeding should be encouraged. Out of Japan has come the results of a pediatric study conducted by Aiiku Hospital in Tokyo on the advantages of breast feeding infants. The 1976 study revealed that the death rate of bottle-fed babies was four times higher than that of breast-fed infants, lending proof to the claim that bottle babies are more susceptible to disease.

Guia Nortell is a radiologist in Houston's Ben Taub Hospital and also on the staff of Jeff Davis Hospital. Now divorced from the American surgeon whose name she bears, she is a graduate of a Philippine medical school where women constituted 30 percent of the class. At the University of Chicago only one woman per year was being accepted when she went there to specialize. "They want you to prove yourself all the time in medical school. They didn't discriminate against women but they're very hard on women. The colleagues make it more difficult by elaborating any mistake you may make. You work harder than a man, and if you come from a minority group as I do, you have to prove yourself to get respect."

How did Nortell, born in poverty, one of seven children, come to study medicine?

"I was reared in a town that did not have a single doctor," she says. "Our family had the only working well in town, and everyone came and took our water until someone broke the pump, and then no one had water." She tells how she determined to become a physician. She was four years old, barefoot, wearing a ragged dress, and she said to her father, "I'm not going to live my life poor...."

When she was eight her mother had her 15th pregnancy. There had been miscarriages and dead babies, and her father had had to do all the deliveries himself. What did he know about delivering a baby?

My mother was 50 years old, and all the kids were standing around while my mother was hemorrhaging. She was lying on the floor in a bed of blood. She was almost dead. I ran through the streets screaming, begging for a doctor to come help her. "Call anybody. Call a doctor. Help, help, my mother is dying. My mother is dying!" My father was frantic. I woke up all the neighbors. But what was the use? Not a single doctor lived in our town. Then someone came with a quack doctor, an old crone who didn't know anything, but she kept falling on my mother's abdomen, and she sang incantations and fell repeatedly on the abdomen until the bleeding stopped because she was contracting the uterus, and she saved my mother.

I made up my mind to be a doctor. I looked

at my poor town, where there was no knowledge of
birth control, no scientific knowledge, and I told
myself that my vow when I was four years old
would be my life's mission. I was not going to
live my life under threat of poverty and hunger and
useless struggle. Just to eat was a struggle.

My father was a smart man. He gave me the
name "Guia" because he believed you had to give
a name to live up to. Mine means "guiding star."
I would be an example or a guiding star to the
other children, he said.

My eldest sister was brilliant, she was class
valedictorian, and my brother was a genius. I was
the third one.

One wonders as one talks to Nortell what she is doing
in Houston, why she has chosen this big city for a place to
practice medicine when in her home town there is still inadequate medical care. She went to Far Eastern University
on a scholarship, and there she made every stitch of her
own clothes and never bought a textbook, but used the books
in the library. Now she drives a $12,000 car and lives in
a plush apartment, and speaks of the terrible poverty in her
Philippine home. "Hunger and anger make terrible hostility
toward the government." And still, in her hometown, children are being delivered by their fathers.

MEDICAL FACTS AND FANTASIES

18. Abortion and the Abused Child

No law can put an end to the soul-searching of a woman who
decides to terminate her pregnancy, and many legislators are
convinced that the condition of a woman's uterus should be
her own concern and not the affair of lawmakers. Should
women be forced by law to bear an unwanted child because
of a shortage of adoptable babies? Or for any other reason?

The emotional response to discussions about abortion
is similar to the earlier excitement about dissemination of
birth-control methods. Look at the history of family
planning--the restriction of conception by mechanical or
chemical means. The expression "birth control" may have
been used first by Margaret Sanger, in her magazine The
Woman Rebel. And because she published birth-control information, she was thrown into prison. H. G. Wells called
her "the greatest woman in the world," and predicted that
within the century the birth-control movement she launched
would be so influential it would control human destiny.

In 1914, when Sanger began her crusade, federal,
state, and local laws were allied against her. She was
jailed eight times, we learn from her biographer, Emily
Taft Douglas. Doctors denounced her. The clergy sermon-
ized against her, summoning the wrath of God on her soul.
Newspapers were unwilling to share the idea of freedom of
the press with her magazine. Even other reformers with-
held comfort and assistance. She was the Joan of Arc of
family planning, and she fought alone. She had no financial
help. All she had was a memory of nursing a new mother
who begged for information to help prevent future pregnancies. Sanger saw in her mind "with photographic clear-
ness," as she wrote in her Autobiography, "women writhing
in travail to bring forth little babies; the babies themselves
naked and hungry, wrapped in newspapers to keep them from
cold; six year old children with pinched, pale, wrinkled

Margaret Sanger (second from left) (photo courtesy of Planned Parenthood)

faces, old in concentrated wretchedness ... in gray, fetid cellars, crouching on stone floors, their small scrawny hands scuttling through rags ... white coffins, black coffins, coffins, coffins, interminably passing in never-ending succession." Her spine froze at the sight of hundreds of poverty-stricken women lined up outside an abortionist's office waiting for the five-dollar curettement that might lead to mutilation, disease, or death.

"It is the big battalions of unwanted babies," Sanger wrote in <u>Family Limitation,</u> "that make life so hard for the working woman and keep her in poverty and stress.... Every mother feels the wrong that the State imposes upon her when it deprives her of information to prevent bringing into the world children she cannot feed or clothe or care for."

Sanger first attracted national attention in the cause of labor. When 25,000 textile workers walked out on strike in Lawrence, Mass., 1,400 soldiers were rushed to the scene. A trigger-happy soldier shot a young woman picket, and labor leaders were arrested.

The strike would have ended there, for parents were prone to return to work when there was no food in the house, but the strikers, mostly Italian, adopted an Old Country practice and gave their children up for temporary adoption into New York homes. Margaret Sanger, a capable nurse, would chaperone the children to their temporary homes. But first, she insisted, the children would have to have physicals. She found one child with diphtheria, some with chicken pox, and all of them undernourished, in mere rags against the bitter winter.

Their generous adoptive parents kept them six weeks, and Sanger was happy to see them warmly dressed, red-cheeked, and well fed. The newspapers recounted Margaret Sanger's role in this Children's Exodus.

Responding to the charge that the Exodus was a publicity stunt, a Socialist member of Congress launched an investigation into conditions in the textile mills. Representative Victor Berger of Milwaukee called on Margaret Sanger to testify, and she took a train to Washington.

In the crowded Rules Committee chamber strikers' testimony was brushed aside as too emotional. But Sanger's nursing had taught her to classify important details, and with her notes she answered the Representatives' questions about the children's ages, weight, and physical conditions: she said they were all undernourished and most had enlarged tonsils and adenoids. Only four out of 119 had overcoats; few had anything but rags.

Across the nation the following day newspaper readers saw the picture of a slim young nurse and read of Margaret Sanger's able testimony (Douglas, p. 28ff).

The high death rate and unending misery she observed in the homes where she nursed new mothers in New York tenements convinced Sanger of the need for birth control. The wasted wretched lives of these people struck her as senseless. In 1921 she organized the first American Birth Control Conference in New York City.

Also in 1921 the Malthusian League established a

clinic for poor mothers in south London. There, another woman, Dr. Marie Stopes, carried on a crusade to inform Great Britain about birth-control methods.

Holland's first woman doctor, Aletta Jacobs, was appalled at the suffering of her patients from too-frequent pregnancies, and applying herself to finding a practical contraceptive, helped develop the world-renowned diaphragm. Dr. Jacobs, in 1878, opened the world's first birth-control clinic, in Amsterdam. Male colleagues condemned her, charging her with causing disease of the pelvis by fitting women with diaphragms. The Scandinavian countries were in the forefront of the support for birth control, with doctors from Norway, Sweden, Denmark, Finland, and Holland urging the establishment of birth-control clinics open to rich and poor alike.

Use of contraceptives had been advocated in England as early as 1877 by Charles Bradlaugh and Annie Besant. They were hauled into court for selling Charles Knowlton's pamphlet The Fruits of Philosophy (subtitled "The Private Companion of Young Married People"). Written by a doctor in an authoritative style, the book was the most important in the field for years, and stressed Knowlton's response to the age-old charge that birth control was unnatural. "Sure it's unnatural," Knowlton agreed, "but so is cutting your hair or fingernails. So is shaving." Knowlton insisted, "Civilization constantly wages war against nature."

Dr. Knowlton, an American, was tracked down in Massachusetts, arrested, tried, and sent to prison for three months at hard labor. Such a severe sentence was a bombshell in the medical community. Few doctors were going to risk informing patients about contraception. But in London Dr. Knowlton's book was reprinted with charts and illustrations. Bradlaugh and Besant brought out a third edition. This led to their arrest.

At her trial Annie Besant declared she was the counsel of poor mothers "worn out with over-frequent childbearing." Both Besant and Charles Bradlaugh were sentenced to six months in jail.

These martyrs like a magnet drew Margaret Sanger to London. She left her husband and children to see what she could learn from the British. A depressing fog and a cheerless lodging house gave her first weeks in London a

sense of desolation.   Thousands of miles from home and
family, she had no job and no plans.   "How lonely it all
is ...," she wrote in her journal.   "Could any prison be
more isolated...?"

Before long Sanger was in the swim of opinion-
formers in England, where birth control was a vital issue.
The Drysdales invited her to contact workers, who had remained alienated.   Unlike Marie Stopes, who was an impressive speaker and enjoyed large audiences, Sanger preferred to address small groups.   In Scotland, on the Fourth
of July, she declared her independence from excess children.
At a Socialist-sponsored forum she responded to Socialist
dogma that refought the battle between Marx and Malthus.
The Socialists held that any reform that made poverty more
tenable retarded the overthrow of capitalism.   The men insisted therefore they should not endorse birth control.
Sanger demanded, "Why do you fight for higher wages?   If
misery is a weapon, why ask for an eight-hour day instead
of a twelve- or fourteen-hour one?"   She also insisted that
women's rights were meaningless without some method of
birth control.

Near Andrew Carnegie's birthplace in Dunfermline
Sanger found poverty unchanged since the Industrial Revolution.   Boys of eight or nine were apprenticed to the mines,
and girls worked ten to 12 hours a day through their adolescence and up to the birth of the first child.

Sanger became obsessed with the need to have cheap,
acceptable contraceptive methods for the poor and uneducated.
Learning of a chemical contraceptive that had been reported
in a German medical journal, she went to Germany to find
out if this might be the beginning of what was needed.

Like a detective, she tracked down the chemist man-
ufacturing the contraceptive jelly in Friedrichshaven.   Disappointed to find that the item was expensive, she nevertheless brought home samples.   Interviewing German doctors,
she found them receptive--until she mentioned her mission.
Then they seemed to turn to ice.   Germany needed babies
to compensate for the men lost in the war.   What about a
woman who might die in pregnancy?   Let her have an abortion.   But abortions are illegal!   Should Germany let mothers determine the future of the master race?   Doctors
should make those decisions.

Back in the United States Sanger saw physicians as

the obstacle to instruction of poor mothers. Before America entered the war the New York Medical Society had been against birth control, but by 1918, doctors, through the Crane decision, had the right to prescribe contraceptives for reasons of the mother's health.

Sanger suggested to her friend Dr. Mary Halton that she make a test of 29 hospitals to see if contraceptives would be given to a charity patient. Even women with tuberculosis and kidney problems were refused such help.

Determined to open a birth-control clinic staffed with doctors, Sanger wrote for support to many child specialists. The cynical replies reminded her that babies were their business.

Sanger, in her first days in London, had heard a lecture about the German philosopher Friedrich Nietzsche, and his philosophy had appealed to her. She had long rejected the unhealthy attitudes of priests toward physical pleasures and particularly toward family planning. She had seen impoverished mothers spending their last dollar to bury a baby with a Mass and then for years paying out precious pennies for candles in remembrance of the dead child. Sanger was convinced that developing God within the individual was better than worshiping "at the shrine of other egos." She concluded her Autobiography with a quote from Nietzsche, "Build thou beyond thyself," and she observed that this was what the birth-control movement was all about. People in the future would have a regard for the equality of body and brain; "birth control will be the cornerstone of that great structure"--future civilization.

Almost half a century would pass before a state law would abandon the tradition that no abortion could be done except to save the life of the mother. Colorado, in 1967, was the first state to legalize abortions. In June 1970 New York passed an "abortion on demand" law, the most liberal in the nation, allowing an operation in the first months of pregnancy. Only the woman and her doctor had to agree to the abortion. Virtually all the state's general, non-sectarian hospitals planned for the anticipated 50,000 to 100,000 applications for abortions annually and the expected invasion from the rest of the country.

Only a few years earlier an epidemic of illegal abortions, including a million a year in the United States, was a major medical problem. Physicians reporting on the abortion

situation in five continents in 1967 at a World Population
Assembly, urged a more liberal legal abortion law and national family-planning programs everywhere to increase
birth-control practices and limit the world's threatening
"population explosion." The reports that year presented to
the Eighth Conference of the International Planned Parenthood
Federation indicated that 15 to 20 million women per year
were undergoing illegal induced abortion to avoid unwanted
pregnancies. Reporting on Europe, Dr. Frank Noval of the
Yugoslavian Faculty of Medicine claimed that countries with
laws limiting access to legal abortion and distribution of
contraceptives were fomenting "more abortions, regardless
of legality." The law, he insisted, "should make it possible
for women to be healthier, and not for abortionists to get
richer."

Almost simultaneously America's Roman Catholic
bishops authorized an intensive campaign to defeat efforts to
liberalize laws on abortions. The budget for the first year
was $50,000. The bishops also voted to conduct a study on
the role and life of the priest, including the problems of
priestly celibacy, reaffirming "clearly and strongly the
Church's traditional rule that priests may not marry."

The views of bishops with strong religious ideals
contribute to sustaining the system that labels abortion a
crime and makes it a source of guilt.

A group of 280 psychiatrists, meeting in 1969, recommended that "abortion when performed by a licensed physician should be entirely removed from the domain of criminal law." Calling the report "The Right to Abortion: A
Psychiatric View," the Committee on Psychiatry and Law of
the Group for the Advancement of Psychiatry, concluded that
"a woman should have the right to abort or not, just as she
has the right to marry or not." These scholars are among
the most influential professionals in psychiatric medicine.
"We want abortion to be as routine a surgical procedure as
an appendectomy," declared Dr. Lawrence Lader, one of the
group's leaders and chair of the National Association for the
Repeal of Abortion Laws. "We suggest that those who believe abortion is murder need not avail themselves of it.
We do not believe such conviction should limit the freedom
of those not bound by such religious convictions."

The Group particularly criticized laws that allow an
abortion to be performed if there is "substantial risk" to the

mother's or baby's physical or mental health. The moral issue should be left to the individual conscience. A woman should control her own body. "We believe it essential," the report noted, "that psychiatrists recognize their own limitations and back away from accepting responsibility for making decisions that rest in the community ... because of the possibility that psychiatric illness as grounds for abortion may lead women either to malinger ... or to emphasize their psychiatric symptoms...."

Other psychiatrists insist there is a moral issue on the side of abortion. "The most deadly of all possible sins is the mutilization of a child's spirit. Nothing is more destructive to a child than the conviction that he's unwanted. Nothing is more disruptive to a woman's spirit than being forced without love or need into motherhood."

Although millions of American women were eager for birth-control information, only one of ten was being reached in the '70s. To the extent that family planning may be improved, as better contraceptives are developed, the incidence of abortion should decrease. But those who fought the dissemination of birth-control methods and made a martyr out of Margaret Sanger are the same people who argue that abortion is murder.

The wheels of progress turn slowly: in 1971 a Florida housewife, 22-year-old Shirley Ann Wheeler, went to prison, convicted of having had an abortion. The maximum penalty under the 1868 law was 20 years, the same as for manslaughter. After a two-day trial Mrs. Wheeler admitted she had had an illegal abortion. Her doctor had informed her that her pregnancy could endanger her life because she had had rheumatic fever. Yet a jury found her guilty.

Have legal restrictions against abortion been more successful than the prohibition of alcohol? Vigorous efforts to enforce laws that seem intolerable cause gradual erosion of morality. Dr. Lonny Myers, of Michael Reese Hospital and president of Illinois Citizens for the Medical Control of Abortion, claimed that with rare exceptions, "women with unwanted pregnancies are forced to accept them or break the law." She went on record as favoring the idea that abortion should be "a private matter between a woman and her physician." Dr. Myers said, "If society is going to designate early abortions as murder, it must deal with a million murders a year. The legal issue involves mass violation of the law by responsible citizens. "

Speaking to a Conference on Abortion Law Reform, John D. Rockefeller III said,

> Basing our laws on the belief that it is morally wrong to abort only serves to create in turn a whole series of social dilemmas. The woman who in desperation seeks abortion poses a difficult moral question.... She feels her entire life situation to be threatened. Shall she be denied relief? If so, what about the unwanted child she bears? The word "unwanted" brings to mind a picture of psychological deprivation, and possibly physical suffering as well. Child abuse cases are steadily increasing in the United States.... All over the world, unwanted children are being permanently harmed both physically and psychologically through hunger, neglect, abuse.
>
> We all want to see children born into this world with every reasonable chance of a life of dignity and self-fulfillment. I believe it is morally indefensible to perpetuate conditions that handicap children from the moment they are born. We must concern ourselves with the fundamental rights of children--to be wanted, loved and given a reasonable start in the world. It seems ironic that society requires the most careful checking and screening of persons who want to adopt children, and at the same time indiscriminately requires parents to go ahead with births they do not want.

Liberalization of the California abortion law dramatically reduced the major cause of death and illness associated with pregnancy. Before the law was revised in 1967 the largest number of maternal deaths in California was from illegal abortions, according to Dr. Edwin M. Gold of the University of California/Berkeley.

Hawaii has also authorized abortion on request, with a 90-day residency requirement and other restrictions. About three-fourths of the women aborted in Hawaii were single, including recent divorcees and widows. Hawaii welfare authorities paid the bills for impoverished patients, since it is less expensive to help a poor woman control the size of her family than force her to have unwanted babies. For women who could pay, the costs were realistic.

In 1975 a National Academy of Sciences committee reported that legal abortions resulted in fewer women dying or being injured by such operations. Estimates of post-abortion psychoses (serious mental breakdowns) range from .2 to .4 per 1,000 legal abortions, fewer than the one or two after every 1,000 normal deliveries. Depression or guilt feelings reported by some women after abortions are described as mild and temporary.

Should restrictive anti-abortion laws be enacted an increase in ill-health of mothers and children is inevitable, said committee chair Dr. Mildred Mitchell Bateman, West Virginia state mental health director. But women must be encouraged to have the abortion early in the pregnancy.

Dr. Alan F. Guttmacher, president of Planned Parent-hood/World Population, observes that Johns Hopkins Hospital in Baltimore was among the first to treat abortion patients on an out-patient basis instead of keeping them overnight at the prohibitive cost of a hospital bed. Often poor women are confronted with the bill for the abortion before they are admitted. For some women this means a delay in getting the money together, and frequently the doctor may then feel it is too late to abort the fetus. When a patient enters the hospital in the morning the Johns Hopkins staff performs the operation soon after admittance. The patient may return home in the afternoon.

Dr. Guttmacher emphasizes that out-patient abortion is a safe procedure when performed with proper medical safeguards by a physician. Statistically, an abortion is safer than a tonsillectomy, and Guttmacher claims that it "presents fewer risks to the mother than normal pregnancy and childbirth."

Everyone agrees that abortion should not replace contraception. "Even if all the women in the country could easily get hold of contraceptives, we must remember that contraceptives fail, people fail, and the circumstances of peoples' lives change," says Dr. Guttmacher.

But the issue of abortion law remains complicated and the subject of much emotion. On February 15, 1975, Dr. Kenneth C. Edelin, coordinator of ambulatory services in the obstetrical and gynecological ward of Boston City Hospital, was found guilty of homicide in the death of a 20- to 24-week-old fetus in the course of a legal abortion. The jury's verdict aroused national debate over what it was that Edelin had murdered.

"A fetus is not a person and not the subject of an indictment for manslaughter," Boston's Superior Court Judge James P. McGuire had instructed the jury. Under the judge's instruction the doctor could not be tried for murder unless he had killed a human being. When does the fetus become a person protected by law?

Edelin worked in a hospital that cares for patients who are mostly black and poor. He was chief resident of his department, one of only two doctors who routinely performed abortions there. He doesn't like to perform abortions. But he believes that a woman has a right to choose whether or not to continue a pregnancy, and if she wants to have the pregnancy terminated, she should have good medical care during the abortion.

"I will continue to do abortions," he promised on television after his conviction. "They are a woman's right. Women since they've been on this earth have been making that choice, whether they want to carry that baby or not. ... The only humane thing we can do is make sure that when they make that choice they have the opportunity to make it under the best conditions possible."

In December 1973 Suffolk County investigators found a fetus in the hospital's morgue when they were looking for evidence for a different case involving four physicians who were performing research on tissues of aborted fetuses. The case rested on an 1814 Massachusetts grave-robbing statute, and on the basis of this statute Edelin was tried.

Edelin had performed the legal abortion in October 1973 for a 17-year-old patient. Three efforts at saline solution had failed, and Dr. Edelin decided to try a hysterectomy. Removing the fetus through an incision in the mother's abdomen, he separated it from the wall of the womb with the afterbirth.

During the trial the issue was not the legality of the abortion. The district attorney argued that the fetus was alive, a child born with all the rights assured by the

Constitution of the United States.   A photograph was passed
among the jurors.   The fetus "looked like a baby, " and constant assurances of the prosecutor that the baby had rights,
that "survival" is a concept that might mean life for a moment, a year, or for a lifetime's participation in society
must have convinced the jury.

Dr. Matthew J. Bulfin of Fort Lauderdale, Fla. ,
president of the American Association of Pro-Life Obstetricians and Gynecologists, questioned, "If the obstetrician has
the right to destroy the live-born infant in an abortion procedure, would he not have the same right to extinguish the
life of a newborn infant with a congenital defect whose
mother may not want him?   The acceptance of this principle
surely would in fact be providing legal endorsement for
euthanasia. "

Many who are opposed to abortion for any reason--
even after rape--ask, "Why punish the baby?" Such opponents view abortion on moral grounds, insisting that the
early fetus, even from the moment of conception is already
a human being.   Other opponents insist that the fetus has
rights because it has the potential to become a human being.
In destroying a fetus, you destroy what it might become.
The rights of the fetus are seen by anti-abortionists as more
important than the rights of the mother.

To these anti-abortionists even the use of an I. U. D.
is murder.   Such contraception is equated with infanticide--
the burden of the guilt of killing a baby.

Those pragmatists who see abortion as merely getting
rid of something as unwanted, like a corn on a toe or the
placenta, which is pitched into the trash after a normal
birth, insist that a woman has the right to be in charge of
her own womb, and if she doesn't want to have a child, her
wish should be the final statement about that fetus.

The fetus in the early months is not a person, med-
ically speaking.   The liver produces blood early in embryonic
development, later to turn this task over to the bone marrow.
The placenta is the most vital organ in fetal metabolism,
responsible for excretion, assimilation, and respiration during pregnancy.

In January 1973 the Supreme Court decided in favor of
the rights of the mother in reproductive decision making

during the first six months of her pregnancy. The decree expressly respected the mother's wishes in regard to the fetus and denied the fetus legal recognition as a human being during the first two trimesters of the pregnancy. Thus the court's ruling seemed to open the door for experimentation on a fetus made available through a legal abortion.

Many people now see the value of bequeathing their bodies to medical schools. Hospitals routinely perform autopsies on the dead. What rationale can there be in forbidding experimentation on a dead fetus? Problems of newborn infants have long been a major area of distinguished research. Some might go so far as to say the death of a fetus is ennobled by having served the cause of humanity, perhaps assuring a healthy future for some much-wanted baby.

An internationally recognized specialist in care of the newborn, Dr. Virginia Apgar* conducted experiments that led to the development of a simple test--to be taken at one minute and at five minutes after a baby's birth--that predicts the infant's chances for healthy survival. This "Apgar Score" sought to understand factors underlying human birth defects and pregnancy failures. Because periodic blood samples were taken from the women involved in Dr. Apgar's enormous project, it was possible to check for infection by 100 known viruses during pregnancy. One virus infection at least, that of German measles, is known to endanger the unborn child. Most people develop immunity to German measles during childhood, but the studies directed by Dr. Apgar revealed that 15 percent of the women had never had the disease.

Exposure to German measles causes serious abnormalities in up to 40 percent of exposed fetuses. Protection for the fetus against measles can be had by immunizing the mother, but doctors were not sure that the rubella vaccine would not harm the fetus itself.

Discussing the controversy over experimentation on

---

*Dr. Apgar was the first woman physician to hold a full professorship at Columbia University, where she taught anesthesiology. She was also Clinical Professor of Pediatrics at Cornell and Research Fellow in Medicine at Johns Hopkins University.

the unborn, Dr. Willard Gaylin and Dr. Marc Lappé of the biological sciences department of the Institute of Society, Ethics and Life Sciences at Hastings-on-the-Hudson, N. Y., refer to the development of the rubella vaccination against German measles as an example of the values and justification for such research. Virtually the only way to discover if the rubella vaccine was safe was through pre-abortion experiments. What alternative was there? To give the vaccine to a pregnant woman who had been exposed to measles but really wanted her child and thus run a risk of seriously damaging the baby, even murdering it, or to withhold the vaccine and let the baby come to term, possibly defective, was the researcher's difficult choice. The alternative was research on the fetus of a woman who did not want to have a baby and had already requested an abortion. Since abortion was already planned, the mother could be injected with rubella vaccine to determine the effect on the unborn child.

"At best," say the doctors, "the vaccine would not affect the child. If the woman changed her mind, the pregnancy would have been protected; at worst, the fetus would have been exposed to an attenuated form of a virus which unquestionably otherwise causes abnormalities in one case out of three."

Rheumatic fever has long been a fear and concern of mothers, and another woman doctor, Rodanthi C. Kitridou, has been studying rheumatoid factors and tests to determine rheumatology symptoms. Dr. Kitridou received her degree from the University of Athens, where she served an internship in the department of clinical therapeutics. She was a rotating intern at St. Luke's and Children's Medical Center in Houston and a resident in internal medicine at Hahnemann Medical College and Hospital in Philadelphia. Now assistant professor of medicine, she directs the division of rheumatology, studying causes and cures of arthritis.

One mother-doctor who insists there should be no laws concerning abortion stressed the need for women with unwanted pregnancies to have good medical care and to understand the contribution the unwanted fetus can make in preventing diseases for future generations.

In an interview she defended fetal research:

Abortion should not be a means of birth control.

But fetal research is vital. This kind of research--
begun while the woman is pregnant and ending with
a study of the aborted fetus--is the object of federal regulations, despite the fact that testing new
vaccines for genetic diseases might prevent congenital abnormalities or fetal death. A wide range of
viral infections and children's diseases, such as
mumps, measles, chicken pox, and hepatitis, when
contracted by a pregnant woman vastly increase
risk of fetal disability or death. An infection during pregnancy causes the birth of 1, 000 to 3, 000
cases of mental retardation annually in the United
States, and while vaccine research is prohibited,
abortions in the case of cytolomegalovirus exposure
will continue. What parents want to risk the birth
of a retarded child?

It may even be immoral and unethical not to carry on
fetal research when the object is saving the lives of wanted
babies. Where abortions are performed on mothers with a
history of hemophilia, the fetus could provide valuable information for the possible studies and development of preventive
measures for future hemophiliacs. If doctors had tested the
thalidomides before aborting unwanted fetuses, there would
have been fewer handicapped children in the world today.

Because this is not the best of all possible worlds
doctors must dedicate themselves to the alleviation of
diseases and deformities of children. If the world were
perfect, babies would be born perfectly beautiful and beauti-
fully perfect. But experimentation is part of progress.
Fetal research may endow the process of abortion with hopes
for better babies in the future. In an article in the Atlantic
(May 1975), Doctors Gaylin and Lappé conclude:

In all of this we must never reduce even the unwanted fetus to the level of an experimental animal. We must recognize the nobility of that which
it might have been; we must honor its potential.
But we must not err in the opposite direction. We
must not guard the "rights" of the about-to-be-
destroyed fetus at the expense of the safety and
health of the wanted, about-to-be-born child.

Psychiatrists have long resented the approach that a
woman had to have her mental health threatened before she
could have an abortion; the doctors are reluctant to testify

that a woman is unbalanced, even when they realize she is in a difficult situation with an unwanted pregnancy.

For many years abortions were only available to the insane, the rich, and the victims of rape. Now all pregnant women have legal rights. As Dr. Alice S. Rossi has observed,

> There is a great deal more satisfaction in showing compassionate empathy toward others and voluntarily extending help to persons in need than there is in reluctantly yielding concessions under human protest. When such empathy is coupled with a recognition of the human rights of those we serve, there is not only a recognition of human rights of those we serve, there is not only a democratic acknowledgement of the dignity of others, but a gain in our own sense of self-worth. It is my hope that the medical and legal professions will realize the relevance of their own work as they deal with problems that touch so intimate a part of women's lives as unwanted pregnancies. If they do, they will further the rights of women to control their own lives.

Women are not likely to use abortion as a substitute for contraceptives, but accidents do happen, and some women, disenchanted with the pill because of the publicity suggesting the pill may cause cancer and other serious side-effects, have stopped using both the I. U. D. and the pill. In the first three years after the U. S. Supreme Court's decision legalizing abortion, about 900,000 women a year had this surgical procedure. Still, there are women who want abortions who can't get them.

By 1978 the crucial issue was no longer whether or not women should be permitted to pay for abortion at will, but rather the problem of the poor woman who could not pay to be relieved of a fetus she did not want to carry to term. Fay Wattleton, president of the Planned Parenthood Federation of America, called for a massive drive to restore free abortion services for poor women--"so cruelly destroyed in two-thirds of the states in recent legal action."

Wattleton, 34, a public health nurse from Dayton, Ohio, pushed for better birth-control methods and national programs to reduce pregnancies among teenagers. Shockingly, 3,000 girls 13 and under bore babies in 1977. Some

3, 265 teenagers became pregnant out of wedlock in America in 1977. In campaigning for free abortions for poor women, Wattleton battles the Right-to-Life crusaders, who would deny anyone--even the victim of a rapist--the right to a safe, dignified abortion.

Many women deny that abortion is murder and regard abortion on demand as being as normal and natural as tonsillectomies or appendectomies, suggesting that those who deny abortion to a mother who does not want to bear her child should be required to adopt and rear the child themselves.

No single organization can accomplish planned parenthood. All who recognize the integral role of reproductive choice in a healthy human life must join forces to guarantee the right of decision for or against abortion being made in a doctor's office, a decision to rest entirely between mother and doctor.

Abortions, after all, are not always induced. More than half of all conceptions result in spontaneous abortion, claims Dr. Dwight P. Cruikshank, obstetrician at the University of Iowa. Some 50 percent of miscarriages are caused by chromosomal abnormalities. About 40 percent of miscarriages occur before a woman even suspects pregnancy, before she misses her first menstrual period. Once a woman realizes she is pregnant, at about six weeks, she still has a 15 to 20 percent chance of aborting spontaneously. However, even though a woman has had one miscarriage, her chance of having a normal child in her next pregnancy is 80 to 85 percent, the same as other women's.

The most common chromosomal abnormality is "trisomy," or the presence of one extra chromosome, which accounts for Down's syndrome (mongolism) should the baby be born at term.

"Nature somehow has an efficient mechanism for getting rid of chromosome errors," commented Cruikshank. Usually nothing a woman can do or refrain from doing will prevent a miscarriage when a defective fetus needs to be aborted.

The medical profession is alert to the necessity for discussing genetic testing and counseling and examining the risk of having a child with Down's syndrome. Pregnant patients may now participate in decisions that affect their lives and families. Many experts predict that in the future there will be fewer births of genetically defective or handicapped children. A New York Court of Appeals ruling held physicians liable for the lifetime care of children born with genetic disorders if they had failed to advise pregnant women adequately. One case involved a 37-year-old woman who was not advised of the risk of bearing a child with Down's syndrome when she became pregnant in 1974. The patient was not given a test to determine if the fetus had the disorder. The baby girl was born with the disease. Another case involved a woman whose first baby was born in 1969 with a kidney disease, and the patient asked the doctor if it "might happen again," and the doctor replied that "the chances were practically nil." In 1970 the patient bore a second child with the kidney disorder, and the child lived in agony for two years.

By examining old medical records, by taking extensive medical history about hereditary diseases and birth defects from the parents and relatives, and by performing a variety of tests, medical geneticists can now calculate the risk that a couple might have a child affected with a birth defect. Tests have been developed to detect chromosomal defects, such as Down's syndrome--performed in conjunction with amniocentesis, in which a thin needle, guided by ultrasound, may be inserted through the mother's abdomen and into the womb. Using the fluid and cells collected in amniocentesis, 60 hereditary biochemical disorders can be detected, disorders that can kill, retard, or otherwise damage the infant. These tests may be made in the early stages of pregnancy when abortions can safely be performed.

Amniocentesis has been widely publicized, and women feel some assurance that they now need not bear a child with a genetic defect such as Down's syndrome. The risk of bearing a Down's syndrome child when the mother is under age 30 is one in 1500; rising to one in 280 between ages 35 and 39, and to one in 130 between 40 and 44. Beyond the age of 45 mothers face the risk of one in 65.

A report in the January 25, 1979, issue of the New England Journal of Medicine evaluated tests on 3,000 women who had had amniocentesis, and the procedure was called "safe, highly reliable and extremely accurate."* Prudent

---

*M. Golbus, pp. 157-63.

physicians, according to Dr. Zena Stein, an epidemiologist
at Columbia University, had questioned the use of the test
in women under age 40 because of the risk to the fetus.

The issue among those who hold with the Right-to-
Life movement is whether or not abortion is murder. The
question among those who believe in the rights of women is:
are you going to charge a woman with involuntary manslaughter if she has a miscarriage?

If a woman is unwilling to be pregnant, should she
be denied relief? If so, what responsibility does society
have to the unwanted child she bears?

Child abandonment and infanticide are serious problems in the United States, and the steady increase in child
abuse is shocking. What happens to an unwanted child
seems to be of less concern to some people than the destruction of a human fetus in abortion.

Dr. Helen Schaffer, a behavioral pediatrician in
Houston says, "Our goal is to make people aware of the
battered child, and the community must set up better and
more effective legislation."

Ironically, the law for the protection of animals was
enacted long before child-protection statutes. In fact, the
successful use of prevention-of-cruelty-to-animals statutes
in behalf of an abused little girl in 1874 provided the impe-
tus for the founding, one year later, of the New York Society for the Prevention of Cruelty to Children.

It was not until 1961 that the professional concern of
physicians brought attention to the problems of the abused
child. That year Dr. C. Henry Kempe, at the University of
Colorado Medical Center, made a study that revealed that
more children are killed by parents than by disease!

Before Dr. Kempe's study was made public California
was the only state in which parental abuse of children was a
criminal offense. Now all states have such laws. By 1969
New York law required that cases of battered children be
reported orally and that a written report be submitted to
local social-service officials within two days.

The terms "battered child" and "abused child" were

coined around 1961, with "battered" pertaining to physical mistreatment and "abused" to neglect and other psychological mistreatment.

The spine-chilling statistic that one child is killed by parents every day in the United States is called "a symptom of the times," by Vincent J. Fontana, a New York pediatrician and a pioneer in trying to safeguard children from inhuman treatment. "It's part of the violence in this country and in the world. Abused and neglected children, if they survive, will strike out at society as future criminals, future murderers--and future child beaters."

Child beating crops up at every level of society. But most often it is found in urban slums, where pressures are greatest. Parents who brutalize their children often are emotionally insecure and have financial or psychological problems. Alcohol, drugs, perversion, broken homes, illegitimacy, and prostitution are the background for child abuse. Abused children, many of them under three years of age, are beaten with leather belts, burned with lit cigarettes, starved, slashed with razors, put into tubs of scalding hot water, hit with any convenient object--hammers, brooms, wire coat hangers, nut crackers, pots, bottles. One stepfather beat a child to death because he couldn't spell "butterfly." A 16-month-old boy was thrown out of a 13th-floor window of a New York apartment. In Houston a mother was charged with suffocating a baby by stuffing the infant's mouth with cotton balls to stop his crying. In Long Branch, N. J., an Army private and his wife were charged with beating a four-year-old son to death. Six weeks earlier the child had been treated for injuries caused by violent abuse. The boy had been returned to his parents.

"There is no one type of personality that will abuse a child," claims Dr. Zidella Brener, a child psychiatrist. "Most often it is the person who has not experienced enough affection and love in his earlier years, or a person who puts a child at the adult level and expects the child to give love and affection to meet the abuser's own emotional needs."

A study conducted at the University of Colorado in 1969 revealed that parents who beat their children are re-enacting the treatment they experienced at the hands of their own parents.

"An abusive act is a symptom rather than a disease,"

is the view of Dr. Elinor F. Downs, associate professor of public health practice at Columbia University. Dr. Downs, a member of the Mayor's Task Force on Child Abuse in New York, began her career as a pediatrician. Besides treating the physical injuries of the abused child, a physician must realize that the child's injuries are a manifestation of the parents'--or the parents' substitutes'--social and psychological problems, maintains Dr. Downs.

Abused children who get to a hospital are only the tip of the iceberg. "Victims of child battering often have death certificates that read 'got near stove and burned,' or 'fell off trike,' or 'fell down stairs,'" according to Dr. James H. Ryan, pediatrician and coroner in Kankakee, Ill.

Sometimes a neighbor may be aware of a parent who beats a child and does nothing to help the child. There may even be a mother or a father who sees a child being brutally treated by the partner and doesn't move to stop the torture.

Doctors who come in contact with child abuse have a dual responsibility, first to treat the child and report abuse to the proper authorities. Then an attempt must be made to understand agencies that may help, and support their efforts. The physician must also aid the parents to get counseling, to see that parents receive treatment as well as the child.

Such organizations as "Mothers Anonymous," much like Alcoholics Anonymous, provide emotional support to parents who are mistreating their children and want to stop.

In New York St. Luke's Hospital has a group of volunteer "grandmothers" befriending parents who are child beaters. The hope is to end the battered-child syndrome in these families. The program--set up by the hospital's department of child psychiatry--is similar to one called "Project Grandmother" at the University of Colorado.

"We're not attempting to discipline the mother or show her how to raise her children," said Dr. Elizabeth B. Watkins, chief of the New York hospital's pediatric clinic. "We try to find people who will accept the mother in spite of the fact that she has hurt her children."

Volunteers are screened by professional staff members. One volunteer will be assigned to a family. Neither a baby-sitter nor a housekeeper, the volunteer visits the home and befriends the mother, keeping in close touch with the clinic to report difficulties and progress.

Accidental burns among small children are common enough that some hospitals have special wards to treat them. But are the burns really accidents? Helen L. Martin, a medical researcher at the Burns unit of London's Hospital for Sick Children, says no. She studied 50 cases over seven months and concluded that most burns are the outcome of emotional problems in which children are victims. Martin matched the patient traffic in the hospital's burns unit, which ranged in age from seven months to 14 years, against a control group of children of similar age, background, and residence who had never been burned. During the seven months she interviewed the parents of both the burned children and the control-group children. Except in five cases all the burn accidents had occurred during emotionally tense situations involving mother and child or other family member or between hostile adults. In only two cases was the burned child alone when injured.

How did these "accidents" happen? What kind of mother would deliberately inflict the anguish of a burn on a child?

Of the 46 mothers involved in the study 44 were anxious about some emotional problem that distracted them from attention to the child. Some 19 mothers confessed they had not wanted to have the child in the first place; 21 classified their attitude toward their husbands as "distant, indifferent, or hostile." Only three women in the control group had those negative feelings.

Martin believes that the burned baby, like the battered baby, is often the innocent pawn in parents' quarrels. But there may be differences, for burned children are not victims of conscious assault. Their injuries appear to be accidents. The mother who accidentally leaves the child where it can reach a pan of boiling water or frying potatoes is perhaps unconsciously wishing for the child to be burned. The parent who beats a child often expresses terrible guilt feelings, but the parents of burned children may feel that the children are at fault, "The kids did it to themselves."

The Fortune Society, a group of former convicts, reports that more than half its membership were severely abused as children. Child abuse is the root cause of much of the violence in society. The abused grow up to abuse others. A New York study of nine juvenile murderers, including one girl who had cut a victim to pieces with a machete, revealed that all nine had been routinely abused and beaten by their parents.

In Chicago, in 1978, increases in reported cases of incest were accompanying more instances of children under age 12 contracting venereal disease. The Chicago Board of Health reported 85 cases of incest-caused V. D., as compared to 49 cases reported in 1977. Social workers contended that the vast majority of venereal disease cases among children stemmed from a severe form of child abuse--sexual advances of adult relatives.

A federal law guaranteeing privacy to V. D. victims prevented social workers from helping the children; the vast majority of V. D. cases go unreported because physicians balk when children are victims. A child-abuse expert said federal privacy regulations on V. D. encouraged treatment because otherwise patients might be afraid to come for medical help. Physicians report cases to the Board of Health, which tries to trace the disease. But the truth is that many children are raped in the home by stepparents or visitors, and some of these children have such low self-esteem that they become prostitutes for the rest of their lives.

MEDICAL FACTS AND FANTASIES

19. Drug Addiction

As we have seen, community medicine is poorly defined and encompasses a multitude of evils: the treatment of drug addicts, as part of "community medicine," is one of the most crucial and frightening problems of the age.

What has caused so many youngsters from every walk of life to turn to drugs? The statistics are appalling and constantly getting worse; they were exacerbated by the thousands of addicts returning from the Indochina war. The United States may have over 250,000 heroin victims.

Dr. Marie Nyswander, a lithe woman who talks with her hands, has been the heroine of storefront psychiatry. Able to create and maintain strong relationships with her patients, East Harlem addicts, she impresses them because she had the courage to move into their neighborhood rather than ask them to come to an impersonal institution.

"To develop a relationship with any stranger is tough," a young Puerto Rican addict confesses,

> especially when the stranger's a professional representing something better than you. Other doctors use strange words and frighten those of us who ain't educated. Doctors can be so damn serious. Tell them what you figure they want to hear. Maybe that's why other doctors think we all have the same story. But Dr. Nyswander won't put us in the same box. She sorted us out, because she got inside. I could blow my top for her, she blows her top too, believe me. If I light up a couple of cigarettes and just talk, she listens. She don't turn her back. Even if she was on her way home to take care of a roast, she'd stop to talk. Look, what it comes down to, I dig her.

> She swings. I mean she's alive. She's really
> alive.

A sociologist on the staff of the East Harlem Protes-
tant Parish Narcotics Committee, Seymour Fiddle maintains,
"The addicts have made an art of guaranteeing their own
failure." Of Marie Nyswander he says,

> Marie compelled these addicts to respond to her as
> total human beings. At first it was a shock for
> them to meet someone like her in a culture in
> which middle-class people either avoid them or
> see them as part of an undifferentiated segment--
> the junky. They've been beaten by policemen,
> hounded by judges, betrayed by lawyers, wept over
> by social workers.... Most of the other psychia-
> trists working with addicts treat them only as ad-
> dicts. But once you start treating them as human
> beings, they begin to feel they're human beings.

Why does Marie Nyswander specialize in addiction?

"I suppose the answer must include my reasons for
being an analyst in the first place. I have a strong feeling
for the beauty and dignity of man ... I have a feeling for
the joy experienced by others, or at least their capacity for
joy, and their desire to be liberated from repression. I
like to be in on the process of release if I can. That's
what motivates me to treat addicts...."

Writing about Dr. Nyswander, Nat Hentoff quotes her
in A Doctor Among Addicts: "In India and throughout the
East, they've had their lotus eaters--their drug addicts--for
centuries. They grow up with them, they feed them, and
they consider the addict part of the whole community as a
balance against the materialistic proclivities of their societies."

Dr. Nyswander sees addiction as being for some a
"mystical experience." Since there's no place for mystics
in a materialistic community, "Addiction becomes a reflec-
tion of failure. Here the addict is forced into the abyss....
Confronting failure so nakedly can bring out an honesty you
rarely find elsewhere in our society." She recalls that every great religious leader, artist, and writer had to go
through horror, agony, torture, and temptation. "I'm not
saying that addicts are poets or religious searchers," she

emphasized, "but many do seek the same quality of feeling poets do. Most don't have the capacity to make the observations of poets, but they do feel an obligation to themselves of a sort that is not common to this society."*

Dr. Nyswander and her partner Dr. Vincent Dole have been controversial figures since 1964, when their program to use methadone to free drug addicts from addiction first began. Methadone programs, which cost an average of $1,500 a year for each addict, as opposed to $5,000 to $10,000 per year to imprison the person, are operated in most U.S. cities. Thousands of addicts clamor to enroll in these life-saving programs. Methadone, when combined with psychiatric help, offers a highly motivated addict a chance to give up heroin. Developed as a morphine substitute in Germany during World War II, methadone relieves pain and eases the symptoms of heroin withdrawal without producing euphoria or the craving for ever-larger doses. Once hooked on heroin, methadone users may have to continue indefinitely, as the heroin habit is said to alter the body's chemistry so crucially that life without opiates becomes impossible.

Heroin addiction was once concentrated in big cities; but now even "clean" cities and affluent suburbs, and sometimes Norman Rockwell hometowns, have pushers and high school addicts, who find themselves hungering for increasing amounts until the drug becomes the object of life. Apathy and loss of appetite deplete them, and such diseases as pneumonia, tuberculosis, and V.D. are contracted. The junkies begin to think of themselves as worthless, and society accepts their view. They can neither study nor hold a job. †

To doctors involved in treating heroin addiction methadone seems to be the most workable weapon. But methadone has its drawbacks. It can be as addictive as the heroin it replaces. Doctors at the University of Chicago Pritzker School of Medicine have experimented with a drug that is like methadone, 1-methadyl acetate, but suppresses withdrawal symptoms and narcotic hunger three times as long as ordinary methadone. The drug reduces temptations to

---

*Science News, 99 (May 15, 1971), p. 332.

†Ibid.

cheat on treatment by selling heroin substitutes for money
to buy drugs.

Dr. Nyswander favors research on addiction that will
help solve the massive problems involved. She claims that
for half a century "the American medical profession has
largely abandoned the drug addict. Because of the laws and
the way they're administered, we've turned him over to the
criminals. "

Dr. Nyswander, critical of the punitive approach to
the addict, claimed that youth were attracted to drugs as an
"adolescent way of rebelling and also of exploring life. " At
least a million sick citizens have been turned into criminals
"virtually by a wave of the legislative wand, " she says. In
her campaign to turn the treatment of addicts over to doctors and do away with the stereotype of the addict, Dr.
Nyswander wrote The Drug Addict as a Patient in 1956.
This country, she insisted, had the harshest laws and at the
same time "the worst narcotic problem of any country in
the world--and the most complicated. "

The American Civil Liberties Union agreed and insisted there had to be changes in Narcotics Bureau regulations to free doctors to treat addicts lawfully with necessary
drugs. Concerned citizens urged less punitive laws regarding rehabilitation, community houses, and half-way homes as
necessities to provide a protected environment.

Dr. Marie Nyswander claims that methadone addicts
receiving daily drugs legally have no need to steal or murder. Crime in the cities may be due largely to heroin addicts, who have to sustain expensive habits. Drugs also
contribute to a high suicide-attempt rate among heroin and
cocaine addicts, perhaps 15 times higher than the non-addicts
in the same age group. Treating addicts requires a close
look at their attitudes toward life and death and some respect
for their real depressions.

Dr. Nyswander revealed that 82 percent of the first
700 addicts who enrolled in her program in 1964 stayed with
it: a remarkable success. Such results stem from social
and economic aid, as well as from medical care. For some
of these addicts the concern and compassion of the physician
is the first charitable care they have had in their lives.

By 1979 a strong shift in drug abuse from heroin and

other opiates toward marijuana had been documented among
urban adolescents. Statistics indicate a flip-flop occurring
in illicit drug use from the first half of the 1967-77 decade,
when opiates were high on the drug-abuse list, to the last
half, when pot popularity surged.

The rising use of pot is thought to be possible because of its lower cost. Relaxed punitive laws against pos-
session in small amounts have contributed to a rapid rise,
so that in 1977 about 75 percent of drug users among adolescents were on pot.

"Opiates were the most frequently reported class of
drug abuse up to 1971," according to Dr. Karen Hein of the
adolescent medicine division, Albert Einstein College of
Medicine, the Bronx, N. Y. "Fifty-eight percent of all drug
users at the detention facility admitted opiate use in 1970,
whereas only 4 percent gave this history in 1977." During
the first half of the decade minimal marijuana use occurred.
However, during the years 1972-77 there was a rapid rise
in the use of marijuana. The cost of cocaine is cited as
the reason for its limited use in 1979. The decline in the
use of L. S. D. and amphetamines, which reached a peak in
1973, is attributed to their severe emotional and physical
hazards.

Drugs have permeated every level of life. So available is marijuana that even elementary school children smoke
it. Police in Austin, Texas, lectured at Doss Elementary
School on the dangers of smoking pot. The next day a ten-
year-old boy brought a marijuana plant for show and tell.
He said that the plants grew around the pool of the apartment complex where he lived. Show-and-tell went to pot
that day.

MEDICAL FACTS AND FANTASIES

20. Death, Pain, and Acne

Pain and death, like troubles, come to all and must be faced in life.

"Ultimately," observes Elisabeth Kubler-Ross, a doctor specializing in death and dying, "it is the knowledge of our own potential destructiveness that forces us today to confront ourselves with the meaning of life and death. "*

Dr. Ross, a Swiss-born psychiatrist for whom the subject of death has been a preoccupation for more than a decade, believes that death is a state of being, the final stage of human growth. She maintains that patients who die in an atmosphere of tenderness and warmth experience peace and wholeness. The blind may see and those who suffered are freed from pain.

In London Dr. Cicely Saunders heads a team developing a remarkably different approach to helping people face death. At St. Christopher's Hospital, which specializes in care of terminal cancer patients, the aim is to relieve the physical, mental, and spiritual distress. "Mostly," said the nursing matron, "the patients know what is the matter with them, but that doesn't mean they accept it. What we are trying to do is make them accept it in their own way and their own time. "

In most hospitals dying people are avoided. Even members of the family get no chance to grieve. People are always telling them to buck up or cheer up.

As part of the effort to make the patient's dying days

---

*Foreword to Jewish Reflections on Death, Schocken Books, 1974, pp. 1-3.

as comfortable as possible, St. Christopher's patients are given an alcoholic drink whenever they request one. Heroin is administered not just to kill pain, but to head off pain and dispel depression.

The religious sense of caring and sharing represented in Christ's plea to his disciples in the Garden of Gethsemane, "Wait with me," is the rule and law of St. Christopher's. "We don't preach at people," said Dr. Saunders, "but we are Christians and believe in the resurrection. Death is not the end."

St. Christopher's is the culmination of a vision Dr. Saunders had in the early '50s, when she attended a young man dying of cancer in a 50-bed ward. Now Dr. Saunders insists that no ward in her hospital have more than four beds. Many dying patients may elect to be out-patients. Some beds are reserved for long-term neurological patients, so that nurses and doctors can look a terminal patient in the eye and say, "Not everyone comes here to die."

Living quarters are provided for families who must manage to be close to the dying patient. The parents of one 18-year-old boy lived at the hospital for months so they could be near him until the end.

At St. Christopher's the responsibility is to "take time" with the patients, talk with them, listen, give them a backrub if they want one--just spend time near them. As for the part alcohol plays in the program, "Spirits should not be underestimated as a great appetizer, a great lifter of mood, a social occasion, and a great sedative." Patients are allowed to see their pets, go home to eat a meal or spend a few days in their own gardens, see a movie, or finish a piece of knitting.

In connection with pain-killers, Dr. Saunders believes that in American hospitals, patients dying of cancer may be either in pain or "slugged," knocked out. Dr. Saunders said that the typical hospital in America allows a patient to be in pain and pleading for relief before giving him an altogether too big a dose of drugs. Sometimes there is too long a gap between drug doses to kill the pain.

Dr. Saunders maintains that at St. Christopher's the patients receive the amount of heroin required to ward off pain and to prevent depression. The drug is given regularly and steadily.   What difference does it make if the dying patient becomes addicted?

Visitors find no signs of pain, fear, or tension in St. Christopher's wards, nor of the gruesome sights so common in American hospitals, patients all but dead hooked up to tubes and other apparatus.

"It's better to have people die holding hands with their family," insists Saunders.   She observes about her work, "A materialistic society doesn't want to face problems, but life is about what you do with what happens to you--and that inevitably includes death."

American hospitals may have lagged behind their British counterparts in helping to better the time that terminal patients have left, but in Cincinnati Dr. Cornelia Dettmer's daily life is pervaded with death.   Dr. Dettmer is head of the department of oncology and president of a hospice program that combats the old stereotype of regarding the doctor's rate of cure as a measure of success. "When death approaches, the patient becomes weak and unattractive," she admits.   "Dying is failure.   It's the opposite of what America is supposed to stand for, so we sweep it under the carpet.

"I have to face patients who are dying.   But I cannot abandon them when I can no longer cure them."

Dr. Dettmer realizes that only one in three of her cancer patients will live five years; there is even less hope for her hospice patients.   She talks cheerfully of her children and her hobbies and is not depressed about death; nor does she ever regard herself as a failure.   "Most medical schools have not taught students how to handle death or dying," she admits.   "With modern technology most people believe that a dying patient means a failure for the doctor."

She has come to believe that there is no threat in treating a dying patient, and she feels comfortable working with patients in the hospice program because she deals with death every day in her practice at the hospital.   The hospice program, which treats the terminally ill, must bring honest recognition to the process of dying.   "The doctor must admit that he can't cure every patient.   It's a part of life we have to accept," she claims.   "I think the hospice program makes it easier for the doctor."   The great need

is to stop playing games. You don't have to say, "Eat this
and you'll get big and strong again." She concludes, "As
I'm more honest, the patient is better able to accept death."

In the early '70s world attention was focused on Dutch
doctor Gertruida Postma-van-Boven, who administered a lethal morphine injection to her 78-year-old mother, who was
dying painfully. The mother had requested repeatedly that
her daughter end her suffering. Dr. Postma-van-Boven and
her doctor husband were general practitioners in a small community, which overwhelmingly supported the doctors in their
belief that someone who is dying in agony has the right to
ask to be allowed to die quickly and quietly. "Nothing in
Jewish or Christian tradition presumes that a physician has
a mandate to impose his or her wishes and skills upon patients for the sake of prolonging the length of their dying
where those patients are terminally ill," said a representative of the United Church of Christ. "We believe there
comes a time in the course of an irreversible terminal illness when, in the interest of love, mercy and compassion,
those who are caring for the patient, should say, 'Enough.'"

"Never be afraid to bother your doctor about a pain,"
is the advice of Dr. Kathleen Foley, a neurologist who is
"Pain Coordinator" at New York City's Memorial Sloan-
Kettering Cancer Center. Dr. Foley emphasized that no one
should be considered "hysterical" for complaining of pain,
even if a physical cause is not immediately apparent, or
even if the cause does prove to be psychosomatic. Any doctor who is annoyed or irritated by a patient because of a
number of seemingly minor complaints may no longer be an
objective observer; that's the doctor's problem, not the patient's, according to Foley, and she recommends looking
around for a different doctor.

"One thing we never do is assume someone who comes
here is crazy," said a member of San Francisco's Mt. Zion
Hospital Pain Center studying, diagnosing, and treating patients who are suffering chronic pain. The center's team
includes neurosurgeons, neurologists, psychiatrists, and
medical anthropologists. Patients under the overall care of
an internist meet for several days with a panel of doctors
from assorted fields. The meetings and conferences that
follow are one of the most important techniques in helping
patients whose life situations are frequently aggravated by
social and psychological problems as well as constant pain.

Many have suffered for ten to 15 years and have undergone
surgery as many as a dozen times.

Sometimes there isn't much correlation between the
amount of money spent by the United States to conquer a
disease and the amount of disability that disease causes.
The question of priorities in medicine must be confronted.
Cancer has had as much as $1,600 million per year for re-
search. There is a tendency for medical research to concentrate on great terminal illnesses, such as cancer and
heart disease. We may be persuaded that attacks on these
diseases and intensive research may save lives. The aim
of medicine is to save life. But another and equally important aim is to relieve suffering. While heart disease and
cancer are the greatest causes of human suffering, they are
mostly diseases of the aged and the affluent. When former
President Harry S Truman died at a ripe old age commen-
tators observed that he was a victim of heart disease. For
a man of that age heart failure is a merciful way to go.

Cancer crusades and heart research have a magnetic
attraction in a country that fears death. Perhaps the problems in this research are beyond solution. We may be
seeking medical answers to questions that involve life itself.

The enormous publicity that surrounded heart trans-
plants in the '60s may one day be looked back upon with
strong distaste, even revulsion. At the time we were hope-
ful and excited by the experiments. Pictures in newspapers
of interns and nurses dashing through hospital halls with organs of a still warm corpse had overtones of ghoulishness.
But what finally appalls was the waste of medical personnel
who should have been trained to relieve the suffering of the
sick--those with routine ailments who were given too little
attention, those undergoing tonsillectomies, appendectomies,
and hysterectomies.

At least one in seven patients suffering from econom-
ically catastrophic illness dies soon after receiving costly
care. Half suffer from chronic illnesses, such as heart
disease or cancer, instead of what we have been led to ex-
pect--an acute condition. These findings in a study done
for the National Center for Health Services Research by a
University of California team on patients with hospital bills
totaling more than $4,000 were published in the New England
Journal of Medicine in 1979 and in various newspapers.
Seventeen San Francisco hospitals were included in the study,
in which catastrophic patients accounted for 20 to 68 percent

of the hospital billings. Researchers concluded that a national catastrophic illness insurance would be devoted to people who would die soon after receiving high-cost medical treatment. The typical patient in the sample suffered from chronic heart disease or cancer and had been under treatment for a long time. Very little of the high costs went for high-technology treatment which is often viewed as the villain in health care inflation.

No one suggests that research on heart disease, cancer, and gerontology should come to a screeching halt. But when funds are limited, priorities must be assigned. How much should be spent to extend life beyond the century mark? How much should be spent on alleviating more prevalent, though admittedly less deadly and perhaps less glamourous, diseases that afflict men and women while they are young?

What could be less glamourous than acne? Yet millions of teenagers are anguished by their appearance as reflected in mirrors, and hundreds of thousands of older people never outgrow inflammation and chronic acne. Research in cancer has certainly affected the lives of many young cancer patients, particularly victims of leukemia--but nothing in recent years has had a more beneficient effect than the research from the National Cancer Institute and the University of Iowa, where testing on a dramatic drug treatment for the most severe and disfiguring form of acne has proven remarkably successful. Some 14 men and women who had suffered from cysts and acne for ten years or more found their skin clearing up after therapy with daily doses of a synthetic derived from vitamin A.

Rare is the teenager who doesn't ever have some attack of acne. For most, it disappears; for some, antibiotics may do the trick. Doctors sometimes inject steroid hormones into acne nodules to reduce inflammation, but there is always the possibility that the treatment may stunt growth. Vitamin A molecule, developed synthetically for cancer research, drastically reduces the amount of sebum, the greasy substance secreted at adolescence. The drug may also prevent skin cells from thickening and clogging the pores.

Medicine will be a more humane and civilized discipline when physicians agree that hospitals are to cure the ill, and failing that, to make the ill as comfortable as humanly possible. Relief from suffering, rather than the prolonging of life or the attempt to abolish death, must be the first order of the medical profession.

MEDICAL FACTS AND FANTASIES

21. Amazing Insights

A woman who is discontented without a profession but insists
on telling her children she is perfectly happy isn't fooling
anyone. The children begin to wonder if their own percep-
tions are inaccurate. Children prefer to have the mother
honest with them and the situation out in the open. They
can then deal with the honest facts.

Many of today's successful career women may have
been steered into professions by a mother who was vocation-
ally frustrated and deeply ambivalent about traditional sex
roles. In a recent study of professional women by two researchers at the U. S. Department of Health, Education and
Welfare, the mothers--many of whom were well educated
themselves--were found to motivate daughters to careers
and non-traditional behaviors and attitudes. These mothers
were often as bright, competent, and intelligent as the fathers, but they were intellectually unfulfilled.

The study dealt with women who faced extreme con-
tradictions of social roles by deciding on high-status professions that are normally dominated by men. Conducted by
two professionals working in the National Institute of Child
Health and Human Development of H. E. W. , psychologist Dr.
Kay Standley and research assistant Dr. Bradley Soule, the
study interviewed 75 women, doctors, lawyers, and archi-
tects. In interviews the women gave vivid accounts of their
parents' preoccupations with academic achievement and as-
sumptions of excellence in their daughters. A majority of
the women confessed they respected their father more than
their mother, and of those who had professional fathers, a
majority of the women followed the same profession, Dr.
Soule concluded.

The women reported that as 16-year-olds they expected to have full-time careers and families or careers

without husbands or children. While parents demonstrated enthusiasm and encouragement in that direction, report the researchers, "there is evidence that many parents did not expect their daughters to embrace such values and behavior so completely."

In one interview a woman doctor noted that her parents lent full support to her academic endeavors and then, to her surprise, when she graduated from medical school, her parents urged her not to practice.

Consistently in this study the desire was evident on the part of the mothers that daughters should limit careers and rear a family. Women were expected to juggle two lives, marriage and a career. One doctor confessed her husband introduced her to everyone with pride, but when she came home from making hospital rounds, he expected her to be a wife, as responsive and fresh as if she hadn't been taking care of patients all day.

Yet the study concludes that these women are, on the whole,

> happy, busy people, very satisfied with their dual roles and ability to live two lives. They have done something worthwhile, and if they feel a price has been paid, they would still unanimously agree that it was well worth it. In our society, at this place in time, we are finally faced with recognizing that "woman" and "professional" don't really go together yet. A small group of highly gifted and advantaged women have managed to make an amalgamation of the two concepts in their lives, but the union is characterized by continuing tension--both psychic and social. The women are not liberated, nor are the professional establishments in which they operate. Change will clearly be required of both as society redefines the sex-typing of its vocations. *

Women at six of the country's most prestigious colleges appear to have lower self-esteem and lower aspirations than men, even when their grades are the same. Women still seem to underestimate themselves, said Lois Monteiro, coordinator of a 1978 Brown University study. "Women are

---

*Elizabeth Bennett, Houston Post, October 4, 1972.

much less likely to think they're well prepared for graduate or professional school. Even women who take that tough physical science major in college are much less likely to say they will go on to medical school, " claims Monteiro, an associate professor in community health at Brown.

Dr. Helen H. Lambert, an expert on brain hormones at Northeastern University in Boston, describes herself as a feminist and has written extensively on sex differences for science journals. She feels that many feminists don't want to listen to statements like, "Women are more likely than men to express emotions and display empathy and compassion in response to the emotions of others." Dr. Lambert claims, "I don't think there's any question that there are sex differences in behavior. There's just too much evidence to deny it." Dr. Lambert stresses that in every case the differences are between the average scores for groups of males and females. "Denying that there are differences is a losing tactic. You can't deny that there are certain biological differences. These may extend to behavior as well. But I don't grant that biological differences are a legitimate basis for unequal social rewards. "*

Scientific evidence largely confirms findings of the past, indicating that there are significant mental and behavioral differences between men and women. But it suggests that nearly all the differences are caused by cultural tradition, not heredity.

This evidence lends continuity to the insights of Karen Horney.

During her life the psychiatrist Karen Horney (1885-1952) was the center of controversy, but her contributions to feminine psychology are now widely recognized and accepted. She practiced and taught in Berlin before coming to the United States in 1932. Eventually she began to question Freud's theories and to reject his biological orientation. She rejected particularly the idea of an innate death instinct. She stressed the early development of a girl's psychology before the girl learns she has no penis; she stood publicly against non-physicians becoming lay analysts, and overall she was more optimistic than Freud about the potential for improvement of individuals and societies.

---

*Houston Chronicle, January 7, 1979, Sec. 9, p. 8.

Horney was among the first women admitted to a medical school in Germany. Admission in 1906 in Germany was difficult, even though Horney had high grades. She had decided on medicine as a career when she was 12. Her father disapproved of her ambition and discouraged her from taking the preparatory courses for a medical school; he refused to help her financially. She determined to teach for a few years and save enough to get to medical school on her own.

Studying in Berlin around 1908, Horney met Oskar Horney, a brilliant student, majoring in economics, who was to become her husband.

In September 1908 Karen passed her Physikum, the examination on preclinical subjects. Her biographer Jack L. Rubins notes that the class photograph shows Karen biting her lip, ill at ease. The six male students carry swagger sticks--that symbol of male arrogance; Horney is holding a skull crooked in her arm--the "symbol of head and intellect."

Karen and Oskar transferred to the University of Göttingen, where he studied economics and she took demanding courses in pathology, pharmacology, and bacteriology and worked in out-patient clinics for the poor. This was her first contact with real patients. Until this experience she had idealized medicine; but the suffering patients brought out in her "the will to heal."

At 24 Karen was mature and knowledgeable when she married Oskar Horney, October 31, 1909. In the Overvaluation of Love, she writes, "It would be going too far to assert that ... conflict confronts every woman who ventures upon a career of her own and who is ... unwilling to pay for her daring with the renunciation of her femininity."

In 1909 in Berlin she seemed happily married, in love, hopefully dedicated to her medicine. Housekeeping may have been more burdensome than she had anticipated. She completed her clinical work by the summer of 1910; preparing for her final examination, she found she was pregnant. Chronically exhausted, she was depressed by indecision between the socially accepted role of homemaker and the defiant role of doctor. Her mother had a stroke and died in February 1911, one month before Horney had her first baby, Brigitte. At the time she was in analysis with Dr. Karl Abraham, but the techniques seem to have made only transitory intellectual therapeutic changes--the effects were not truly integrated into the patient's experience and personality.

The analysis seemed to heighten Horney's depressions, and she lost some of her youthful spontaneity and exuberance. She took on the semantics of analysis as a substitute for her earlier, more poetic, way of expressing herself.

Horney took her state medical examination in 1911, and despite the palpable prejudices of professors against women in medicine, she was given a specially lenient examination schedule so she could have time between the tests to nurse Brigitte. Horney's friend Lisa Honroth admired her persistence and offered her (ironically) what she regarded as the greatest compliment: "Karen thinks and works like a man" (Rubins, p. 40).

The Lankwitz Kuranstalt, the neuropsychiatric hospital where Dr. Horney went to work, had many poor clients, but Karen Horney tended patients in the small private sanatorium treating women's mental illnesses. The famed Sigmund Freud consulted cases among the patients. Even though she had passed her medical qualifying examinations, she still had to write a doctoral thesis. She turned to Karl Bonhoeffer to direct her thesis, and suggested post-traumatic syndromes as a topic. She had a second daughter in 1913. Now her social life and studies gave her great insight into philosophy, psychoanalysis, politics, and religion--although she became family oriented. Working at the Kuranstalt, which was close to home, she was able to combine attention to her daughters (a third was born in 1916) and to her thesis. Accepted and published in 1915, it dealt with psychosis as the result of head injury.

Germany had entered the war in August 1914, and Karen Horney's schedule at the Lankwitz Kuranstalt became difficult, as psychiatric war casualties were brought in. Her husband became the family disciplinarian, and despite her thorough understanding of child psychology, she distanced herself from Oskar's severity in punishing the girls with beatings with a leather strap, a crop, or a stick. Hunger and illness due to the hardships of the war plagued the family.

While other psychiatrists, like Auguste Ferel, Richard von Krafft-Ebing, and Havelock Ellis, were studying sexual relationships and problems, Karen Horney, too, was deeply involved in her own marriage and looking at analysis through the light of her own experience. "Many a marriage," she observed, "that might have floundered because of the neurosis

of one of the partners has become more healthy through
analysis because the patient became able to direct his forces
toward his marital partner, forces previously fixated upon
infantile models."

She held that analysis could liberate a person who
felt tied down. She was examining and rejecting Freudian
theories and introducing new concepts of human growth, an
innate constructive force. Her theories were optimistic and
life-affirming, and already she was speaking of the capacity
"to wish and to will" the part of oneself which grows, ex-
pands, and fulfills. This, she maintained, was the real self.
Knowing this real self leads to genuine integration and a
sound sense of wholeness, oneness, and self-acceptance.
The woman who finds her real self can function without serious inner conflict. There is no doubt she is a better mother, a better wife, and a better human being.

To be an analyst in the years before the First World
War was to be regarded as a sexual pervert. Analysis was
generally misinterpreted as advocating complete sexual license. (Dr. Horney knew that patients sometimes deliberately misguided the doctor; one of her private patients worked
as a gardener. He pretended to be a male transvestite, and
donned women's clothing to do maid's work. Dr. Horney
was hoodwinked until she discovered he was only trying to
avoid the draft!)

She began to examine cases of women whose fears
were traceable to conflicts with fathers. She lectured on
the value of psychoanalysis for social workers. Berlin
after the war--like all of Germany--was depressed and de-
moralized, and unemployment was high. With the men
away at war, women had taken over the operation of trol-
leys, buses, construction, street cleaning, and garbage collecting. After the war women enrolled in college in great
numbers, some attending classes at night after heavy work
all day. Returning soldiers eased the women out of jobs
and classes. A women's rights movement began, but it was
not until 1922 that official equality for women in universities
was finally achieved. But German women still had a long
row to hoe.

The German economy hit the skids, the poor getting
poorer, the rich richer. Dr. Horney was questioning her
marriage, and she wrote about typical conflicts, observing
that a man may be said to have a "happy marriage" even if

he ruins his wife's life and makes her into a drudge. A
man's work--when it takes precedence over his marriage--
can have "life-destroying effects." She noted that independent women and civilized men had "a limited fitness for marriage." People in Germany were in a spontaneous social
revolution, where inflation had wiped out daughters' dowries
and the system of traditional marriage had died. Marriage
was considered bourgeois, and Horney, whose husband had
declared financial bankruptcy, may have regarded her husband as having also declared emotional bankruptcy.

By 1932 she was considered an authority on marriage,
and her paper "The Problem of the Monogamous Ideal" attracted attention to the question of why couples remain married after love is gone, and why people seek extramarital
affairs. This paper, coming so soon after her own separation from her husband, may have originated in her own experiences and emotions. Disagreeing with Freud's theory of
penis envy, Horney explored the view of a child's potential
to be complete, the boy with a penis, the girl with a vagina--
rather than only as a penis-proud or a penis-lacking individual. She claimed that girls do have early awareness of vaginal sensations, which are repressed out of anxiety.

Dr. Horney's reputation--particularly among women--
was widespread. She was included among nine German
analysts invited to America for the 1930 international congress of psychiatrists in Washington. Although she could
not make the trip, she must have begun to think of moving
to the United States at this time, because within a few years
she was associated with the Chicago Institute.

Eventually Karen Horney came to believe that life itself is the best therapist. She hoped to repudiate Freudian
emphasis on infantile instinctive urges, and she wanted to
point to cultural factors as equally significant.

Long self-supporting, she was now divorced. In her
teaching at the New School in New York she explored "Types
of Personality" and "Power, Domination and Freedom."
With fabulous trips and three grown daughters and a successful career, her life seemed harmonious and happy. Yet she
wrote about women's need for affection and love, need for a
partner, and she was constantly involved in her own self-
analysis.

As a flower leans to the sun, the innate tendency of

an individual is to grow in a healthy direction. This was Karen Horney's ultimate concept of self-realization. She believed that social and cultural factors could cause emotional illness, but she certainly would never point to society as the culprit for all mental sickness. She came to have a strongly holistic view of the dynamic interaction between culture, interpersonal relations, and emotional experiences--a "systems-theory"; eventually she focused on the concept, "On Feeling Abused. " She maintained that the neurotic may be inviting abuse from others and responding with disproportionate feelings of hurt, victimization, and vulnerability. Then the neurotic takes pride in not showing anger, in false serenity. Carried to extremes, the neurotic's self-hate may lead to contemplation of suicide.

Oriental religions came to have a great magnetism for her, and she seemed to accept the belief, finally, that the spiritual powers in people develop as people cease to violate their true and beautiful nature.

We have as yet no psychology of women; as psychologist Naomi Weisstein bluntly put it, "Psychology has nothing to say about what women are really like, what they need and what they want, essentially because psychology does not know.... The evidence is collecting that what a person does and who he believes himself to be, will in general, be a function of what people around him expect him to be, and what the overall situation in which he is acting implies that he is" (Weisstein, p. 135).

From platforms all over America women denounce Freud, who looked at society in the restricted light of nineteenth-century male attitudes. "Am I to believe my little wife, my helpmate, my child, is my intellectual equal?" (You'd better believe it, in the twentieth century!)

Speaking at the American Association for the Advancement of Science in 1979, Dr. Barbara DuBois of Goddard College spoke of "Passionate Scholarship, " insisting

> In science as in society, the power of naming is at least twofold: Naming defines the quality and value of that which is named--and it also denies reality and value to that which is never named, never uttered. That which has no name, that for which we have no words or concepts, is rendered

mute and invisible: powerless to inform or trans-
form our consciousness of our experience, our
understanding, our vision; powerless to claim its
own existence....

This has been the situation of women in our
world; and this silence, this invisibility, has been
confirmed and perpetuated by the ways in which
social science has looked at--and not seen--women.
But in this silence and invisibility is to be found
the reality of women, of our lives, our experience,
our vision--and the potential for new understand-
ings and constructions of ourselves and our world.
To address women's lives and experience in their
own terms, to create theory grounded in the actual
experience and language of women, is the central
agenda for feminist scholarship....

"Many women now seek out a woman therapist in an
attempt to clarify their role as women and to remove themselves from the traditional 'man in power--woman subservi-
ent' model. In therapy, these women focus on their ambiv-
alence about the nurturing capabilities of the therapist, their
ingrained belief that women are basically second-rate persons, and their ingrained socially conditioned attitude that
women are only rivals for men and are therefore not to be
trusted," according to Dr. Nancy A. Roeske, professor in
the Department of Psychiatry, Indiana University school of
medicine. She sees women's personality characteristics as
particularly suitable for the role of psychiatrist, intuitive,
patient, verbally skillful and empathetic (Roeske, a).

In 1979 male therapists were experiencing an "empty
couch syndrome." Women make up two-thirds of all psycho-
therapy patients, but male therapists outnumber female
therapists three to one. Fascinating.

Women are looking at psychiatry not only as potential
patients but as practicing physicians. Take Dr. Irene Kassoria. In 1968 Dr. Kassoria, an American psychiatrist
practicing in the United Kingdom, won the Italia prize, one
of the top British radio awards. She had described how she
had nursed a patient out of a "vegetable" state. A professional code had always discouraged psychiatrists from discussing patients' problems in public. But Dr. Kassoria had
asked herself, should the public benefit from the research
and success of what doctors and psychiatrists were doing?

A standard-bearer and crusader, Dr. Kassoria had a small private practice at the back of the Science Museum in London. She treated her patients to a 30-hour crash course. No Freudian excesses on couches dredging up the dream life of the patient before five years of age. Dr. Kassoria is not a silent type: she listened, but she also talked. Her patients often hummed or whistled when they left her office and walked down London's busy streets--happy!

In 1962 Kassoria began work with a helpless nine-year-old girl. The doctor applied "common sense" and the same loving discipline with which she had reared her own two children. The accepted way for 60 years of treating mentally sick children who banged their heads on the floor and defecated all over the place was to pick them up and hug them. If they broke a window, if they punched a neighbor, you treated them kindly.

It seemed to Irene Kassoria that no normal mother rewarded a child for shitting on the floor. Something wrong there. "I thought, from a mother's experience, what you reward keeps going, and what you ignore stops. So medicine was being practiced contrary to the principles of every mother who scolds a boy who is naughty. "

The nine-year-old patient was a head-banger. She was covered with welts. "I rewarded her and hugged her and kissed her when she didn't bang her head, and ignored her when she did. She got better. She was banging her head for attention. The girl didn't become completely normal. But she was able to read and to return home. She became a child instead of something bizarre. "

When Dr. Kassoria received a grant to practice in England, she sought out the most difficult patient she could find. The man she chose, a Mr. Blake, became the subject of a fascinating documentary. He was a man who had not spoken a word for 30 years. Within two weeks, with Dr. Kassoria's constant encouragement, Mr. Blake was responding verbally. By the end of a month he was giving quick correct answers to her questions. From a man who had retreated entirely from life, a man who had become strange, forbidding, and silent, he changed into an animated human being who would jump up when she arrived with her team of interning students.

Dr. Kassoria admits it is not always possible to

retrieve these lost souls. But the insights that psychiatrists gain from trying to redeem the hard cases is valuable. She studied how effective people operate, and she interviewed dozens of Britons to see what makes them tick. "But I haven't met anyone yet who could not make themselves 20 percent more effective."

Dr. Kassoria observed that many people fall short because of a failure to love and appreciate others around them, who are, after all, those they depend on to get things done. If "effective" people could operate more efficiently, what are we to think of women who come to a time of life when they devote themselves entirely to shopping and playing cards or eating? Psychologist Phyllis Chesler notes that many more women than men are considered "sick" by psychologists. She believes that if continual disappointments and rejections cause a woman to become more active or more aggressive, the woman may seek psychiatric help. If her psychiatrist is a Freudian, she will certainly be considered "sick."

Dr. David G. Rice and Dr. Joseph G. Kepecs report that the women's liberation movement may be responsible for the fact that female psychiatric patients seem sicker in the '70s than they seemed in the '60s. A University of Wisconsin study revealed that in 1972 "women patients show greater anxiety, deeper depression, less ability to cope with stress and increased alienation." The doctors conclude that "the change in sexual and social role expectations during the past decade seem to be greater and somewhat more ambiguous for women than for men."

Denver cardiologist Dr. John T. Kimball claims that women are now more likely to have heart attacks, and as they compete in "a man's world," they "are showing an earlier incidence of vascular problems. They are eating more, smoking more, and increasing stress situations. More women under 40 are having strokes and heart attacks," observes Dr. Kimball, and "they are also causing their husband's heart attacks!"

A Los Angeles urologist at Cedars of Lebanon Hospital, Dr. B. Lyman Steward blames the women's rights movement for increasing impotency in young men! Hear this: "The normally aggressive male eventually becomes impotent because of unconscious fear or hostility toward women."

American medicine has performed technical miracles.

We have not done so well in convincing male doctors that women are people. The women's rights movement is not an effort to dominate males; the idea is equality. Unequal pay, discrimination in promotion, segregation of professions, and the assumption that higher education is wasted on women because they will abandon their careers for marriage are rank injustices. Women have not had what Gertrude Stein ironically called "simple rights in a sane and simple world." Reasonable men respect women for standing up for dignity and justice.

In 1976 a study of women doctors in Detroit found that 59 percent of the women, ranging in age from 30 to 86, had worked without interruption since their medical-school graduation. Some 84 percent were working at the time of the study. Even among married women with children, 53 percent had never dropped out of medical practice for family reasons. Some had worked to the very day of childbirth and returned to practice within two weeks of delivery. Of the women interviewed, 67 percent were married (43 percent to doctors) and 69 percent had children. Among those who did not work five were retired, two were disabled, and one had dropped out of practice because of job conflicts. Four of the women were not working because they had young children, and two had given up their careers at the request of their husbands. The study revealed that 90 percent of the doctors practiced medicine full time; even the mothers worked--80 percent of them--and put in 40 hours or more per week. Many had no domestic help and continued to do most of the household chores. Child care and homemaking put too many demands on time and energy, women doctors say; the study concludes, "Now that we are approaching a time in which a fourth of physicians will be women, we must ask whether women physicians must also have full responsibility for a household. The assumption that women automatically have total responsibility for housework and child care needs to be challenged. Shared responsibility of these important tasks seem to be a crucial issue."

In 1979 an article in Medical Mrs. (a magazine for doctor's wives) revealed that one out of six young doctors who marry in medical school will find him- or herself in divorce court within ten years of graduation. Medical school changes the young scholar. Neither husband nor wife is prepared for the tremendous demands on time and emotions, according to Dr. Myra Hatterer, a psychiatrist with Columbia University College of Physicians and Surgeons. The strain may be attributable to the person putting the doctor through--what used to be called "P. H. T. ": Putting Hubby Through--with one person carrying the financial burden. The time has come for a system of universal public medicine that will open wide the doors of medical schools to qualified young scholars, male and female. America can afford the best medical system in the world. Women doctors may help to bring to fruition a concept of medical care embracing all who need care and concern. We must insist on nothing less.

In the final analysis, both men and women must question those who look on a medical career as a business enterprise, and must look to moral reciprocity, political involvement, and human responsibility. Good health is the promise of grace, a zest for life, joy in the morning, exuberance in work and play, a gift that calls for gratitude. We require not more mechanization of medicine, but more humanization, where doctors are offering not orders, but hope, courage, and compassion. Then in this human community, good medicine will be available to all, and good medical training available to all who qualify.

BIBLIOGRAPHY

Addams, Jane. Twenty Years at Hull-House. New York: Macmillan, 1929.

"Alpha Wave of the Future, " Time, (January 4, 1974), p. 22 (Barbara Brown).

Alsop, Gulielma Fell. History of the Woman's Medical College: Philadelphia, Pa. , 1850-1950. Philadelphia: Lippincott, 1950.

"Amalgamation, Not Segregation, " Woman's Medical Journal, 26 (May 1916). Editorial.

Anderson, Louisa Garrett. Elizabeth Garrett Anderson: 1836-1917. London: Faber and Faber, 1939.

Austin, Anne L. History of Nursing Source Book. New York: Putnam, 1957.

Banks, J. and O. Feminism and Family Planning in Victorian England. Liverpool: Liverpool University Press, 1964.

Barringer, Emily Dunning. Bowery to Bellevue: The Story of New York's First Woman Ambulance Driver. New York: Norton, 1950.

Bartholow, Roberts. New York Medical Journal, 5 (May 1867). Letters to the Editor.

Bass, Elizabeth. "Leisure Hours, " Women in Medicine, 66 (October 1937), pp. 9-12.

Bell, Enid M. (a) Storming the Citadel: the Rise of the Woman Doctor. London: Constable, 1953.

_____. (b) Josephine Butler. London: Constable, 1963.

Blackwell, Elizabeth. (a) Pioneer Work in Opening the Medical Profession to Women. London: Longmans, Green, 1895.

_____. (b) The Laws of Life. New York: Putnam, 1852.

Blake, John B. "Women and Medicine in Anti-Bellum America," Bulletin of the History of Medicine, 32 (1965).

Block, J. L. "Dr. Kelsey's Stubborn Triumph," Good Housekeeping, 155 (November 1962).

Bluemel, Elinor. Florence Sabin, Colorado Woman of the Century. Boulder: University of Colorado Press, 1959.

Böhmert, Victor. Women's Studies in the Experience of the University of Zurich. Leipzig: 1874 (German).

Brockett, Linus Pierpont, and Mary C. Vaughn. Woman's Work in the Civil War. Boston: Curran, 1867.

Brussel, James A. "Pants, Politics, Postage, and Physic," Psychiatric Quarterly Supplement, 35 (Part I, 1971), pp. 332-45.

Cartwright, L. K. "Personality and Family Background of a Sample of Women Medical Students at the University of California," Journal of American Medican Women's Association, 27 (1972), pp. 260ff.

Chaff, Sandra L., Ruth Haimbach, Carol Fenichel, and Nina B. Woodside. Women in Medicine: A Bibliography of the Literature on Women Physicians. Metuchen, N. J.: Scarecrow Press, 1977.

Clymer, Eleanor, and Lillian Erlich. "Helen B. Taussig, Physician." In Modern American Career Women. New York: Dodd, Mead, 1959.

Cohen, Lysbeth. Rachel Forster Hospital: The First Fifty Years. Sydney, New South Wales: Rachel Forster Hospital, 1972.

Cole, Margaret. Women of Today. New York: Nelson, 1930.

Cooperstock, Ruth. "Sex Differences in the Use of Mood Altering Drugs: An Explanatory Model," Journal of Health and Social Behavior, 12 (1971), pp. 238-44.

Corea, Gena. Hidden Malpractice. New York: Morrow, 1977.

Cunnington, Cecil W. Feminine Attitudes in the 19th Century. New York: Macmillan, 1936.

Curie, Eve. Madame Curie (translated by Vincent Sheean). New York: Doubleday, 1938.

Curie, Marie. Pierre Curie (translated by Vernon and Charlotte Kellogg). New ed. New York: Dover, 1963.

Dally, Ann. Cicely: The Story of a Doctor. London: Gollancz, 1968.

Dionesov, S. M. "Russian Female Medical Students in Zurich," Sovetskoe Zdravookrhranenie, 32 (1973), pp. 68-72 (Russian).

"Doctor and the Drug: Kelsey," Newsweek, (June 24, 1963), p. 70.

"Dr. Helen Taussig: Pediatrician with a Heart." Medical World News (October 22, 1965), pp. 94ff (photos).

Douglas, Emily Taft. Margaret Sanger: Pioneer of the Future. New York: Holt, Rinehart and Winston, 1969.

Dube, W. F. "Datagram: U. S. Medical School Enrollment," 1969-1970 through 1973-4." Journal of Medical Education, 49 (March 1974), pp. 302-7.

DuBois, Barbara. Paper read before the American Association for the Advancement of Science, Symposium on Feminism, Houston, January 6, 1979.

Edwards, Linden F. "Dr. Mary Edwards Walker (1832-1919); Charlatan or Martyr? Part II." Ohio State Medical Journal, 54 (1958), pp. 1296, 1298.

Ehrenreich, Barbara, and Deirdre English. Witches, Midwives, and Nurses; A History of Women Healers. Old Westbury, N. Y.: The Feminist Press, 1973.

Eulenburg, Albert. "Women Medical Students in German Universities during the Summer Semester, 1901," Deutsche Medicinische Wochenschrift, 27 (July 11, 1901), p. 472 (German).

Falto, Charles. "Barefoot Doctors of China." Los Angeles Times (June 16, 1972).

Fay, Marion. "Women in Medicine: Letters from Other Desks," Journal of the American Medical Women's Association, 16 (May 1961), p. 394.

Fickert, Auguste K. "Women and Medical Studies," Wiener Klinische Rundschau, 13 (April 9, 1899) (German).

Fidell, Linda, and Jane Prather. "Mood Modifying Drug Use in Middle Class Women," paper presented at Western Psychological Assn. Meeting, Sacramento, California, April 25, 1975.

"Fighting Breast Cancer," Time (May 22, 1972), p. 103.

Flexner, Simon, and James Thomas Flexner. William Henry Welch and the Heroic Age of American Medicine. New York: Dover, 1961, 1966.

Freud, Sigmund. "Feminity," New Introductory Lectures on Psychoanalysis, (translated and edited by James Strachey). New York: W. W. Norton, 1933 (Freud), 1964, 1965 (Strachey). See also Sigmund Freud, "Three Contributions to the Theory of Sex," The Basic Writings of Sigmund Freud (translated and edited by A. A. Brill). New York: Random House, 1938.

Froslid, E. Kenneth. "Helen Taussig, A Woman of Science." New York: World Book Science Annual, 1967, p. 389.

Garrison, Fielding Hudson. Introduction to a History of Medicine. Philadelphia. London: Saunders, 1914.

Golbus, M. "Prenatal Genetic Diagnosis," New England Journal of Medicine, 300 (January 25, 1979), pp. 157-63.

Gordon, Barbara. I'm Dancing as Fast as I Can. New York: Harper & Row, 1979.

Gramont, Sanche de. The French, Portrait of a People. New York: Putnam, 1969.

Greene, J. W., Jr. "Maternal and Fetal Outcome of Lamaze-Prepared Patients," Journal of Obstetrics and Gynecology, 51 (June 1978), pp. 723-24.

Gregory, S. Man-Midwifery Exposed and Corrected. Boston: George Gregory, 1948, pp. 18ff. See also his Letters in Favor of Female Physicians. New York: Fowler and Wells, 1850.

Gutentag, M., and H. Bray. Undoing Sex Stereotypes. New York: McGraw-Hill, 1976.

Hahn, Otto. A Scientific Autobiography. New York: Scribner's, 1966.

Hamilton, Alice. Exploring the Dangerous Trades. Boston: Little, Brown, 1943.

Haseltine, F., and Y. Yaw. Woman Doctor. Boston: Houghton Mifflin, 1976.

Heckford, Sarah. Voluntaries for an East London Hospital. London: David Scott, 1887.

Hentoff, Nat. A Doctor Among the Addicts. New York: Rand McNally, 1968.

Hoover, Nancy. "Dr. Anna Easton Lake: First Lady Physician Appointed to the White House," Journal of the American Medical Women's Association, (November 1962), pp. 906-07.

Horney, Karen. (a) Are You Considering Psychoanalysis? New York: Norton, 1946.

_____. (b) Neurosis and Human Growth. New York: Norton, 1950.

_____. (c) The Neurotic Personality of Our Time. New York: Norton, 1937.

Hughes, Marija M. The Sexual Barrier: Legal, Medical, Economic and Social Aspects of Sex Discrimination. New York: Hughes Press, 1977.

Hughey, M. J.; T. W. McElin, and T. Young. "Maternal and Fetal Outcome of Lamaze-Prepared Patients," Obstetrics and Gynecology, 51 (June 1978), pp. 643-47.

Hume, Ruth Fox. Great Women of Medicine. New York: Random House, 1964.

238 / Women and Medicine

Huntley, E. A. The Study and Practice of Medicine by Women. London: Lewes Farncombe, 1886.

Jacobi, Mary Putnam. Mary Putnam Jacobi, M. D., a Pathfinder in Medicine. Her writings edited by the Women's Medical Association of New York. Putnam, 1925.

Jelliffe, Derrick Brian, and E. F. Patrice Jelliffe. "Human Milk, Nutrition and the World Resource Crisis," Science, (May 9, 1975), pp. 557ff.

Jex-Blake, Sophia. Medical Women, a Thesis and a History. London: Oliphant, 1886.

Johnson, Davis G., and Edwin B. Hutchins. "Doctor or Dropout? A Study of Medical School Attrition," Journal of Medical Education, 41 (December 1966), pp. 1097-1260.

Johnson, Davis G., and William E. Sedlacedk. "Retraining by Sex and Race of 1968-72 U. S. Medical School Entrants," Journal of Medical Education, 50 (October 1975), pp. 925-33.

Johnson, Jeanette. "Medical Schools Show Upsurge in Women Students," Houston Chronicle (AP), (August 26, 1973), Sec. 3, p. 7.

Johnston, Malcolm S. Elizabeth Blackwell and Her Alma Mater: the Story in the Documents. Humphrey, 1947.

Kaplan, H. I. "Woman Physicians: The More Effective Recruitment and Utilization of Their Talents and the Resistance to It--The Final Conclusions of a Seven-Year Study," Woman Physician, 25 (1970).

Keleman, Stanley. Living Your Dying. New York: Random House, 1976.

Kelman, Harold, ed. New Perspectives in Psychoanalysis: Karen Horney's Holistic Approach. New York: Norton, 1964.

Kent, Elaine. "Swedish Visitor to Hope Haven," Florida Times Union, (March 31, 1972), p. 8.

Kitridou, Rodanthi. "Synovianalysis," American Family Practice, 5 (May 1972), pp. 106ff.

Knight, William. Some Nineteenth Century Scotsmen. London: Oliphant, 1903.

Kubie, Lawrence S. "Florence Rena Sabin," Perspectives in Biology and Medicine, 5, pp. 306-14.

Lader, Lawrence. The Margaret Sanger Story. New York: Doubleday, 1955.

The Lancet. February 15, 1964, pp. 345-48 (Cicely Williams).

Landau, G. M. "Rosalyn Sussman Yalow: Interview," Parents Magazine, 53 (January 1978).

Lear, J. "Kelsey's Reward," Saturday Review, 46 (February 2, 1963).

Leuchtag, H. F. "Yalow Wins Half of Nobel Prize in Medicine," Physics Today, 30 (December 1977), pp. 78-79.

Lipinska, M. Histoire des Femmes Medecins. Paris: Jacques, 1900.

Lopate, Carol. Women in Medicine. Baltimore: Johns Hopkins, 1968.

Lorber, J. "Women in Medical Sociology: Invisible Professional and Ubiquitous Patient." In Another Voice, edited by K. Millman and R. M. Kanter. New York: Doubleday, 1975.

Lovejoy, Esther Pohl. (a) "American Women's Hospitals Overseas Service (Medical Service Committee of the American Medical Women's Association)," Medical Woman's Journal, 51 (October 1944), pp. 20-22.

_____. (b) Certain Samaritans. New York: Macmillan, 1933 (rev. ed.).

_____. (c) House of the Good Neighbor. New York: Macmillan, 1919.

_____. (d) Women Doctors of the World. New York: Macmillan, 1957.

Lutzker, Edythe. Women Gain a Place in Medicine. New York: McGraw-Hill, 1969.

Manton, Jo. Elizabeth Garrett Anderson. London: Methuen & Co., Ltd., 1965.

Martindale, Louisa. (a) The Woman Doctor. London: Mills & Boon, 1922.

_____. (b) A Woman Surgeon. London: Gollancz, 1951.

Mattman, Lida Holmes. "Cell Wall--Deficient Forms of Mycobacteria," Annals of the New York Academy of Sciences, 174 (October 30, 1970), pp. 852-61.

Mayer, Jean. "Let's Put Women in Their Place Like, for Instance, City Hall," McCall's, (February 1971), pp. 74ff.

Mead, Kate Campbell Hurd. Women in Medicine. Haddam, Conn.: Haddam Press, 1938. New York: AMS Press, 1977 (reprint).

Medicine as a Career for Women. Booklet. American Medical Women's Association, 1740 Broadway, New York 10019.

"Medicine: The Bars Against Women," Time, (January 11, 1971), p. 31.

Meeker, Frances. "At Meharry, They're Learning Doctor-Type Skills," The Nashville Banner, (April 15, 1974), p. 28.

Meites, J. "Nobel Prize in Physiology or Medicine" (Yalow), Science, 198 (November 11, 1977), pp. 594-96.

Modern Medicine, (November 9, 1964), p. 75 (Leona Baumgartner).

"Modern Midwives," Newsweek, (September 1, 1975), p. 59.

Moore, N. History of St. Bartholomew's Hospital. London: Arthur Pearson, 1918.

Morris, E. W. The History of the London Hospital. London: Arnold, 1910.

Morton, Rosalie Slaughter. (a) A Doctor's Holiday in Iran. New York: Funk & Wagnalls, 1940.

_____. (b) A Woman Surgeon. London: Robert Hale, 1937.

Mosher, E. "Portrayal of Women in Drug Advertising: A Medical Betrayal," Journal of Drug Issues, 6 (1976).

Mulliken, J. "Woman Doctor Who Would Not Be Hurried," Life, 53 (August 10, 1962), pp. 28-29.

Murray, Flora. Women as Army Surgeons. London: Hodder, 1920.

Nelson, Harry. "Researchers Link Lack of Chemical to Obesity" (Rosalyn Yalow), Houston Chronicle, Sec. 3.

New York Infirmary: A Century of Devoted Service. New York: (privately printed), 1954.

Newman, Charles. The Evolution of Medical Education in the Nineteenth Century. London: Oxford University Press, 1957.

Nutting, M. Adelaide, and L. L. Dock. History of Nursing. New York: Putnam, 1907.

Nyswander, Marie. The Drug Addict as Patient. New York: Gruen and Stratton, 1956.

"Nyswander, Marie," Time, (January 4, 1971), p. 60.

"Nyswander, Marie," Vogue, 151 (May 1968), pp. 210-11.

O'Faolain, Julia, and Lauro Martines. Not in God's Image. New York: Harper & Row, 1973.

O'Malley, Ida Beatrice. (a) Florence Nightingale, 1820-1856. London: Thornton Butterworth, 1931.

_____. (b) Women in Subjection: A Study of the Lives of Englishwomen Before 1832. London: Thornton Butterworth, 1933.

Packard, Francis R. History of Medicine in the United States. New York: Hafner, 1963.

Parker, Beulah. A Mingled Yarn. New Haven: Yale University Press, 1972.

Peterson, Houston, and Havelock Ellis. Philosopher of Love. Boston: Houghton Mifflin, 1928.

Pfister, Shirley. "Dr. Janet Butel, Virologist," Houston Chronicle, (April 20, 1975), Sec. 8, p. 2.

Phillips, B. "Mary Walker, First Woman Doctor in the Army," New York Times Magazine, (July 11, 1943), p. 28.

Piercy, Harry D. "Marie Zakrzewska, Class of 1856," Case Western Reserve Medical Alumni Bulletin, 33 (Fourth Quarter 1969), pp. 14-15.

Power, E. "Women Practitioners of Medicine in the Middle Ages," Proceedings of the Royal Society of Medicine, 1921.

Poynter, Lida. "Dr. Mary Walker, M.D., Pioneer Woman Physician," Medical Woman's Journal, 53 (October 1946), pp. 43-51. (History of Women in Medicine.)

"Psychiatric Lecture Series Honors Dr. Hilde Bruch," BCM: Inside Baylor Medicine, 5 (April 1974), 1. port. (Four tributes to Dr. Bruch with brief biographical information.)

Putnam, Ruth, ed. Life and Letters of Mary Putnam Jacobi. New York: Putnam, 1925.

Ramey, Estelle. (a) "An Interview," Georgetown Medical Bulletin, 24 (August 1970), pp. 5-11.

_____. (b) "Well, Fellows, What Did Happen at the Bay of Pigs?" McCall's Magazine, (January 1971), pp. 26ff.

Ratner, Herbert. "Birth Control Pills." Speech given at St. John's University, Collegeville, Minn., June 18, 1979.

Raven, Clara. "Achievements of Women in Medicine, Past and Present--Women in the Medical Corps of the Army," Military Medicine 125 (February 1960), pp. 105-11.

Ravitch, Mark, ed. Summing Up. The Papers of Alfred Blalock, VI. Baltimore: Johns Hopkins, 1966.

Reynolds, Arthur R., M.D. Commissioner of Health. Biennial Report of the Department of Health of the City of Chicago. 1897.

Rich, Adrienne. "Foreword: Conditions for Work: The
Common World of Women. " In Sara Ruddick and Pamela
Daniels, eds. , Working It Out. New York: Pantheon,
1977, p. xxiii.

Riemer, Jack, ed. Jewish Reflections on Death. New
York: Schocken Books, 1974. Foreword by Elisabeth
Kubler-Ross.

Roeske, Nancy A. , M. D. (a) "Women in Medicine--Looking
to the Future. " Pre-publication draft. Dept. of Psychiatry, Indiana University School of Medicine.

_____. (b) "Women in Psychiatry: A Review, " American
Journal of Psychiatry, 133 (April 1976), pp. 365-72.

_____, and Karen Lake. "Role Models for Women Medi-
cal Students, " Journal of Medical Education, 52 (June
1977), pp. 459-66.

Ross, Ishbel. Child of Destiny. New York: Harper &
Row, 1949.

Ross, Nancy L. "The Battle of Raging Hormones, "
Washington Post, (August 26, 1970), Sec. B, p. 1.

Rossi, B. "Florence Sabin, " Baltimore: The Johns Hopkins Magazine, 7 (1959).

Rossiter, Margaret. "Florence Sabin. " Speech delivered
to the American Association for the Advancement of Science Conference, Boston, February 20, 1976.

Rubins, Jack L. Karen Horney, Gentle Rebel of Psychoanalysis. New York: Dial, 1978.

Samuels, Gertrude. "Methadone: Fighting Fire with Fire, "
New York Times Magazine, (October 15, 1967), pp. 44-
45. (Discussion about Marie Nyswander, November 12,
1967, pp. 22ff.)

Sanger, Margaret. (a) An Autobiography. New York:
Norton, 1938.

_____. (b) Family Limitation. London: Rose Witcop, 1924.

Schmeck, Harold M., Jr. (a) "Testing System Gauges Infants' Survival Chances," New York Times, (June 23, 1963), p. 10.

_____. (b) "Study Backs Charges of Sexism in Medicine," New York Times, (June 5, 1979).

Seidenberg, R. "Images of Health, Illness and Women in Drug Advertising," Journal of Drug Issues, 4 (1974), pp. 264-67.

Shapiro, C. S.; B. J. Stibler; A. A. Zelkovic; and J. S. Mausner. "Careers of Women Physicians: A Survey of Women Graduates from Seven Medical Schools, 1945-1951," Journal of Medical Education, 43 (1968), p. 1033.

Sherfey, Mary Jane. The Nature and Evolution of Female Sexuality. New York: Vintage Books, 1973.

Shryock, R. H., ed. (a) The Arnold Letters. Durham, N. C.: Duke University Press, 1929, vol. 17, p. 18.

_____. (b) Medicine in America. Baltimore: Johns Hopkins, 1966.

Simpson, James Young. Obstetric Memoirs, 2 vols. London: Black, 1855.

Smith, Brenda Beust. "Dr. Priori Makes Another Discovery: Cancer Virology," Houston Chronicle, July 11, 1971, Sec. 7, p. 4.

Snell, Elsie K. "Dr. Marie Zakrzewska, Memorial Member," Women in Medicine, 58 (October 1937), p. 25.

Snow, Edgar. "Population Care and Control," The New Republic, (May 1, 1971), pp. 20ff.

Snyder, Charles McCool. Dr. Mary Walker: The Little Lady in Pants. New York: Vantage Press, 1964.

Spieler, Carolyn, ed. Women in Medicine--1976. Report of a Macy Conference. Baltimore: Waverly Press, 1977.

Standley, Kay, Ph. D., and Bradley Soule, M. D. Women in Professions: Historic Antecedents and Current Lifestyles. Bethesda, Md.: Social and Behavioral Sciences Branch, National Institute of Child Health and Human Development.

Starchey, R. (a) Millicent Garrett Fawcette. London: John Murray, 1931.

_____. (b) The Cause. London: Bell & Sons, 1928.

Stinson, Robert and Peggy. "On the Death of a Baby," The Atlantic, 244 (July 1979), pp. 64-72.

"Thalidomide Disaster," Time, 80 (August 10, 1962).

"Thalidomide Heroine Seeks New Culprits," Science Digest, 53 (May 1963).

"Thalidomide: Kelsey's Struggle," Saturday Review, 45 (September 1, 1962).

Thomson, H. Campbell. The Middlesex Hospital Medical School. London: John Murray, 1935.

Thorne, Isabel. The Foundation and Development of the London School of Medicine for Women. London: G. Sharrow, 1905.

Tiburtius, Franziska. Memories of an Octogenarian. Berlin: C. A. Schwelschke and Sohn, 1925. (German).

Todd, Margaret. The Life of Sophia Jex-Blake, M.D. London: Macmillan, 1918.

Travell, Janet. Autobiography: Office Hours, Day and Night. New York: World, 1968.

_____, and Marion Fay. "Letters from Other Desks," Journal of the American Medical Women's Association, 16 (May 1961), pp. 394-96.

_____, and Louise Oftedal Wensel. "Doctor, Wife and Mother," Wellesley Alumnae Magazine, 36 (November 1953), pp. 13-15.

Truax, Rhoda. The Doctors Jacobi. Boston: Little, Brown, 1952.

Valdes-Dapena, Marie, M.D. "Crib Death," Medical World News: Pediatrics, (special issue, 1970), pp. 67-69.

Varro, Barbara. "Withdrawal from Valium," Houston Chronicle, (May 31, 1979), Sec. 9, p. 4.

Vaughan, Paul. Doctors Commons, a History of the British Medical Association. London: Heinemann, 1959.

Vaughan, Victor C. A Doctor's Memories. New York: Bobbs-Merrill, 1926.

"Vigilant Doctor Gets a Medal: Kelsey, " U. S. News, 53 (August 20, 1962).

Walsh, James. History of Medicine in New York. New York: National American Society, 1919.

Weideger, Paula. Menstruation and Menopause. New York: Knopf, 1976.

Weisstein, Naomi. "Psychology Constructs the Female." In Vivian Gornick and Barbara K. Moran, eds. Woman in Sexist Society: Studies in Power and Powerlessness. New York: Basic Books, 1971, p. 135.

Welsh, M. R. Doctors Wanted; No Women Need Apply: Sexual Barriers in the Medical Profession 1835-1975. New Haven: Yale University Press, 1977.

Williams, Cicely D. (a) "Maternal and Child Health Services in Developing Countries." (Lecture to the Ceylon Public Health Assn., September 1963.) The Lancet, (February 15, 1964), pp. 345-48.

_____. (b) Address delivered at the Royal Sanitary Institute Health Congress, Bournemouth, England, April 1955.

Williams, P. A. "Women in Medicine: Some Themes and Variations, " Journal of Medical Education, 46 (1971).

Wilson, Dorothy Clarke. (a) Lone Woman: The Story of Elizabeth Blackwell. Boston: Little, Brown, 1970.

_____. (b) Stranger and Traveler, Story of Dorothea Dix. Boston: Little, Brown, 1975.

"Women M. D. 's Join the Fight, " Medical World News, (October 23, 1970), pp. 22-28.

Women's Leadership and Authority in the Health Profession. Program for Women in Health Sciences. University of California, San Francisco, 1977.

Woodham-Smith, Cecil. Florence Nightingale. New York: McGraw-Hill, 1951.

Woodward, Helen Beal. "The Right to Wear Pants: Dr. Mary Walker." In The Bold Women. New York: Farrar, Straus and Young, 1953, pp. 281-98.

Woolsey, Jane Stuart. Hospital Days. New York: N. p., 1870.

Yalow, Rosalyn S. "What's Ahead for Women in Medicine?" Parents Magazine, 53 (January 1978), pp. 38-39.

Zakrzewska, Marie. A Woman's Quest. New York: Appleton, 1924.

INDEX

Answer to popular puzzler:

Of course.   The surgeon is his mother.

Biology class, Purdue University, 1907